Italian Grammar Drills

SECOND EDITION

Paola Nanni-Tate

McGraw Hill

New York   Chicago   San Francisco   Lisbon   London   Madrid   Mexico City
Milan   New Delhi   San Juan   Seoul   Singapore   Sydney   Toronto

The McGraw·Hill Companies

Copyright © 2012 by The McGraw-Hill Companies, Inc. All rights reserved. Printed in the United States of America. Except as permitted under the United States Copyright Act of 1976, no part of this publication may be reproduced or distributed in any form or by any means, or stored in a database or retrieval system, without the prior written permission of the publisher.

1 2 3 4 5 6 7 8 9 10 10 11 12 13 14 15   QDB/QDB   1 9 8 7 6 5 4 3 2

ISBN   978-0-07-178967-7
MHID   0-07-178967-7

e-ISBN 978-0-07-178968-4
e-MHID   0-07-178968-5

Library of Congress Control Number 2012931391

McGraw-Hill products are available at special quantity discounts to use as premiums and sales promotions or for use in corporate training programs. To contact a representative, please e-mail us at bulksales@mcgraw-hill.com.

This book is printed on acid-free paper.

This book is printed on acid-free paper.

Contents

Preface

If you've picked up this book, you probably already know that to learn a language well—to have the ability to read it and write it and to understand others in that language and be understood yourself—you must at some point deal with the grammar. *Italian Grammar Drills* will give you a better command of Italian grammar by providing plenty of writing drills that will reinforce your knowledge and enhance your ability to speak, read, and write with finesse. You will be able to work at your own pace while focusing on those aspects of grammar that you feel require most of your attention.

Each of the book's nineteen chapters features concise explanations of various grammar topics. And each chapter includes a variety of exercises that will reinforce your ability to manipulate the Italian language and give you an opportunity to immediately apply what you have learned. You can find answers to all exercises in the Answer Key at the back of this book. When using this book, you can follow the order presented or skip a chapter and return to it at a later time.

Once you've worked your way through *Italian Grammar Drills*, not only will you find yourself confidently on your way to fluency, but you will also find that this book will remain a unique resource any time you need to clarify or review essential grammatical concepts.

Sometimes learning a new language may appear to be an insurmountable and tedious task, but the students who stay with it and master the grammar will find it a satisfactory and gratifying experience. How exciting to be able to communicate in Italian and appreciate the language of Italy and its people! My hope and intent in writing *Italian Grammar Drills* is to give you a basic tool for understanding, speaking, reading, and writing basic Italian, whether you are learning the language on your own or with an instructor.

I am proud and excited to help students learn such a beautiful language. I will never tire of the excitement I feel when I see students wanting to learn Italian and then mastering it through study and practice. It has been my pleasure and privilege to have written *Italian Grammar Drills*. I wish to thank my editor, Garret Lemoi, for his guidance and many useful suggestions; my husband, Bob Tate, for proofreading the text; and the many students who encouraged me to write a grammar book.

1

Nouns

A noun is used in a sentence to refer to people, animals, and objects that can be real or imaginary.

Gender

All nouns in Italian are either masculine or feminine, whether they refer to people, animals, or things. It is important to know the gender of a noun in order to accompany it with the right article—**il, lo,** or **la** (*the*) or **uno** or **una** (*a*)—and the right adjective (definite and indefinite articles are discussed in depth in Chapter 2 and adjectives in Chapter 5). The other words in a sentence that refer to the noun must agree in gender and number with that noun.

Italian makes it easy to learn the gender of a noun: The noun's ending often reveals whether it is masculine or feminine. Most nouns ending in **-o** are masculine and most nouns ending in **-a** are feminine.

masculine		**feminine**	
il cielo	*sky*	la casa	*house*
il libro	*book*	la finestra	*window*
l'uccello	*bird*	la porta	*door*
il violino	*violin*	la tazza	*cup*

There are a few exceptions. Some nouns ending in **-a** are masculine such as:

il papa	*pope*
il pianeta	*planet*
il poeta	*poet*
il pilota	*pilot*

Nouns of Greek origin ending in **-ma** are also masculine. For example:

il clima	*climate*
il fantasma	*ghost*
il panorama	*landscape*

| il problema | *problem* |
| il programma | *program* |

And some nouns ending in **-o** are feminine:

l'auto	*car*
la foto	*photo*
la mano	*hand*
la moto	*motorcycle*
la radio	*radio*

L'auto, la foto, and **la moto** are abbreviations of **l'automobile, la fotografia,** and **la motocicletta.**

Nouns with the following endings are generally masculine:

- **-ore** and **-tore**

il difensore	*defender*
il dottore	*doctor*
il professore	*professor*
lo sciatore	*skier*

- **-ere** and **-iere**

il cameriere	*waiter*
il corriere	*courier*
l'ingegnere	*engineer*

- **-ame** and **-ale**

il catrame	*tar*
il falegname	*carpenter*
il temporale	*storm*

Nouns with the following endings are generally feminine:

- **-ione**

| la colazione | *breakfast* |
| l'opinione | *opinion* |

| la pens**ione** | *pension* |
| la staz**ione** | *station* |

(Most of these nouns correspond with English words ending in *-tion* or *-sion*.)

- **-udine** and **-igine**

l'abit**udine**	*habit*
l'or**igine**	*origin*
la solit**udine**	*loneliness*

- **-ice**

l'attr**ice**	*actress*
la copiatr**ice**	*copying machine*
la direttr**ice**	*female manager/director*

- **-tà** and **-tù**

la gioven**tù**	*youth*
la ones**tà**	*honesty*
la veri**tà**	*truth*
la vir**tù**	*virtue*

(Most of these nouns correspond with English words ending in *-ty* and *-th*.)

- **-i**

| la cris**i** | *crisis* |
| la tis**i** | *tuberculosis* |

Exercise 1

Translate the following nouns into Italian. Don't worry about putting in the articles; just pay attention to the endings.

1. book _____

2. flower _____

3. window _____

4. door _____

5. house _____

6. cup _____

7. bird _____

Exercise 2

Translate the following nouns into Italian. Don't worry about putting in the articles; just pay attention to the endings.

1. planet _____

2. climate _____

3. ghost _____

4. pope _____

5. pilot _____

6. landscape _____

7. hand _____

8. photo _____

9. car _____

10. radio _____

11. professor _____

12. doctor _____

Exercise 3

Translate the following nouns into Italian. Don't worry about putting in the articles; just pay attention to the endings.

1. breakfast _____

2. station _____

3. opinion _____

4. pension _____

5. habit _____

6. origin _____

7. actress _____

8. city _____

9. honesty _____

10. youth _____

11. truth _____

12. crisis _____

Change of gender

Sometimes changing the gender of a noun also changes its meaning. For example:

il baleno	*sudden light, flash*	la balena	*whale*
il caso	*case*	la casa	*house, home*
il collo	*neck*	la colla	*glue*
il gambo	*stem*	la gamba	*leg*
il lama	*llama*	la lama	*blade*
il manico	*handle*	la manica	*sleeve*
il mento	*chin*	la menta	*mint*
il modo	*manner*	la moda	*fashion*
il pianto	*cry*	la pianta	*plant*
il pizzo	*lace*	la pizza	*pizza*
il porto	*port*	la porta	*door*
il posto	*place*	la posta	*mail*
il testo	*text*	la testa	*head*
il torto	*fault, guilt*	la torta	*cake*

Exercise 4

Translate the following nouns into Italian. Don't worry about putting in the articles, just pay attention to the endings.

1. case _____

2. home _____

3. text _____

4. head _____

5. place _____

6. mail _____

7. lace _____

8. pizza _____

9. fashion _____

10. mint _____

11. cake _____

12. chin _____

13. door _____

14. neck _____

Many nouns referring to people can be both masculine or feminine depending on whether they refer to a male or a female. However, the definite article preceding the noun (see Chapter 2) and the adjective following it (see Chapter 5) must be either masculine or feminine, depending on the gender of the noun they are referring to.

l'artista	*artist*
il/la cantante	*singer*
il/la collega	*colleague*
il/la consorte	*spouse*
il/la dirigente	*manager*
il/la fisiatra	*physical therapist*
il/la nipote	*nephew, niece*
il/la pediatra	*pediatrician*
il/la pianista	*pianist*
il/la turista	*tourist*

Some nouns referring to animals, however, have only one form to indicate male or female. For example:

la balena	*whale*
l'elefante	*elephant*
il falco	*hawk*
il giaguaro	*jaguar*
la giraffa	*giraffe*
il pesce	*fish*

la rana	*frog*
la tartaruga	*turtle*
la tigre	*tiger*
il topo	*mouse*

When one needs to distinguish whether an animal is male or female, the term **maschio** (*male*) or **femmina** (*female*) is added. It looks like this: **l'elefante femmina** (*female elephant*), **la giraffa maschio** (*male giraffe*).

Some nouns ending in **-a** can be used to refer either to males or females but are considered feminine nouns, such as:

la folla	*crowd*
la guida	*guide*
la persona	*person*
la vittima	*victim*

Exercise 5

Translate the following nouns into Italian, this time including the definite articles. (The letters in parentheses refer to masculine [m.] and feminine [f.].)

1. tourist (m.) _____
2. colleague (f.) _____
3. nephew _____
4. niece _____
5. singer (m.) _____
6. patient (f.) _____
7. spouse (m.) _____
8. elephant (m.) _____
9. hawk _____
10. turtle _____
11. crowd _____
12. victim _____
13. physical therapist _____

Many masculine nouns referring to people or to occupations and professions have a separate feminine gender using an **-a** ending.

masculine		feminine	
il cassiere	*cashier*	la cassiera	*cashier*
il figlio	*son*	la figlia	*daughter*
il nonno	*grandfather*	la nonna	*grandmother*
il parrucchiere	*hair stylist*	la parrucchiera	*hair stylist*
il signore	*gentleman*	la signora	*lady*

Other masculine nouns add the suffix **-essa** in the feminine form.

masculine		feminine	
l'avvocato	*lawyer*	l'avvocatessa	*female lawyer*
il dottore	*doctor*	la dottoressa	*female doctor*
il poeta	*poet*	la poetessa	*female poet*
il principe	*prince*	la principessa	*princess*

And some masculine nouns change the **-tore** ending to **-trice** in the feminine version.

masculine		feminine	
l'attore	*actor*	l'attrice	*actress*
il direttore	*director*	la direttrice	*female director*
il redattore	*editor*	la redattrice	*female editor*
lo sciatore	*skier*	la sciatrice	*female skier*

Sometimes the feminine forms are significantly modified from the masculine. These are usually words inherited from Latin.

masculine		feminine	
l'abate	*head priest, abbot*	la badessa	*head of a nunnery*
il dio	*god*	la dea	*goddess*
l'eroe	*hero*	l'eroina	*heroine*
il gallo	*rooster*	la gallina	*chicken*
il re	*king*	la regina	*queen*

A few nouns have completely different forms in the masculine and in the feminine.

masculine		feminine	
il frate	*monk*	la suora	*nun*
il fratello	*brother*	la sorella	*sister*
il genero	*son-in-law*	la nuora	*daughter-in-law*

il marito	*husband*	la moglie	*wife*
il maschio	*male*	la femmina	*female*
il padre	*father*	la madre	*mother*
l'uomo	*man*	la donna	*woman*

Exercise 6

Translate the following nouns into Italian using the definite articles.

1. son _____

2. uncle _____

3. daughter _____

4. grandmother _____

5. gentleman _____

6. poet (m.) _____

7. doctor (f.) _____

8. actor (m.) _____

9. skier (m.) _____

10. skier (f.) _____

There are other words in Italian that are always treated as masculine. The following list will help you get a feel for some of these nouns.

- Days of the week (except for **la domenica**, *Sunday*)

lunedì	*Monday*
martedì	*Tuesday*
mercoledì	*Wednesday*
giovedì	*Thursday*
venerdì	*Friday*
sabato	*Saturday*
domenica	*Sunday*

- Months of the year

| gennaio | *January* |
| febbraio | *February* |

marzo	*March*
aprile	*April*
maggio	*May*
giugno	*June*
luglio	*July*
agosto	*August*
settembre	*September*
ottobre	*October*
novembre	*November*
dicembre	*December*

- Names of metals and chemical elements

l'argento	*silver*
il calcio	*calcium*
l'oro	*gold*

- Nouns taken from other languages

il computer	*computer*
il film	*film, movie*
il manager	*manager*

- Most names of trees

il melo	*apple tree*
il pino	*pine tree*
il platano	*plane tree*

(However, **la palma**, *palm*, and **la betulla**, *birch*, are feminine.)

- Compass points

il nord	*north*
il sud	*south*
l'est	*east*
l'ovest	*west*

- Other direction-related terms

il settentrione	*north*
il meridione	*south*
l'oriente	*east*
l'occidente	*west*

- Proper names of major geographical features (rivers, lakes, etc.)

l'Arno	*Arno River*
il lago di Como	*Lake Como*
il Monte Bianco	*Mont Blanc*
il Mediterraneo	*Mediterranean Sea*
il Tevere	*Tiber River*

(But **le Alpi,** *the Alps.*)

- All languages

l'arabo	*Arabic*
l'italiano	*Italian*
il tedesco	*German*

Exercise 7

Translate the following nouns into Italian using the definite articles.

1. singer (m.) _____

2. pediatrician (m.) _____

3. Monday _____

4. Sunday _____

5. January _____

6. July _____

7. gold _____

8. iron _____

9. calcium _____

10. apple tree _____

Nouns that are generally feminine follow these guidelines:

- Names of most fruits

la banana	*banana*
la mela	*apple*
la pera	*pear*

(However, **il fico**, *fig*, **l'ananas**, *pineapple*, and **il mango**, *mango* are masculine.)

- Most names of cities, regions, islands, countries, and continents

Bologna	*Bologna*
l'Europa	*Europe*
la Lombardia	*Lombardy*
le Maldive	*Maldives*
Roma	*Rome*
la Sicilia	*Sicily*
la Svizzera	*Switzerland*
la Toscana	*Tuscany*

(However, **il Lazio**, *Lazio*; **il Perù**, *Peru*; **il Brasile**, *Brazil*; and **gli Stati Uniti**, *United States*, are masculine.)

- School subjects

la fisica	*physics*
la geografia	*geography*
la matematica	*mathematics*
la musica	*music*
la storia	*history*

Italian nouns ending in -e can be either masculine or feminine. When one of these nouns refers to a person, the gender of the noun is the same as the person it refers to.

masculine		**feminine**	
il cantante	*singer*	la cantante	*female singer*
il consorte	*husband*	la consorte	*wife*
il nipote	*nephew*	la nipote	*niece*
il paziente	*patient*	la paziente	*female patient*

Note: **Il/la nipote** is also used for the terms *grandson* and *granddaughter*.

When a noun ending in -e does not refer to a person, determining its gender can be difficult. These nouns must be learned by practice and memorization. Remember, it is important to know the genders of nouns so that the articles and adjective endings are used correctly.

Il **canale** è pieno di acqua.	*The **canal** is full of water.*
Il **paziente** è molto ammala**to**.	*The **patient** is very ill.*
La **paziente** è molto ammala**ta**.	*The **patient** is very ill.*

The following table shows some common nouns that end in -e:

masculine		feminine	
il canale	*canal*	la canzone	*song*
il fiore	*flower*	la capitale	*capital*
il fiume	*river*	la carne	*meat*
il giornale	*newspaper*	la chiave	*key*
il mare	*sea*	la classe	*class*
il nome	*name*	la fame	*hunger*
il pane	*bread*	la fine	*end*
il piede	*foot*	la frase	*phrase; sentence*
il ponte	*bridge*	la gente	*people*

Exercise 8

Translate the following nouns into Italian using the definite articles.

1. apple _____
2. strawberry _____
3. fig _____
4. pineapple _____
5. Rome _____
6. Tuscany _____
7. Maldives _____
8. Switzerland _____
9. Asia _____
10. Brazil _____

Plural of nouns

In Italian the plural of masculine nouns ending in **-o** or **-a** is formed by changing the final vowel to **-i**.

singular		plural	
il libro	*book*	i libri	*books*
il poeta	*poet*	i poeti	*poets*
il programma	*program*	i programmi	*programs*

To form the plural of feminine nouns ending in **-a**, change the **-a** to **-e**.

singular		plural	
la casa	*house*	le case	*houses*

Masculine and feminine nouns ending in **-e** form the plural by changing the **-e** to an **-i**.

singular		plural	
il nome	*noun*	i nomi	*nouns*
la cenere	*ash*	le ceneri	*ashes*

Some nouns ending in **-a** change the **-a** to an **-i** in their plural forms.

singular		plural	
l'ala	*wing*	le ali	*wings*
l'arma	*arm*	le armi	*arms (weapons)*
il clima	*climate*	i climi	*climates*

However, not all nouns follow these rules. In the following table you will see that there are some nouns ending in **-o** that are feminine, but that only the noun **mano** changes its form in the plural. The others (some of them abbreviations of their fuller forms) do not change. It is easy to tell that these nouns are in their plural forms by looking at the definite article before them. Definite articles change to show singular or plural forms.

singular		plural	
l'auto	*car*	le auto	*cars*
la foto	*photo*	le foto	*photos*
la mano	*hand*	le mani	*hands*

la moto	*motorcycle*	le moto	*motorcycles*
la radio	*radio*	le radio	*radios*

Other nouns that do not change in the plural are those ending in **-i** or **-ie**.

singular		**plural**	
la bici	*bicycle*	le bici	*bicycles*
il brindisi	*toast*	i brindisi	*toasts* (congratulatory)
la crisi	*crisis*	le crisi	*crises*
la serie	*series*	le serie	*series*
la tesi	*thesis*	le tesi	*theses*

Feminine nouns ending in accented vowels also remain unchanged in the plural.

singular		**plural**	
la città	*city*	le città	*cities*
la gioventù	*youth*	le gioventù	*youths*
la tribù	*tribe*	le tribù	*tribes*

Exercise 9

Write the plural forms of the following words.

1. la casa _____

2. il libro _____

3. il programma _____

4. il poeta _____

5. la polvere _____

6. la mano _____

7. l'auto _____

8. la foto _____

9. la crisi _____

10. la bici _____

11. la verità _____

12. la città _____

There are still more nouns that do not make a change in their plural forms, such as:

singular		plural	
l'autobus	*bus*	gli autobus	*buses*

Masculine and feminine nouns accented in the final vowel, and monosyllable nouns, do not change in the plural.

singular		plural	
il bar	*bar*	i bar	*bars*
il caffè	*coffee*	i caffè	*coffees*
la gru	*crane*	le gru	*cranes*
il lunedì	*Monday*	i lunedì	*Mondays*
il martedì	*Tuesday*	i martedì	*Tuesdays*
il re	*king*	i re	*kings*
lo sci	*ski*	gli sci	*skis*
il tè	*tea*	i tè	*teas*

There are even some masculine nouns that become feminine in the plural.

singular		plural	
il braccio	*arm*	le braccia	*arms*
centinaio	*hundred*	centinaia	*hundreds*
il dito	*finger*	le dita	*fingers*
il ginocchio	*knee*	le ginocchia	*knees*
il lenzuolo	*sheet*	le lenzuola	*sheets*
migliaio	*thousand*	migliaia	*thousands*
il miglio	*mile*	le miglia	*miles*
mille	*thousand*	mila	*thousands*
l'orecchio	*ear*	le orecchie	*ears*
il paio	*pair*	le paia	*pairs*
l'uovo	*egg*	le uova	*eggs*

Exercise 10

Write the plural forms of the following nouns.

1. lo sci _____

2. il re _____

3. il bar _____

4. la gru _____

5. il lunedì _____

6. il caffè _____

7. il braccio _____

8. l'uovo _____

9. l'orecchio _____

10. il ginocchio _____

11. il dito _____

12. il lenzuolo _____

13. centinaio _____

14. migliaio _____

Feminine and masculine nouns ending in **-ca/-co**, or **-ga/-go**, form the plural by replacing the endings with **-che/-chi** or **-ghe/-ghi** respectively, in order to preserve the hard sound of the **-c** and the **-g** that is in the singular.

singular		plural	
l'albico**cco**	*apricot tree*	gli albico**cchi**	*apricot trees*
l'ami**ca**	*girlfriend*	le ami**che**	*girlfriends*
la ban**ca**	*bank*	le ban**che**	*banks*
il catalo**go**	*catalog*	i catalo**ghi**	*catalogs*
il colle**ga**	*colleague*	i colle**ghi**	*colleagues*
la di**ga**	*dam*	le di**ghe**	*dams*
il du**ca**	*duke*	i du**chi**	*dukes*
il fi**co**	*fig*	i fi**chi**	*figs*
il la**go**	*lake*	i la**ghi**	*lakes*
la mani**ca**	*sleeve*	le mani**che**	*sleeves*
la mona**ca**	*nun*	le mona**che**	*nuns*
il monar**ca**	*monarch*	i monar**chi**	*monarchs*
l'o**ca**	*goose*	le o**che**	*geese*
il par**co**	*park*	i par**chi**	*parks*
il sa**cco**	*bag*	i sa**cchi**	*bags*
la tecni**ca**	*technique*	le tecni**che**	*techniques*

However, some nouns ending in -co/-go, do not keep the hard sound in the plural. In these words the -ci and -gi retain a soft sound, as in the English words *cheese* and *jeep*.

singular		**plural**	
l'amico	*friend*	gli amici	*friends*
l'asparago	*asparagus*	gli asparagi	*asparagus*
il chirurgo	*surgeon*	i chirurgi	*surgeons*
il medico	*doctor*	i medici	*doctors*
il nemico	*enemy*	i nemici	*enemies*
il parroco	*priest*	i parroci	*priests*

Of course, some masculine nouns have a completely irregular plural. For example:

singular		**plural**	
il bue	*ox*	i buoi	*oxen*
l'uomo	*man*	gli uomini	*men*

Exercise 11

Write the plural forms of the following nouns.

1. l'amica _____

2. la banca _____

3. la mosca _____

4. la diga _____

5. il lago _____

6. il fico _____

7. l'albicocco _____

8. il cuoco _____

9. il catalogo _____

10. la manica _____

11. l'oca _____

12. il medico _____

13. il nemico _____

The plural of nouns taken from other languages is formed by using the plural form of the definite article. The noun itself is unchanged.

singular	plural
il bar	i bar
il film	i film
il gas	i gas
lo sport	**gli** sport
il tram (trolley)	i tram
il weekend	i weekend

Masculine nouns ending in **-io** use an **-ii** ending if the final **-i** in the word is a stressed syllable. If it is not stressed only one **-i** is used.

singular		plural	
il fruscio	*rustle*	i fruscii	*rustles*
il ronzio	*buzzing*	i ronzii	*buzzings*
lo zio	*uncle*	gli zii	*uncles*

But:

il bacio	*kiss*	i baci	*kisses*
l'inizio	*beginning*	gli inizi	*beginnings*
l'operaio	*worker*	gli operai	*workers*
l'orologio	*watch, clock*	gli orologi	*watches, clocks*
lo studio	*study*	gli studi	*studies*
l'ufficio	*office*	gli uffici	*offices*

Feminine nouns ending in **-cia** and **-gia** usually omit the **-ia** and add an **-e** in the plural.

singular		plural	
l'arancia	*orange*	le arance	*oranges*
la doccia	*shower*	le docce	*showers*
la faccia	*face*	le facce	*faces*
la frangia	*fringe*	le frange	*fringes*
la pioggia	*rain*	le piogge	*rains*
la valigia	*suitcase*	le valige	*suitcases*

But **la camicia** (*shirt*) and **la ciliegia** (*cherry*) are two exceptions; they keep the **-i** in the plural: **camicie, ciliegie.**

Another exception to this rule are nouns that stress the **-i** in **-cia** and **-gia**. They make their plural form by using **-cie** and **-gie**.

singular		plural	
la bugia	*lie*	le bugie	*lies*
la farma**cia**	*pharmacy*	le farma**cie**	*pharmacies*
la s**cia**	*trail*	le s**cie**	*trails*

Exercise 12

Write the plural forms of the following nouns.

1. il film _____

2. il gas _____

3. lo zio _____

4. il fruscio _____

5. il bacio _____

6. lo specchio _____

7. l'orologio _____

8. il giornalaio _____

9. l'arancia _____

10. la guancia _____

Compound nouns

Sometimes a word in Italian combines the root of the third person singular present tense conjugation of a verb with a noun. Together they form one word, called a compound noun. In some cases the plural form of compound nouns remains the same and the definite article will indicate if it is plural or singular. (See Chapter 2.) In other cases the ending of the compound noun changes to indicate a plural form. There is no rule to follow here, so it is best if these nouns are practiced and memorized.

singular		plural	
il cacciavite	*screwdriver*	i cacciaviti	*screwdrivers*
il cantastorie	*ballad singer*	i cantastorie	*ballad singers*
il paracadute	*parachute*	i paracaduti	*parachutes*
il parafulmine	*lightning rod*	i parafulmini	*lightning rods*
il paraurti	*bumper*	i paraurti	*bumpers*
il paravento	*screen*	i paravento	*screens*
il portafoglio	*wallet*	i portafogli	*wallets*
il portavoce	*spokesperson*	i portavoce	*spokespersons*

Other compound nouns combine two nouns to form one word, much like a compound word in English. The gender of such nouns is determined by the gender of the second noun and their plural is usually formed by changing the second noun to its plural form.

singular		plural	
l'arcobaleno	*rainbow*	gli arcobaleni	*rainbows*
la banconota	*bill, banknote*	le banconote	*bills, banknotes*
il capolavoro	*masterpiece*	i capolavori	*masterpieces*
il cavolfiore	*cauliflower*	i cavolfiori	*cauliflowers*
la ferrovia	*railway*	le ferrovie	*railways*
il pomodoro	*tomato*	i pomodori	*tomatoes*

Sometimes, however, there are compound nouns that will change the first noun to its plural form.

singular		plural	
il capofamiglia	*head of the family*	i capifamiglia	*heads of the family*
il capofila	*head of the line*	i capifila	*heads of the line*
il caposquadra	*team leader*	i capisquadra	*team leaders*
il capostazione	*station master*	i capistazione	*station masters*

Some compound nouns combine a noun and an adjective. The plural for this type of noun is formed by using the plural of both elements.

singular		plural	
la cassaforte	*safe*	le casseforti	*safes*
la terracotta	*clay*	le terrecotte	*clays*

An exception to this rule is **il palcoscenico** (*stage*). Its plural form is **i palcoscenici** (*stages*).

Compound nouns that combine an adjective with a masculine noun ending in **-o** change the noun as follows:

singular		plural	
il biancospino	*hawthorn, white bush*	i biancospini	*hawthorns, white bushes*
il francobollo	*stamp*	i francobolli	*stamps*
il gentiluomo	*gentleman*	i gentiluomini	*gentlemen*

But:

singular		plural	
l'altopiano	*plateau*	gli altopiani	*plateaus*
		or altipiani	

Compound nouns that combine an adjective with a feminine noun change the endings of both elements.

singular		plural	
la malalingua	*bad mouth*	le malelingue	*bad mouths*
la mezzaluna	*half-moon*	le mezzelune	*half-moons*

But:

singular		plural	
la piattaforma	*platform*	le piattaforme	*platforms*

When two adjectives combine to create a compound noun, the plural is formed by changing the ending of the second adjective.

singular		plural	
il chiaroscuro	*chiaroscuro*	i chiaroscuri	*chiaroscuros*
il pianoforte	*piano*	i pianoforti	*pianos*
il sordomuto	*deaf mute*	i sordomuti	*deaf mutes*

Exercise 13

Fill in the blanks using the words in parentheses.

1. Ho bisogno di un _____ (*screwdriver*).

2. I _____ (*parachutes*) sono fatti di seta.

3. Le hanno rubato il _____ (*wallet*).

4. L'_____ (*rainbow*) si vede dopo la pioggia.

5. I _____ (*tomatoes*) sono molto buoni in estate.

6. I _____ (*masterpieces*) di Michelangelo sono molto famosi.

7. Ci piace mangiare il _____ (*swordfish*).

8. Mio padre era il _____ (*head of the family*).

9. I ladri hanno rotto la _____ (*safe*).

10. Vorrei vedere i soldati di _____ (*clay*) in Cina.

11. Devono comprare dei _____ (*stamps*).

12. È un vero _____ (*gentleman*).

Diminutive nouns

Nouns with suffixes that indicate *smallness* are called diminutives. These suffixes are: **-ino, -icino, -etto, -ello, -erello, -otto** (for the masculine), and **-ina, -icina, -etta, -ella, -erella,** and **otta** (for the feminine). The following table shows how diminutive endings are used:

noun		diminutive noun	
l'albero	*tree*	l'alber**ello**	*small tree*
la camicia	*shirt*	la camic**ina**	*small shirt*
la casa	*house*	la cas**ina**	*small house*
il cuore	*heart*	il cuor**icino**	*small heart*
il pane	*bread*	la pagn**otta**	*small bread loaf*
la pazza	*crazy woman*	la pazz**erella**	*small crazy woman*
il prato	*meadow*	il prat**icello**	*small meadow*
l'uccello	*bird*	l'uccell**ino**	*small bird*
l'uomo	*man*	l'om**etto**	*small man*
la vecchia	*old lady*	la vecchi**etta**	*small old lady*

Exercise 14

Fill in the blanks using the diminutive nouns in parentheses.

1. Ho visto un _____ (*small bird*) morto sotto un albero.

2. Lei abita in una _____ (*small house*).

3. Abbiamo visto una _____ (*small old lady*) per la strada.

4. Mia zia è una bella _____ (*small old lady*).

5. Mangerei tutta la _____ (*small bread loaf*).

6. Gli piace sedersi sul _____ (*small meadow*) sulla collina.

7. Ci sono molti _____ (*small trees*) dove abito.

8. Hanno comprato delle _____ (*small bread loaves*) per la festa.

9. L'amica di Eric è una _____ (*small old lady*).

10. Maria ha comprato una _____ (*small shirt*) per il bambino.

11. Luigi è un bell'_____ (*small man*).

Pejorative nouns

Nouns with the suffixes **-accio, -astro, -ucolo** (for the masculine), and **-accia, -astra, -ucola, -iciattola** (for the feminine), are used to convey a feeling of dislike, bad quality, and contempt and are called pejoratives. The following list shows how pejorative endings are used:

il giovin**astro**	*lazy young man*
il poet**ucolo**	*untalented poet*
il ragazz**accio**	*brat; bad boy*
il cagn**accio**	*big, bad dog*
la cas**accia**	*big, ugly house*
la donn**accia**	*bad, ugly woman*
la stanz**accia**	*lousy room*
la strad**accia**	*bad road*

Exercise 15

Translate each sentence into Italian using a pejorative noun.

1. He is a bad boy.

_____.

2. This is a lousy room.

_____.

3. He is a poor poet.

_____.

4. He is a lazy young man.

_____.

5. That is a bad dog.

_____.

6. That is a big, ugly house.

_____.

7. She is a bad woman.

_____.

8. That is a bad road.

_____.

9. She is a bad girl.

_____.

Augmentative nouns

Nouns with the suffixes **-one** and **-ione**, used to convey size, are called augmentative. The following examples show how augmentative endings are used. They are usually used in the masculine form even when referring to feminine subjects: **-omone** (*large* or *tall man*), **mattacchione** (*big joker; big rascal*). Note the change of the definite articles for some of these words.

il gatto	*cat*	il gatt**one**	*large cat*
il matto	*crazy person*	il mattacchi**one**	*big joker*
il palazzo	*palace*	il palazz**one**	*large building*
la porta	*door*	il port**one**	*large door*
la strada	*street*	lo strad**one**	*large street*
la tenda	*drape*	il tend**one**	*large drape, awning*

Exercise 16

Translate the following sentences into Italian using augmentative nouns.

1. He is a real big man.

_____.

2. There is a large road in front of her house.

_____.

3. They live in a large building.

_____.

4. She is a large woman.

_____.

5. That is a big cat.

_____.

6. Luigi is a real joker.

_____.

7. They often use big words.

_____.

8. Please close the large door at the bottom of the stairs.

_____.

9. In the living room there are three large windows.

_____.

10. Lower the awning!

_____.

Exercise 17

Change each noun into a diminutive, pejorative, and augmentative noun. For example:

la casa: la casina   la casaccia   la casona

	diminutive	pejorative	augmentative
1. l'uomo	_____	_____	_____
2. la ragazza	_____	_____	_____

3. il gatto   _____   _____   _____

4. la parola   _____   _____   _____

5. il palazzo   _____   _____   _____

6. la stanza   _____   _____   _____

7. la vecchia   _____   _____   _____

8. la scarpa   _____   _____   _____

9. l'uccello   _____   _____   _____

10. la sorella   _____   _____   _____

11. la macchina   _____   _____   _____

12. il libro   _____   _____   _____

Nouns from adjectives

Many adjectives become nouns when preceded by a definite article. These often describe people or a group of people in a general way. For example:

gli americani/le americane	*the Americans* (m./f.)
gli antichi	*the ancients*
gli aristocratici	*the aristocrats*
gli avari	*the greedy*
i belli	*the beautiful*
i buoni	*the good* (*people*)
i cattivi	*the bad* (*people*)
i duri	*the hard ones*
i forti	*the strong*
i francesi/le francesi	*the French* (m./f.)
i generosi	*the generous*
i giovani/le giovani	*the young* (m./f.)
i grandi	*the greats*
gli ignoranti	*the ignorant*
gli intelligenti	*the intelligent*
i nobili	*the nobles*
i piccoli	*the small*
i poveri	*the poor*
i timidi	*the shy*
gli umili	*the humble*

Nouns of quantity

Some nouns expressing quantity or measure are followed by the preposition **di** (*of*). The following are some of the most commonly used nouns of quantity:

un bicchiere di	*a glass of*
un chilogrammo di	*a kilogram of*
una dozzina di	*a dozen of*
una fetta di	*a slice of*
una libbra di	*a pound of*
un litro di	*a liter of*
un metro di	*a meter of*
un paio di	*a pair of*
un pezzo di	*a piece of*

Compro **un paio di** guanti.	*I buy **a pair of** gloves.*
Vorrei **una fetta di** formaggio.	*I would like **a slice of** cheese.*
Bevo **un bicchiere di** vino.	*I am drinking **a glass of** wine.*
Un chilogrammo di patate.	***A kilogram of** potatoes.*

Exercise 18

Fill in the blanks with the appropriate forms of the nouns in parentheses.

1. _____ (*The generous*) aiutano molta gente.

2. _____ (*French women*) sono sempre eleganti.

3. _____ (*The greedy*) non godono del loro benessere.

4. _____ (*The beautiful*) sono sempre sulle copertine delle riviste.

5. _____ (*The small ones*) devono andare a letto presto.

6. _____ (*The Americans*) sono molto competitivi.

7. _____ (*The aristocrats*) oggi non sono più considerati.

8. _____ (*The shy*) non si fanno mai sentire.

9. _____ (*The poor*) vivono in case piccole.

10. Vorrei _____ (*a dozen*) di uova.

11. Compro _____ (*a slice*) di formaggio.

12. Mi occorre _____ (*a meter*) di stoffa.

2

Articles

Articles in Italian, just as in English, refer to something known and specific.

Mi piace **il** gatto. *I like **the** cat.*

Articles can be definite, indefinite, and partitive. In this chapter you will learn about the different types of articles, their genders, and numbers.

Definite articles

In Italian the definite article has seven forms for the equivalent of *the* in English. In addition, the definite article in Italian is used in many places where it is omitted in English.

masculine singular	masculine plural	feminine singular	feminine plural
il libro	**i** libri	**la** macchina	**le** macchine
lo zio	**gli** zii	**l'**oca	**le** oche
l'amico	**gli** amici		

Also unlike English, the definite article in Italian must be used with all general nouns (**la casa**, *the house*), abstract nouns (**la speranza**, *hope*), and titles (**il signor Giovanni**, *Mr. Giovanni*).

La speranza è l'ultima a morire. *Hope is the last to die.*
Il signor De Pietro viaggia molto. *Mr. De Pietro travels a lot.*

Gender and number of the definite articles

In Italian the definite article agrees in gender and number with the noun. There are two singular masculine forms of the definite article and one singular feminine form. In addition, there are two plural masculine forms and one plural feminine form of the definite article.

masculine singular		masculine plural	
il		i	
lo		gli	
l'		gli	

il ragazzo	*the boy*	**i** ragazzi	*the boys*
lo zio	*the uncle*	**gli** zii	*the uncles*
l'inverno	*the winter*	**gli** inverni	*the winters*

The definite article **il** is used with masculine words beginning with a consonant, **i** is used for the plural forms of those words. For example: **il ristorante, i ristoranti.** Use **lo** (singular) or **gli** (plural) with nouns that begin with:

- s + a consonant

lo studente	*the student*	**gli** studenti	*the students*
lo sceriffo	*the sheriff*	**gli** sceriffi	*the sheriffs*

- z

lo zaino	*the backpack*	**gli** zaini	*the backpacks*

- ps, gn

lo psicologo	*the psychologist*	**gli** psicologi	*the psychologists*
lo gnomo	*the gnome*	**gli** gnomi	*the gnomes*

- y

lo yogurt	*the yogurt*	**gli** yogurt	*the yogurts*

- a vowel, in which case the article **lo** loses the vowel **-o** and becomes **l'**

l'amico	*the friend*	**gli** amici	*the friends*

The definite article **la** is used with feminine words beginning with a consonant. Use **le** with feminine words in the plural.

feminine singular		feminine plural	
la		*le*	
la mamma	*the mother*	le mamme	*the mothers*
la casa	*the house, home*	le case	*the houses, homes*
la pensione	*the pension*	le pensioni	*the pensions*

If the article is followed by a noun starting with a vowel, **la** loses the **-a** and becomes **l'**. This is true only in the singular form.

feminine singular		feminine plural	
la		*le*	
l'ombra	*the shadow*	le ombre	*the shadows*
l'amica	*the girlfriend*	le amiche	*the girlfriends*
l'ora	*the hour*	le ore	*the hours*

In Italian there are some rules regarding when to use definite articles:

• Omit definite articles when addressing someone directly.

Buon giorno, Signor Giovanni.   *Good morning, Mr. Giovanni.*

• Use definite articles with names of languages unless the language follows the verb **parlare** or the prepositions **di** (*of*) or **in** (*in*).

Lui parla bene l'italiano.	*He speaks Italian well.*
Parlo italiano.	*I speak Italian.*
È un libro **di** francese.	*It is a French book.*

• Use definite articles with geographical terms such as names of continents, countries, large islands, regions, seas, oceans, rivers, lakes, and mountains.

Il Garda è molto bello.	*Lake Garda is very beautiful.*
Il Pacifico è un grande oceano.	*The Pacific is a big ocean.*
L'America è un grande paese.	*America is a large country.*
La Sicilia è un'isola italiana.	*Sicily is an Italian island.*

• Definite articles are omitted when the name of the continent, island, country, and so on is preceded by the preposition **in** or **di**.

Sono **in** America.   *I am **in** America.*

La capitale **d'**Italia è Roma.   *The capital **of** Italy is Rome.*

- However, definite articles are used with **di** and **in** when the name of a continent, island, or country is masculine.

La capitale **del** Canadà è Ottawa.   *The capital **of** Canada is Ottawa.*

- Definite articles are used when **di** means *than* in comparative expressions such as **più... di**. (Comparative expressions will be discussed further in Chapter 7.)

La Francia è più grande **della** Svizzera.   *France is bigger **than** Switzerland.*

L'Italia è più piccola **della** Germania.   *Italy is smaller **than** Germany.*

- In sentences using **andare in** or **andare a**, omit the definite article with singular names or when the name of a country is not qualified by an adjective. A definite article is used if the noun is plural, however.

Il mese scorso **sono andato in** Europa.   *Last month **I went to** Europe.*

L'anno prossimo **andrò a** San Francisco.   *Next year **I will go to** San Francisco.*

Il mese scorso **sono andato negli** Stati Uniti.   *Last month **I went to the** United States.*

Exercise 19

Fill in the blanks with the correct definite articles or prepositions.

1. _____ Australia è il continente il più piccolo.

2. Io conosco bene _____ bella Firenze.

3. Io vado spesso _____ Italia.

4. L'Italia è _____ Europa.

5. Le strade _____ America sono immense.

6. Madrid è _____ capitale _____ Spagna.

7. _____ seta cinese è molto famosa.

8. Mia nonna vive _____ America.

9. Mia nonna è _____ Stati Uniti.

10. I canguri vivono _____ Australia.

11. La casa di Giovanni è _____ Svizzera.

There are a few rules for when definite articles are always omitted:

- Do not use a definite article with singular nouns of family members and relatives preceded by a possessive adjective (**mio, mia,** etc.), except with **loro.** In the plural forms, the article must be used, however.

<table>
<tr><td>**Mia** sorella è bella.</td><td>*My sister is beautiful.*</td></tr>
<tr><td>**Le mie** sorelle sono belle.</td><td>*My sisters are beautiful.*</td></tr>
<tr><td>Come si chiama **tuo** fratello?</td><td>*What is **your** brother's name?*</td></tr>
<tr><td>Come si chiamano **i tuoi** fratelli?</td><td>*What are **your** brothers' names?*</td></tr>
</table>

- Do not use definite articles with proper nouns if the noun is not preceded by a qualifying adjective.

<table>
<tr><td>Ho visto **Maria.**</td><td>*I saw Maria.*</td></tr>
<tr><td>Ho visto **la** bella Maria.</td><td>*I saw beautiful Maria.*</td></tr>
</table>

- Do not use definite articles with a man's last name.

<table>
<tr><td>Ho visto **Marchi.**</td><td>*I saw Marchi.*</td></tr>
</table>

- Do not use definite articles with the last name of famous men.

<table>
<tr><td>**Manzoni** è stato un gran scrittore e poeta.</td><td>*Manzoni was a great writer and poet.*</td></tr>
</table>

- Do not use definite articles with names of cities.

<table>
<tr><td>**Venezia, Roma,** e **Firenze** sono città molto belle.</td><td>*Venice, Florence, and Rome are very beautiful cities.*</td></tr>
</table>

Exceptions to this rule are **La Spezia, L'Aquila, l'Avana, la Mecca,** and **la Valletta.** In these cases, the articles are part of the nouns.

- Do not use a definite article with names of small islands.

    Tahiti è un'isola tropicale.   *Tahiti is a tropical island.*

Exceptions to this rule are the names of some islands in the Mediterranean Sea and some groups of islands such as: **l'Elba, il Giglio, le Eolie, le Canarie, la Corsica, le Antille,** and **le Bahama.**

Exercise 20

Fill in the blanks with the correct forms of the definite articles when necessary.

1. _____ miei nonni sono italiani.
2. Maria va al cinema con _____ sua amica.
3. _____ suo zio non vuole viaggiare.
4. _____ loro zii non vogliono viaggiare.
5. Roberto gioca con _____ nostro fratello.
6. Roberto gioca con _____ nostri fratelli.
7. _____ tue sorelle hanno tanti libri da leggere.
8. _____ tuoi genitori hanno l'aspetto giovane.
9. _____ vostre zie non vivono più a Chicago.
10. _____ miei parenti vivono a Chicago.
11. _____ mia madre lavora sempre.
12. Tutte _____ madri lavorano molto.

There are still more rules to learn about definite articles. Use them:

- with possessive adjectives when a singular noun of a close family member is expressed as a diminutive

    Sara è **la mia** sorellina.   *Sara is **my** little sister.*

- with expressions of time

    Sono **le** sei e venti.   *It is twenty past six.*
    La settimana prossima andiamo   *Next week we'll go camping.*
        al campeggio.

- with proper nouns preceded by a common noun or an adjective

Il marchese Enrico IV ha visitato il Vaticano.	*Marquis Henry the IV visited the Vatican.*
La cara Giovanna mi chiama spesso.	*Dear Giovanna calls me often.*

- when using a last name to refer to a family or to a husband and wife

Ci hanno telefonato i Fortina.	*The Fortinas called us.*

- when referring to a woman by her last name

La Maffei è una brava professoressa.	*Maffei is a good professor.*

- with nicknames

Il Caravaggio è molto conosciuto.	*Caravaggio is very well known.*

- with nouns denoting parts of the body, clothing, and belongings (In these sentences English uses the possessive, but Italian does not follow the same pattern.)

Il ragazzo ha le gambe lunghe e magre.	*The boy has long and skinny legs.*
Mi lavo le mani.	*I wash my hands.*
Ho perso la borsa.	*I lost my purse.*

- with nouns expressing illnesses

la tosse	*cough*
il raffreddore	*cold*
l'influenza	*flu*
la pressione alta	*high blood pressure*

However, the definite article is not used when expressing aches and pains.

Ho mal di testa.	*I have a headache.*
Ha mal di denti.	*She has a toothache.*
Hai mal di schiena.	*You have a backache.*

Exercise 21

Fill in the blanks with the correct forms of the definite articles when necessary.

1. _____ due fratellini camminavano tenendosi per mano.

2. Sono _____ sette e dobbiamo andare a scuola.

3. _____ signori Di Pietro ci hanno chiesto se vogliamo andare al cinema con loro.

4. _____ Di Pietro ci hanno invitati a cena.

5. _____ Collodi ha scritto la storia di Pinocchio.

6. Ci si deve lavare _____ mani prima di toccare il cibo.

7. _____ mia borsa è stata rubata al mercato.

8. Sono a casa dal lavoro per tutta la settimana perché ho _____ influenza.

9. In inverno è facile prendere _____ raffreddore.

10. Ho spesso _____ mal di testa.

11. È andato dal dentista perché aveva _____ mal di denti.

12. _____ settimana prossima andremo a comprare _____ stivali per _____ inverno.

13. Quando finisco di giocare al tennis, mi fanno male _____ gambe.

The definite article is not used with several common expressions that include the prepositions **a**, **da**, **in**, and **per**.

a casa	*at home*
a destra	*to the right*
a piedi	*by foot*
a scuola	*to/at school*
a tavola	*at the table*
a teatro	*to/at the theater*
a sinistra	*to the left*
da casa	*from home*
in aereo	*by plane*
in biblioteca	*to/at the library*
in bicicletta	*by bicycle*
in campagna	*to/in the country*
in cantina	*to/in the cellar*
in casa	*at home*
in chiesa	*to/in church*

in città	*in town*
in giardino	*in the garden*
in macchina	*by car*
in montagna	*to/in the mountains*
in piazza	*in the square*
in pigiama	*in (wearing) pajamas*
in treno	*by train*
per terra	*on the floor; on the ground*
per via aerea	*by airmail*

When referring to a specific place, a definite article is used.

Oggi pomeriggio andiamo **alla** chiesa di San Paolo Fuori dalle Mura.	*This afternoon we'll go **to the** Church of Saint Paul Outside the Walls.*
I ragazzi vanno **alla** scuola di via Muratti.	*The boys go **to the** school on Muratti Street.*

The definite article is not used before **cento** (*one hundred*) and **mille** (*one thousand*).

Ho solo **cento** euro.	*I have only **one hundred** euros.*
Ci sono **mille** persone in quella sala.	*There are **a thousand** people in that hall.*

Exercise 22

Translate the following sentences into Italian.

1. Last night we went to the theater.

_____.

2. She went shopping by foot.

_____.

3. My dog is at home.

_____.

4. I like to go to school by bicycle.

_____.

5. I sent the letter by airmail.

_____.

6. There are one hundred students at this school.

_____.

7. She has planted many flowers in the garden.

_____.

8. He likes to go to the library.

_____.

9. There are many papers on the ground.

_____.

10. There are many people in church.

_____.

11. Every weekend we drive in the country.

_____.

12. We travel by car.

_____.

Exercise 23

Fill in the blanks with the appropriate definite articles.

1. _____ ragazzo è intelligente e studioso.
2. _____ occhi di Lisa sono verdi.
3. _____ suoi occhi sono molto belli.
4. _____ studenti in Italia portano _____ zaino a casa tutti i giorni.
5. _____ zaini dei soldati sono molto pesanti.
6. _____ gnomo è nelle favole per bambini.
7. _____ yogurt di frutta fa bene alla salute.
8. _____ amico di Giovanni abita a Roma.
9. _____ amici di Giovanni vanno in montagna tutti _____ anni.
10. _____ persone anziane prendono _____ pensione.
11. Mi siedo sotto _____ ombra degli alberi.

Exercise 24

The following sentences tell what Pietro does in the morning. Circle the correct definite article in each sentence.

1. La/Le mattina beve lo/il cappuccino.

2. Legge la/il giornale.

3. Prende la/il valigetta.

4. Saluta il/lo figlio e la/l' moglie.

5. Compra lo/il biglietto dell'autobus.

6. Aspetta lo/l' autobus.

7. Saluta i/le colleghi di lavoro.

8. Accende il/lo computer.

9. Legge la/le posta elettronica.

10. Manda i/gli messaggi.

11. Parla con il/lo suo capo.

12. Prepara la/le relazione.

13. Invita a pranzo il/i clienti.

14. Passa il/lo pomeriggio in riunioni.

15. Ritorna a casa tardi con lo/il lavoro da finire.

Exercise 25

Fill in the blanks with the correct forms of the definite articles.

1. A colazione _____ italiani bevono solo _____ caffè.

2. _____ italiani bevono _____ cappuccino solo alla mattina.

3. Prima di pranzare molti italiani prendono _____ aperitivo al bar.

4. In estate molti italiani mangiano _____ melone con _____ prosciutto.

5. Gli italiani prima mangiano _____ pasta e poi _____ carne e alla fine _____ insalata.

6. Alle 17,00 _____ bambini fanno _____ merenda.

7. A tutti _____ italiani piacciono _____ spaghetti.

8. Con _____ pesce bevono _____ vino bianco.

9. A Capodanno _____ italiani bevono _____ spumante.

10. In agosto tutti vanno in vacanza con _____ famiglia.

11. _____ italiani prendono _____ ferie e vanno al mare o in montagna.

12. Alla sera si rilassano e guardano _____ televisione.

13. Alla domenica guardano _____ partite di football.

Definite articles in combination with prepositions

The definite articles can sometimes be combined with some simple prepositions to form new single words. (You will study the prepositions and their uses in Chapter 4.) For example: **di + il** becomes **del**. The meaning remains the same, but the word becomes a contraction of the two. The following table shows how these new words look.

	di of	*a* at; to	*da* from; at	*in* in	*con* with	*su* on
singular						
il	del	al	dal	nel	con il (col)	sul
lo	dello	allo	dallo	nello	con lo (collo)	sullo
la	della	alla	dalla	nella	con la (colla)	sulla
l'	dell'	all'	dall'	nell'	con l' (coll')	sull'
plural						
i	dei	ai	dai	nei	con i (coi)	sui
gli	degli	agli	dagli	negli	con gli (cogli)	sugli
le	delle	alle	dalle	nelle	con le (colle)	sulle

Exercise 26

Fill in the blanks with the correct forms of the combined prepositions for the sentences below.

1. Ho bisogno _____ chiavi della scrivania.

2. Oggi andiamo _____ zio Giovanni.

3. Mio fratello è andato _____ stadio.

4. Siamo andati in viaggio _____ zii.

5. Sabato sera andremo _____ cinema.

6. La lezione finisce _____ sette.

7. La palestra _____ scuola è molto grande.

8. Il libro di italiano è _____ tavolo.

9. Sono in macchina _____ mattina _____ sera.

10. Maria ha comprato il pollo _____ macellaio.

11. Tutti i venerdì vado _____ mercato a comprare la frutta.

12. Gli americani vivono _____ Stati Uniti.

Indefinite articles

The Italian indefinite articles correspond to the English *a/an* and also to *one*. Indefinite articles refer to nonspecific persons or things. There are four indefinite articles in Italian: two masculine—**un, uno**—and two feminine—**un', una**. Indefinite articles are used before singular nouns.

un gatto	*a cat*
uno scoiattolo	*a squirrel*
un'ombra	*a shadow*
una pianta	*a plant*

Indefinite articles are also used before accompanying adjectives as in:

un bel gatto	*a **nice** cat*
una bella pianta	*a **beautiful** plant*

In Italian indefinite articles are affected by the gender and spelling of the nouns or adjectives that follow them. **Un** (*a, an*) is used before masculine nouns and adjectives beginning with most consonants and vowels.

un aereo	*a plane*
un amico	*a friend*
un bambino	*a child*

Vedo **il** cane.	*I see* the *dog*. (specific)
Vedo **un** cane.	*I see* a *dog*. (vague)

Uno (*a, an*) is used before masculine nouns starting with s + a consonant, **ps, z, y, gn**, and a few French words used in Italian, starting with **ch**.

uno studente	*a student*
uno sciopero	*a strike*
uno psicologo	*a psychologist*
uno zio	*an uncle*
uno yogurt	*a yogurt*
uno gnomo	*a gnome*
uno chalet	*a chalet*

Sono andato da **uno ps**icologo.	*I went to a psychologist.*
A colazione ho mangiato **uno** yogurt.	*For breakfast I ate a yogurt.*
Ho affittato **uno ch**alet a Cortina d'Ampezzo.	*I rented a chalet in Cortina d'Ampezzo.*

Indefinite articles are not used before nouns referring to occupations or religions.

| Sono **dottore**. | *I am a doctor.* |
| Mario è **cattolico**. | *Mario is a Catholic.* |

Also omit indefinite articles in exclamations and before **mezzo**(-a).

Che vergogna!	*What a shame!*
Che bella ragazza!	*What a beautiful girl!*
Vorrei **mezzo** litro di vino rosso.	*I would like half a liter of red wine.*

The indefinite article is used if the noun is preceded by an adjective.

| È **un bravo** professore. | *He is a good professor.* |
| È **una devota** cattolica. | *She is a devoted Catholic.* |

Exercise 27

Translate the following nouns into Italian using the indefinite articles.

1. a dog _____

2. a pharmacy _____

3. a hotel _____

4. a car _____

5. a park _____

6. a city square _____

7. a museum _____

8. a clock _____

9. a plant _____

10. a suitcase _____

Exercise 28

Translate the words into Italian giving the definite and indefinite articles and placing them in the proper columns.

> house, table, museum, book, wife, evening, family, letter, lawyer, architect, backpack, zoo

	definite article	indefinite article
1.	_____	_____
2.	_____	_____
3.	_____	_____
4.	_____	_____
5.	_____	_____
6.	_____	_____
7.	_____	_____
8.	_____	_____
9.	_____	_____
10.	_____	_____
11.	_____	_____
12.	_____	_____

Partitive articles

A partitive article (*some, any*) expresses an indeterminate part of the noun it precedes. In Italian a partitive article is formed by combining the preposition **di** + a definite article. Note that **di** becomes de before forming a contraction. Sometimes the partitive article **di** is part of an expression: **un po' di** (*some*), **un certo numero di** (*some*), **una certa quantità di** (*some*).

Mi occorre **della** (un po' di) farina.	*I need **some** flour.*
Aggiungi **della** (una certa quantità di) farina alla pasta.	*Add **some** flour to the dough.*
Vuoi che prepari **dei** (un certo numero di) panini?	*Would you like me to prepare **some** sandwiches?*

The following list shows when to use the various partitive articles:

- **del.** Use with masculine nouns starting with consonants other than **ps**, **gn**, **z**, **s** + consonant, or a vowel.

    del pane   *some bread*

- **dello.** Use with masculine singular nouns beginning with **ps**, **gn**, **z**, or **s** + consonant.

    dello zucchero   *some sugar*

- **dell'.** Use with any singular masculine noun starting with a vowel.

    dell'orzo   *some barley*

- **della.** Use with feminine singular nouns beginning with a consonant.

    della frutta   *some fruit*

- **dell'.** Use with any singular feminine noun starting with a vowel.

    dell'acqua   *some water*

- **dei.** Use with masculine plural nouns starting with consonants other than **ps**, **gn**, **z**, or **s** + consonant.

    dei polli   *some chickens*

- **degli.** Use with masculine plural nouns starting with **ps**, **gn**, **z**, or **s** + consonant.

    degli aeroplani   *some airplanes*

- **delle.** Use with feminine plural nouns.

      delle scarpe   *some shoes*

Partitive articles are repeated before each noun in a sentence.

Mangiamo **del** pesce, **dell'**insalata, **dei** fagiolini e **delle** patate.	*We'll eat some fish, salad, green beans, and potatoes.*
Volete **del** caffè o **del** tè?	*Do you want some coffee or tea?*
No, vogliamo **della** cioccolata calda.	*No, we would like some hot chocolate.*

Exercise 29

The following sentences tell what Mrs. Bassani is doing while shopping. Translate the sentences into Italian using the partitive articles where needed.

1. She puts some money in the wallet.

_____.

2. She buys some bread rolls.

_____.

3. She buys some whole wheat bread, breadsticks, and cookies for breakfast.

_____.

4. Then, Mrs. Bassani goes to the butcher shop.

_____.

5. The Bassanis do not eat much meat.

_____.

6. She buys some veal.

_____.

7. She buys some asparagus, carrots, peas, and potatoes.

_____.

8. She goes in the bar and orders a cup of coffee.

_____.

9. She wants some sugar and milk.

_____.

10. Before leaving she buys some pastries.

_____.

11. She goes to the bank to get some money.

_____.

12. She goes home to cook.

_____.

13. When she arrives home she remembers that she was supposed to buy some stamps.

_____.

Partitive articles are usually omitted in negative sentences.

Non leggono mai (**dei**) libri.	*They never read (**any**) books.*
Non hanno (**dei**) francobolli.	*They don't have (**any**) stamps.*

Partitive articles are also omitted in interrogative sentences.

Cercano (**dei**) libri di avventura?	*Are they looking for (**some**) action books?*
Avete (**dei**) soldi?	*Do you have (**any**) money?*

A contraction of **di** + the article may be used in place of terms that are in the plural such as **alcuni(-e)**.

Vorrei **alcuni** CD di musica italiana.	*I would like **some** CDs of Italian music.*
Vorrei **dei** CD di musica italiana.	*I would like **some** CDs of Italian music.*
Vorrei vedere **alcune** fotografie della tua famiglia.	*I would like to see **some** pictures of your family.*
Vorrei vedere **delle** fotografie della tua famiglia.	*I would like to see **some** pictures of your family.*
Sono andata ad **alcune** conferenze.	*I went to **some** lectures.*
Sono andata a **delle** conferenze.	*I went to **some** lectures.*
Ho comprato dei libri per **alcuni** amici.	*I bought some books for **some** friends.*
Ho comprato dei libri per **degli amici**.	*I bought some books for **some** friends.*

Partitive articles are also used in place of **qualche** (*some*), which is always followed by a singular noun or adjective, even if it expresses a plural concept. Both **alcuni(-e)** and **qualche** are used only when *some* or *any* mean *several* and not when *some* or *any* mean *a little*. They are used with nouns that are quantifiable. In this case **un po' di** (*a little*) is used, especially with food terms.

Compriamo **qualche** pasta per i bambini.	*Let's buy **some** pastries for the children.*
Compriamo **alcune** paste per i bambini.	*Let's buy **some** pastries for the children.*
Vorrei **un po' di** pane.	*I would like **some** (**a little**) bread.*

The adjective **nessuno** (*nobody*) may replace the partitive article in a negative sentence but only when followed by a singular noun.

Non c'è **nessun** posto libero nello stadio.	*There are **no** free seats in the stadium.*
Non ci sono **dei** posti liberi nello stadio.	*There are **no** free seats in the stadium.*
Non c'è **nessuna** casa libera al momento.	*There is **no** available home at the moment.*
Non ci sono **delle** case libere al momento.	*There are **no** available homes at the moment.*

Exercise 30

Fill in the blanks with the correct partitive in parentheses.

1. Lara dammi _____ (alcuno, un po' di, qualche) pepe, per favore.

2. Non avevano _____ (alcuna, nessuna, qualche) busta abbastanza grande.

3. Mio marito ha bevuto _____ (del, qualche, alcuno) buon vino rosso.

4. Compro _____ (qualche, della, alcuna) bottiglia di acqua minerale per mia figlia.

5. Nell'album c'erano _____ (qualche, alcune, un po' di) fotografie molto vecchie.

6. Questo negozio non ha _____ (alcune, delle, un po' di) belle cose.

7. Ho dato _____ (alcuno, un po' di, dei) libri alla mia amica.

8. Giovanna, mi compri _____ (alcuno, dei, qualche) francobolli?

9. Marco dipinge sempre _____ (alcuno, dei, qualche) bei quadri.

10. Portami _____ (alcuni, qualche, un po' di) pacchetti di mastica.

11. Vorrei comprare _____ (alcuna, qualche, della) frutta.

12. A pranzo preferisco mangiare _____ (qualche, alcuna, dell') insalata.

13. Ogni mattina prendo _____ (qualche, alcune, un po' di) vitamine.

14. Non c'è _____ (nessuno, nessuna, nessuni) allo stadio.

15. Non ho visto _____ (nessuno, nessuna, nessun) bel film quest'anno.

3

Pronouns

While adjectives precede or follow the noun, pronouns are used in place of the noun. There are many types of pronouns: subject pronouns, direct and indirect object pronouns, demonstrative pronouns, possessive pronouns, disjunctive pronouns, reflexive pronouns, relative pronouns, and indefinite pronouns. This chapter will cover all of them and their various uses.

Personal pronouns

Personal pronouns are used in place of a subject noun and refer to specific people, objects, or animals. In Italian there are five types of personal pronouns: subject, direct object, indirect object, disjunctive or stressed pronouns, and reflexive.

Subject pronouns

Subject pronouns refer to the subject of a sentence.

io	*I*
tu	*you* (sing.)
lui	*he*
lei	*she*
Lei	*you* (formal sing., m. or f.)
noi	*we*
voi	*you* (pl.)
loro	*they* (informal pl., m. or f.)
Loro	*you* (formal pl.)

Italian has four ways to express the English term *you*. The informal subject pronouns **tu** (sing.) and **voi** (pl.) are used for relatives, friends, children, and animals. The formal pronouns **Lei** (sing.) and **Loro** (pl.) are used for strangers, acquaintances, and older people.

49

Subject pronouns are often omitted in Italian, because for the most part, the verb endings and other references within the sentence reveal the subject.

Con chi **parlate**?	*With whom **are you speaking**?*
Parliamo con i nostri amici.	*We **are speaking** with our friends.*

Subject pronouns are used in the following situations:

- To place emphasis on the subject. Even more emphasis can be given to the subject by using **stesso(-a/-i/-e)**. This word agrees with the subject in gender and number and can precede or follow the verb.

Tu hai mangiato tutto.	***You** ate everything.*
Hai detto **tu stesso** che non era un bel film.	*You said it **yourself**, that the movie was not good.*

- To contrast two different subjects

Noi siamo italiani, **voi** siete francesi.	*We are Italians, you are French.*

- To avoid ambiguity or possible confusion. It is especially necessary to use the subject pronoun with the singular form of the subjunctive tense, when the verb endings are identical. Otherwise there would be confusion.

Voglio che **tu** vada con tua figlia.	*I want **you** to go with your daughter.*

- When there is no verb

Come stai? Bene, e **tu**?	*How are you? Fine and **you**?*

- After **nemmeno** (*neither*), **anche** (*also, too*), **neanche** (*not even*), and **neppure** (*not even*)

Mangi **anche tu**?	*Do **you** eat, too?*

- After the relevant verb form. In English a disjunctive pronoun is used with *is* or *was*.

Avete chiamato **voi** l'ambulanza?	*Was it **you** who called the ambulance?*
No, sono stati **loro**.	*No, it was **them**.*

- When the subject pronoun stands alone

Vuoi aiutare tua madre? Chi, **io**?   *Do you want to help your mother? Who **me**?*

The following subject pronouns are almost exclusively used in written Italian, but it is important to be familiar with them.

masculine		feminine	
egli	*he*	ella	*she*
esso	*he; it*	essa	*she; it*
essi	*they*	esse	*they*

Exercise 31

Translate the sentences into Italian using or omitting the subject pronouns as necessary.

1. What did you (sing.) see?

_____?

2. I saw the solar eclipse.

_____.

3. Did you (sing.) see it, too?

_____.

4. No, I did not see it.

_____.

5. They are Chinese, and we are Indians.

_____.

6. Do you (sing.) want to buy the tickets?

_____?

7. He works a lot, she sleeps a lot.

_____.

8. I made this sweater.

_____.

9. They talk about the elections.

_____.

Direct object pronouns

A direct object pronoun receives the action of the verb in a sentence. Direct object pronouns can only be used with transitive verbs, however. These are verbs that answer the questions *what?* or *whom?* Verbs that do not take a direct object pronoun are called intransitive verbs. These are verbs of motion or of a state of being, such as **andare**, *to go*; **arrivare**, *to arrive*; **essere**, *to be*. The direct object pronoun replaces the direct object noun in a sentence.

Leggo il **libro**.	*I read the **book**.* (direct object noun)
Lo leggo.	*I read **it**.* (direct object pronoun)

The forms of the direct object pronoun in Italian are as follows:

singular		**plural**	
mi	*me*	ci	*us*
ti	*you* (informal)	vi	*you* (informal)
lo	*him; it*	li	*them* (m.)
la	*her; it*	le	*them* (f.)

The direct object pronoun is usually placed immediately before a conjugated verb. In a negative sentence the word **non** is placed before the direct object pronoun.

Exercise 32

Fill in the blanks with the appropriate direct object pronouns.

1. Carlo, mangi la carne? Sì, _____ mangio.

2. Dov'è la rivista? Non _____ vedo.

3. Domani invito i miei amici. Domani _____ invito.

4. Vincenzo beve la birra. _____ beve.

5. Invito Mario a pranzo. _____ invito.

6. Perché non leggi il libro? Perché non _____ leggi?

7. Capisco la lezione. _____ capisco.

8. Non capisco la lezione. Non _____ capisco.

9. Ripeto le frasi. _____ ripeto.

10. Guardiamo le stelle. _____ guardiamo.

11. Scrivete le lettere. _____ scrivete.

12. Parlano bene l'italiano. _____ parlano bene.

13. Guardano voi. _____ guardano.

The direct object pronoun can also be attached to the end of the verb infinitive. In this case the final **-e** of the infinitive is dropped.

È importante studiare **la geografia**.	*It is important to study **geography**.*
È importante studiar**la**.	*It is important to study **it**.*
È impossibile vedere i miei **amici**.	*It is impossible to see my **friends**.*
È impossibile veder**li**.	*It is impossible to see **them**.*

When the infinitive is preceded by **dovere**, **potere**, or **volere**, the direct object pronoun may either precede the verb or be attached to the infinitive (after dropping the **-e** of the infinitive).

Voglio pulir**lo** bene.	*I want to clean **it** well.*
Lo voglio pulire bene.	*I want to clean **it** well.*
Devo invitar**li** a cena.	*I have to invite **them** for dinner.*
Li devo invitare a cena.	*I have to invite **them** for dinner.*

Exercise 33

Replace the underlined noun in each sentence with a direct object pronoun by using both methods discussed above.

1. Voglio vedere l'opera.

   Voglio _____.

   _____ voglio vedere.

2. Devi leggere il giornale.

   Devi _____.

   _____ devi leggere.

3. Lui può comprare la macchina.

   Può _____.

   _____ può comprare.

4. Lei vuole comprare la pianta.

Vuole _____.

_____ vuole comprare.

5. Dobbiamo guardare i bambini.

Dobbiamo _____.

_____ dobbiamo guardare.

6. Devi pulire i vetri.

Devi _____.

_____ devi pulire.

7. Devono leggere i giornali.

Devono _____.

_____ devono leggere.

8. Dovresti vedere il film.

Dovresti _____.

_____ dovresti vedere.

9. Dovrei scrivere le lettere.

Dovrei _____.

_____ dovrei scrivere.

10. Non vuole bere il latte.

Non vuole _____.

Non _____ vuole bere.

Direct object pronouns can also be attached to the word **ecco** to express *here*: **eccomi** (*here I am*), **eccoti** (*here you are*), **eccolo** (*here he is*), **eccola** (*here she is*), and so on. However, with impersonal expressions such as: è **importante** (*it is important*), è **possibile** (*it is possible*), è **magnifico** (*it is wonderful*), and so on, the direct object pronoun can only be attached to the infinitive.

Dov'è tua **figlia? Eccola!**	*Where is your **daughter? Here she is!***
Dov'è il **portafoglio? Eccolo!**	*Where is the **wallet? Here it is!***
È importante **studiare i verbi.**	*It is important **to study the verbs.***
È importante **studiarli.**	*It is important **to study them.***

Exercise 34

Fill in the blanks using the correct forms of the direct object pronouns.

1. Dov'è il cane? _____! (*Here it is!*)

2. Dove sono i negozi? _____! (*Here they are!*)

3. Dov'è la scuola? _____! (*Here it is!*)

4. Dove sei? _____! (*Here you are!*)

5. Dove sei? _____! (*Here I am!*)

6. Dove siete? _____! (*Here we are!*)

7. È importante firmare la carta di credito. È importante _____.

8. È possibile cantare la canzone. È possibile _____.

9. È importante studiare la geometria. È importante _____.

10. È meraviglioso vedere le Olimpiadi. È meraviglioso _____.

In compound tenses conjugated with **avere** (*to have*), the past participle agrees in gender and number with the direct object pronouns **lo, la, le, li**. Agreement with **mi, ti, ci, vi** is optional.

Hai spedito **le lettere?**	*Have you mailed **the letters?***
Sì, **le** ho già spedite.	*Yes, I have already mailed **them.***
Avete ascoltato **i CD?**	*Have you listened to **the CDs?***
Sì, **li** abbiamo ascoltati ieri.	*Yes, we listened to **them** yesterday.*

When an infinitive follows a conjugated form of the verbs **fare** (*to do; make*), **lasciare** (*to leave*), **ascoltare** (*to listen*), **guardare** (*to look*), **sentire** (*to hear, listen*), or **vedere** (*to see*), the direct object pronoun precedes the conjugated verb.

La sento suonare il piano tutti i giorni.	*I hear **her** playing the piano every day.*
Li vedo partire.	*I see **them** leaving.*

Position of direct object pronouns with commands. With commands, direct object pronouns are positioned in the following ways:

- With affirmative commands using the familiar form, direct object pronouns usually follow and are attached to the verb.

Compra il **pane**!	*Buy **the bread**!*
Compra**lo**!	*Buy **it**!*
Leggi **i libri**!	*Read **the books**!*
Leggi**li**!	*Read **them**!*

- With negative familiar commands, direct object pronouns may either precede or follow the verb.

Non comprare **la pasta**!	*Do not buy **pasta**!*
Non comprar**la**!	*Do not buy **it**!*
Non **la** comprare!	*Do not buy **it**!*

- With affirmative and negative formal commands (**Lei, Loro**), the direct object pronouns can only precede the verb.

Signora Lolli, prenda **il caffè**!	*Mrs. Lolli, have a **cup of coffee**!*
Signora Lolli, **lo** prenda!	*Mrs. Lolli, take **it**!*
Signorina Geli, metta **le scarpe** nuove!	*Miss Geli, put the **new shoes** on!*
Signorina Geli, **le** metta!	*Miss Geli, put **them** on!*

- If the command consists of a single syllable verb, such as **da', va', di** (or **di'**), **fa'**, or **sta'**, the initial consonant of the direct object pronoun in the second person singular (**tu**) form is doubled, except with **gli**.

Da' un pezzo di pane a Gino.	*Give a piece of bread to Gino.*
Dallo a Gino.	*Give **it** to Gino.*
Fa' gli auguri a Giovanni.	*Wish Giovanni Happy Birthday!*
	*(**Give my best wishes to Giovanni**!)*
Fagli gli auguri.	***Wish him** Happy Birthday!*
	*(**Give him** my best!)*

- When verbs have more than one syllable, direct object pronouns can be attached to the first person plural command (**noi** form) in the affirmative. Direct object pronouns usually come before the verb in the negative form, but they also have the option of being attached to the end of the verb.

Scriviamo**la**!	*Let's write **it**!*
Non **la** scriviamo!	*Let's not write **it**!*
Non scriviamo**la**!	*Let's not write **it**!*

Exercise 35

Translate the sentences into Italian using the appropriate forms of the direct object pronouns.

1. I have not bought it.

_____.

2. Laura has read them (f., pl.).

_____.

3. Laura has not read them (f., pl.).

_____.

4. Don't buy them (m., pl.)!

_____!

5. I mailed them (f.) yesterday.

_____.

6. We did not study them (m., pl.).

_____.

7. She lets him go.

_____.

8. I watch her from the window.

_____.

9. I have someone make it (m.).

_____.

10. Mrs. Fanti, finish them (m., pl.)!

_____!

Exercise 36

Translate the sentences into Italian.

1. Give it (m., sing.) to Maria!

_____!

2. Go to get it (f., sing.)!

_____!

3. Do it (m., sing.) well!

_____!

4. Give them (m., pl.) to Luigi!

_____!

5. Say it (m., sing.) aloud!

_____!

6. Let Giovanna see it (m., sing.)!

_____!

7. Give them (m., pl.) to Pietro!

_____!

8. Let's give it (m., sing.) to Maria!

_____!

9. Let's go to get it (m., sing.)!

_____!

10. Let's write them (f., pl.)!

_____!

Indirect object pronouns

Indirect object pronouns answer the question **a chi?** (*to whom?*) or **per chi?** (*for whom?*). In English the prepositions *to*, *for*, and *from* are often omitted in this construction, but in Italian **a** (*to*) is almost always used before the indirect object noun, making it easy to spot in a sentence. The indirect object pronoun replaces the indirect object noun and omits the prepositions *to* (**a**), *for* (**per**), and *from* (**da**). The indirect object pronouns in Italian are as follows:

singular		**plural**	
mi	*to/for me*	ci	*to/for us*
ti	*to/for you* (informal, sing.)	vi	*to/for you* (pl.)
Le	*to/for you* (formal, m. or f.)	Loro	*to/for you* (formal, pl.)
gli	*to/for him*	loro	*to/for them*
le	*to/for her*		

Do il libro nuovo **a Maria**.	*I give the new book **to Maria.***
or	*I give **Maria** the new book.*
Le do il libro nuovo.	*I give **her** the new book.*

Today **gli** is often used in place of **loro,** so it is being used for the singular masculine and for the plural masculine and feminine.

Ho chiesto **loro** di venire con noi.	*I asked **them** to come with us.*
Gli ho chiesto di venire con noi.	*I asked **them** to come with us.*

Just as with direct object pronouns, not all verbs will take an indirect object pronoun. The following list shows some common Italian verbs that take the indirect object pronouns.

assomigliare a	*to resemble*
bastare a	*to be enough*
chiedere a	*to ask*
dare a	*to give*
dire a	*to tell, say*
dispiacere a	*to be sorry*
domandare a	*to ask*
donare a	*to donate*
fare male a	*to hurt*
insegnare a	*to teach*
mandare a	*to send*
mostrare a	*to show*
piacere a	*to like, to be pleasing*
portare a	*to bring*
preparare a	*to prepare*
rassomigliare a	*to resemble*
regalare a	*to give a present*
riportare a	*to bring back*
rispondere a	*to answer*
scrivere a	*to write*
sembrare a	*to appear*
telefonare a	*to call (*telephone*)*
volere bene a	*to love*

Chiedo un favore **a Carla**.	*I ask **Carla** a favor.*
Le chiedo un favore.	*I ask **her** a favor.*
Non rispondo **alla sua lettera**.	*I will not answer **her letter.***
Non **le** rispondo.	*I will not answer **her**.*

Exercise 37

Translate the sentences into Italian.

1. Luigi looks at me.

_____.

2. I wrote him a long letter.

_____.

3. You (sing.) speak to her.

_____.

4. He speaks to them.

_____.

5. Maria writes him a letter.

_____.

6. I send her a gift.

_____.

7. You (sing.) send them a gift.

_____.

8. You (sing.) sent them a gift.

_____.

9. You (sing.) have to send them a gift.

_____.

10. She wants to send her a gift.

_____.

Position of the indirect object pronouns. Indirect object pronouns normally precede a conjugated verb, except for **loro** which follows the verb.

Le mando un invito.	*I send **her** an invitation.*
Gli mando un invito.	*I send **them** an invitation.*

But:

Mando **loro** un invito.	*I send **them** an invitation.*

When indirect object pronouns are attached to the end of an infinitive, the final -e of the infinitive is dropped.

Non ho voglia di parlar**gli**.   *I don't feel like talking to **him**.*

If the infinitive is preceded by a form of **dovere**, **potere**, or **volere**, the indirect object pronoun can either be attached to the infinitive, or can be placed before the conjugated verb.

Devo telefonar**le**.   *I have to call **her**.*

Or:

Le devo telefonare.   *I have to call her.*

In compound tenses the indirect object pronouns precede the auxiliary verb, but they *do not* agree with the past participle as do the direct object pronouns.

Hai visto Maria?   *Have you seen Maria?*
Sì, l'ho vist**a**, ma non **le** ho parlato.   *Yes, I have seen **her**, but I have not spoken to **her**.*

L'ho vista agrees with the direct object pronoun. **Le ho parlato** does not agree with the indirect object pronoun.

Exercise 38

Rewrite the following sentences, replacing the indirect object nouns in parentheses with the corresponding indirect object pronouns.

1. Mando un regalo (al bambino).

_____.

2. Telefoni (alla mamma).

_____.

3. Lui risponde (a Luisa).

_____.

4. Il professore fa una domanda (agli studenti).

_____.

5. Vogliono parlare (al professore).

_____.

6. Pensiamo di telefonare (a Teresa).

_____.

7. Diamo il pacco (alla signora).

_____.

8. Tu scrivi (agli amici).

_____.

9. Lei parla (a Olga).

_____.

10. Lui parla (a Pietro).

_____.

The following verbs take indirect object pronouns, but are only conjugated in two forms. When the subject is singular, the third person singular conjugation of the verb is used; when the subject is plural, the third person plural conjugation of the verb is used.

bastare	*to be enough*
fare male	*to hurt*
interessare	*to be interested in*
occorrere	*to be necessary*
piacere	*to like, be pleasing*
sembrare	*to appear*

Mi basta un foglio di carta.   *One sheet of paper **is enough**.*
Mi bastano due fogli di carta.   *Two sheets of paper **are enough**.*

Exercise 39

Answer the questions using the direct or indirect object pronouns as required.

1. Hai telefonato a Maria?

Sì, _____.

2. Hai visto i tuoi amici ieri?

No, _____.

3. Avete comprato la verdura?

   Sì, _____.

4. Hai portato la frutta a casa?

   Sì, _____.

5. Hai telefonato a Luisa?

   Sì, _____.

6. Hai chiesto la ricetta?

   No, _____.

7. Avete finito i biscotti?

   Sì, _____.

8. Hai mandato l'invito?

   Sì, _____.

9. Tua mamma, ha ricevuto i fiori?

   Sì, _____.

10. Quella ragazza vuole bene a tuo figlio?

    Sì, _____.

When verbs have more than one syllable, the indirect object pronouns are attached to the first person plural form in both the affirmative and the negative commands.

Facciamo**gli** una sorpresa!	*Let's surprise **him**!*
Non facciamo**le** una sorpresa!	*Let's not surprise **her**!*

Disjunctive (stressed) pronouns

Unlike the direct or indirect object pronouns previously studied, disjunctive or stressed pronouns in Italian follow a preposition or a verb. They are in the same position in the sentence as their English equivalent.

singular		plural	
me	*me*	noi	*us*
te	*you*	voi	*you*
Lei	*you* (formal)	Loro	*you* (formal pl.)
lui	*him*	loro	*them*
lei	*her*	loro	*them*
sé	*yourself, himself, herself*	sé	*yourselves, themselves*

As previously mentioned, the disjunctive or stressed pronouns are used after a preposition. Some prepositions are followed by **di** before a disjunctive pronoun. The following list shows some of the most commonly used prepositions that take **di** before a disjunctive pronoun:

contro di	*against*
dietro di	*behind*
dopo di	*after*
prima di	*before*
senza di	*without*
sopra di	*above*
sotto di	*under*
su di	*on*
verso di	*toward*

Il gatto è **dietro di te**.	*The cat is **behind you**.*
Tuo fratello è uscito **senza di te**.	*Your brother went out **without you**.*
Il libro è **per me**.	*The book is **for me**.*
Ho ricevuto una lettera da **lei**.	*I received a letter **from her**.*
Non vado al cinema **con loro**.	*I am not going to the movies **with them**.*

The preposition **da** (*at, to, in*) followed by a stressed pronoun may mean: **a casa di** (*at the home of*), or **da te** (*by yourself, at your house*), **da me** (*by myself, at my house*), **da sé stesso** (*by himself*), and so on.

Perché non dormi **da me**?	*Why don't you sleep **at my house**?*
Devi studiare **da te**.	*You have to study **by yourself**.*

Stressed pronouns are used when there are two direct or indirect object pronouns in a sentence.

Devo fare un regalo **a te** e **a Maria**.	*I have to give a present **to you** and **to Maria**.*
Hanno invitato **me** e **te**.	*They invited **me** and **you**.*

Stressed pronouns are also used after adjectives in exclamations.

Povera **me**!	*Poor **me**!*
Beato **lui**!	*Lucky **him**!*

Stressed pronouns may be followed by **stesso(-a/-i/-e)** (*oneself*) for emphasis. **Stesso** agrees in gender and number with the stressed pronoun.

Lui pensa sempre a **sé stesso**.   *He always thinks of **himself**.*

L'hanno fatto **loro stessi**.   *They did it **themselves**.*

The stressed pronouns **me, te, lei, lui, noi, voi,** and **loro** are preceded by the preposition **di** in comparatives.

*Loro parlano più **di me**.*   *They talk more than I.*

*Tu mangi più **di lui**.*   *You eat more than he.*

Exercise 40

Fill in the blanks with the appropriate forms of the stressed pronouns in parentheses.

1. Ho imparato molto da _____. (*him*)

2. La lettera è per _____. (*me*)

3. Andiamo a scuola con _____. (*them*)

4. Siamo dietro di _____. (*him*)

5. Parlano sempre di _____. (*you,* pl.)

6. Telefoniamo a _____. (*them*)

7. Sono usciti senza di _____. (*us*)

8. È arrivata prima di _____. (*him*)

9. Io penso solamente a _____. (*him*)

10. Andiamo a casa di _____. (*her*)

Reflexive and reciprocal pronouns

Reflexive pronouns are used with verbs that express an action executed and received by the subject. (These pronouns will be covered more in depth in Chapter 10.) Reciprocal pronouns are used when two or more people execute an action to each other and not to themselves. The following list shows the various reflexive/reciprocal pronouns:

io—mi	*myself*
tu—ti	*yourself*
lui—si	*himself*
lei—si	*herself*
noi—ci	*ourselves; each other* (reciprocal)

| voi—vi | *yourselves; each other (reciprocal)* |
| loro—si | *themselves; yourselves (reciprocal)* |

Io **mi** sveglio.	*I wake (myself) up.*
Tu **ti** alzi.	*You get (yourself) up.*
Lui **si** lava.	*He washes **himself**.*
Lei **si** pettina.	*She combs **herself** (her hair).*
Noi **ci** vestiamo.	*We dress **ourselves**.*
Voi **vi** preparate.	*You prepare **yourself**.*
Loro **si** salutano.	*They greet **each other**.*

| **Mi** sveglio alle otto, **mi** alzo, **mi** lavo, faccio colazione e **mi** preparo per andare a lavorare. | *I wake up at eight o'clock, I get up, I wash **myself**, I eat breakfast, and I prepare to go to work.* |

Exercise 41

Fill in the blanks with the appropriate reflexive and reciprocal pronouns.

1. Io _____ chiamo Giovanni.

2. A che ora _____ alzi?

3. Dove _____ siede?

4. Pietro _____ mette i pantaloni nuovi.

5. Noi _____ vediamo alle quattro.

6. Teresa _____ addormenta tardi.

7. Voi non _____ sentite bene.

8. Il bambino _____ veste da solo.

9. Loro _____ vedono e _____ salutano.

10. Tu _____ metti la giacca pesante.

Double object pronouns

In Italian a direct object pronoun and an indirect object pronoun can be combined and precede the verb. In most cases the indirect object pronoun precedes the direct object pronoun and **mi**, **ti**, **gli**, **ci**, and **vi** are changed to **me**, **te**, **glie**, **ce**, and **ve**. The one exception is when using **loro/Loro**, which follows the verb and remains unchanged. The resulting double object pronouns are:

	lo	la	li	le	ne
mi—me	me lo	me la	me li	me le	me ne
ti—te	te lo	te la	te li	te le	te ne
gli—glie	glielo	gliela	glieli	gliele	gliene
ci—ce	ce lo	ce la	ce li	ce le	ce ne
vi—ve	ve lo	ve la	ve li	ve le	ve ne
loro—loro	lo loro	la loro	li loro	le loro	ne loro

Giovanni **me lo** porta.	*Giovanni brings **it to me**.*
Giovanni **te lo** dice.	*Giovanni tells **it to you**.*
Giovanni **ce lo** regala.	*Giovanni gives **it to us**.*
Giovanni **ve lo** regala.	*Giovanni gives **it to you**.*

As seen in the previous table, the indirect pronoun **gli**, becomes **glie** and combines with the direct object pronouns **lo, la, li, le,** and **ne** to form one word: **glielo, gliela, glieli, gliele,** and **gliene.**

Io porto **il libro a Maria**.	*I bring **Maria the book**.*
Io **lo** porto **a Maria**.	*I bring **it to Maria**.*
Io **glielo** porto.	*I bring **it to her**.*

In a negative sentence the word **non** goes directly before the direct and indirect pronoun combination.

Io **non** glielo porto.	*I will **not** bring it to her.*

Exercise 42

Rewrite each sentence substituting the noun with a direct and indirect object pronoun combination.

1. Do il mio libro a Pietro.

_____.

2. Io darei la mia macchina a Luca.

_____.

3. Maria insegna la danza classica a noi.

_____.

4. Loro insegnano l'italiano a Paolo.

_____.

5. Io insegno l'italiano a Paolo e Giovanna.

_____.

6. Lui mi dà le lettere.

_____.

7. Carla mostra le foto a Luisa.

_____.

8. Luisa mostra le foto a noi.

_____.

9. Io porto il libro ai miei amici.

_____.

10. Maurizio porta il pacco ai gemelli.

_____.

Exercise 43

Rewrite the following sentences changing them from the affirmative to the negative and combining the object pronouns when appropriate.

1. Io te lo do.

_____.

2. Noi glielo regaliamo.

_____.

3. Me l'ha regalato.

_____.

4. Voi ce lo avete dato.

_____.

5. Loro te l'hanno portata.

_____.

6. Lui gliele scrive.

_____.

7. Io le do a loro.

_____.

8. Tu le dai a loro.

_____.

9. Tu glielo compri.

_____.

10. Lui ve lo dice.

_____.

11. Io glielo porto.

_____.

12. Tu glieli compri.

_____.

Generally an infinitive follows a conjugated form of **potere**, **volere**, **dovere**, **sapere**, or **preferire**. The direct and indirect object pronouns may either follow or precede the conjugation If following, however, they are attached to the infinitive and the final -e of the infinitive is dropped.

Puoi portar**melo**?	_Can you bring **it to me**?_

Or:

Me lo puoi portare?	_Can you bring **it to me**?_

When an infinitive follows the verbs **lasciare** or **fare**, the double pronoun can _only_ be used before the conjugated verb.

Te l'ho lasciato comprare.	_I let **you** buy **it**._
Gliel'ho fatta mangiare.	_I made **her** eat **it**._

Exercise 44

Rewrite each sentence putting the combined object pronoun in a different position within the sentence.

1. Puoi darmelo.

_____.

2. Lui vuole insegnarmelo.

_____.

3. Preferiamo chiedervelo.

_____.

4. Devo comprarmeli.

_____.

5. Lei voleva regalartelo.

_____.

6. Devo portartelo.

_____.

7. Dobbiamo venderteli.

_____.

8. Lei non poteva mostrarmela.

_____.

9. Vuoi darmeli?

_____?

10. Possono regalarmelo.

_____.

11. Vogliamo mostrarglielo.

_____.

12. Lei può leggertelo.

_____.

13. Volevano vendergliela.

_____.

Exercise 45

Translate each sentence into Italian substituting the direct object with the pronoun **ne** and combining it with the indirect object pronoun.

1. I will speak to her about it tonight.

_____.

2. Gianni will bring a few magazines to me.

_____.

3. Don will send him two or three books.

_____.

4. She has given me some cherries.

_____.

5. We will bring him some chestnuts.

_____.

6. You went away without saying good-bye.

_____.

7. I am not going to give him one.

_____.

8. He brings home two for himself.

_____.

9. She wants to send me two of them.

_____.

10. He doesn't care about it at all.

_____.

11. He owes him a lot of money.

_____.

12. She will buy two of them for herself.

_____.

13. You should buy him a pair of shoes.

_____.

When using the word **ecco** (*here*) with double object pronouns, the pronouns always follow it, which, when combined in expressions, is usually used to emphasize something.

Eccotela!	*Here it is for you!*
Eccoglieli!	*Here they are for him!*

Single-syllable commands always precede double object pronouns and the first consonant of the pronoun is doubled if it begins with **c, l,** or **m**. In negative commands, double object pronouns can either precede the verb or be attached to the infinitive, in which case the final **-e** of the infinitive is omitted and the first consonant is not doubled.

affirmative		negative	
Daccelo!	*Give it to us.*	Non darcelo! *or*	*Don't give it to us.*
		Non **ce lo** dare!	
Daglielo!	*Give it to her/*	Non darglielo! *or*	*Don't give it to her/*
	him/them.	Non **glielo** dare!	*him/them.*
Fammelo!	*Do it for me.*	Non farmelo! *or*	*Don't do it for me.*
		Non **me lo** fare!	
Diccelo!	*Tell it to us.*	Non dircelo! *or*	*Don't tell it to us.*
		Non **ce lo** dire!	

Object pronoun combinations are attached to the infinitives of first person plural (**noi**) affirmative commands. They generally come before the verb in a negative command, but in today's Italian you may often hear the double object pronoun attached to the infinitive in the negative form as well.

Scriviamo**gliela**!	*Let's write it to her/him/them.*
Non scriviamo**gliela**!	*Let's not write it to her/him/them.*
Non **gliela** scriviamo!	*Let's not write it to her/him/them.*

Exercise 46

Rewrite each sentence replacing the direct and indirect objects with a double object pronoun.

1. Maria, da' la palla a tuo fratello!

_____!

2. Carlo, porta la bicicletta a Erica, per favore!

_____!

3. Signorina, mi porti una sedia, per favore!

_____!

4. Signorina, non mi porti la sedia adesso!

_____!

5. Voglio telefonare la notizia a Elena.

_____.

6. Signore, mi porti un cappuccino, per favore!

_____!

7. Marco, dai i soldi alla bambina!

_____!

8. Carla, non raccontare la storia ai bambini!

_____!

9. Giovanna, chiedi a Paolo di prestarti la macchina!

_____!

10. Posso mandare tutti i conti a Pietro.

_____.

11. Facciamo una sorpresa a Elda!

_____!

12. No, non facciamo la sorpresa a Elda!

_____!

Direct and indirect object pronouns *mi*, *ti*, *ci*, and *vi*

The pronouns **mi, ti, ci,** and **vi** function as either direct or indirect object pronouns. **Mi, ti,** and **vi** can be contracted (**m', t',** and **v'**) before verbs starting with a vowel or **-h. Ci** contracts only before verbs starting with **-i.** It is more common to use these contractions in spoken Italian than in written Italian.

Maria **mi** risponde.	*Maria answers **me**.*
Luigi **ci** telefona.	*Luigi calls **us**.*
Loro **c'**invitano.	*They invite **us**.*
Maria e Carlo non **ci** chiamano.	*Maria and Carlo don't call **us**.*

When a direct object pronoun is placed before a verb, it is considered *weak*. When placed after the verb, however, it is *emphatic*. When using emphatic pronouns, **mi** becomes **me; ti** becomes **te; lo** becomes **lui; la** becomes **lei; ci** becomes **noi; vi** becomes **voi;** and **le** and **li** become **loro.** Emphatic pronouns are often accompanied by **anche, proprio, solo,** or **solamente.**

weak	emphatic	
Luigi **mi** invita.	Luigi invita **me**.	*Luigi invites **me**.*
Paola **ti** chiama.	Paola chiama **te**.	*Paola is calling **you**.*
Io **l'**accompagno.	Io accompagno **lui**.	*I accompany **him**.*
Tu **l'**accompagni.	Tu accompagni **lei**.	*You accompany **her**.*
Lei **ci** accompagna.	Lei accompagna **noi**.	*She accompanies **us**.*
Pietro **vi** saluta.	Pietro saluta **voi**.	*Pietro greets **you**.*
Noi **li** salutiamo.	Noi salutiamo **loro**.	*We greet **them**.*

Rewrite the following sentences using the emphatic pronouns.

1. Luisa mi chiama dalla finestra.

_____.

2. Pietro ti invita.

_____.

3. Luigi non vi invita.

_____.

4. Loro ci invitano.

_____.

5. Loro ci telefonano.

_____.

6. Tu le inviti.

_____.

7. Io lo chiamo.

_____.

8. Noi non li vediamo.

_____.

9. Io ti amo.

_____.

10. Pietro e Luisa vi invitano.

_____.

Demonstrative pronouns

Demonstrative pronouns are the same as demonstrative adjectives in that they refer to people, animals, or things. They agree in gender and number with the noun they replace. The demonstrative pronouns **questo** and **quello** have four forms:

masculine singular	feminine singular		masculine plural	feminine plural	
questo	questa	*this one*	questi	queste	*these ones*
quello	quella	*that one*	quelli	quelle	*those ones*

Quale libro vuoi leggere?	*Which book do you want to read?*
Voglio leggere **quello**.	*I want to read **that one**.*
Voglio leggere **questo**.	*I want to read **this one**.*

For emphasis **questo**(-a/-i/-e) and **quello**(-a/-i/-e), may be followed by **qui** (*here*) and **lì** (*there*). **Quì** is used with **questo** and **lì** is used with **quello**. You would say **questo qui** (*this one here*), or **quello lì** (*that one there*).

Quale vuoi?	*Which one do you want?*
Quello lì sulla destra.	*__That one__ there on the right.*

Desidera delle pere? Sì, **queste qui** a destra.	*Would you like some pears? Yes, __these__ here on the right.*

Often **quello** is followed by **che**, meaning *the one who* or *the one that*.

Quella casa in collina è **quella che** abbiamo comprato noi.	*That house on the hill is **the one that** we bought.*

When the pronoun **quello** is followed by **di** (**quello di, quella di, quelli di,** and **quelle di**), it is used to express possession.

I nipoti di Maria guardano la televisione, **quelli di** Giovanna sono fuori a giocare.	*Maria's grandchildren are watching television, **Giovanna's** are playing outside.*

Exercise 48

Translate the sentences into Italian using the appropriate demonstrative adjectives and pronouns.

1. This is my brother, and these are my sisters.

_____.

2. That house is mine, and this is my sister's.

_____.

3. Who is that (m.)?

_____?

4. That one (m.) is a famous singer.

_____.

5. That book is very interesting, but this one is boring.

_____.

6. This student is intelligent, but that one is very lazy.

_____.

7. These people come from Africa, those come from South America.

_____.

8. Those apples are more expensive than these.

_____.

9. This rose is very beautiful, but that one is wilted.

_____.

10. These children are lucky, those are neglected.

_____.

Ciò che (*that, what*) is an invariable demonstrative pronoun. It is used more in writing than in speaking.

Ho detto **ciò che** voglio.   *I said **what** I want.*
Ho comprato **ciò che** desideravo.   *I bought **what** I wished.*

Exercise 49

Translate the following paragraph into Italian using **ciò che** where the demonstrative pronoun is needed.

I don't know what Peter said. He talks all the time, but I don't understand what he says. It is difficult to follow what Peter says and do what he wants. I would prefer to have him write down what he wants to say. This way, there would be no misunderstanding and everybody could do what Peter wishes.

_____

_____

_____

_____

_____

_____

_____

Exercise 50

Fill in the blanks with the appropriate demonstrative pronouns or adjectives.

1. Vorrei delle banane. _____ (_These_) qui, sono più belle di _____ (_those_) lì.

2. Poi ho bisogno di un chilogrammo di patate. Mi dia _____ (_these_) per favore.

3. _____ (_Those_) fragole sembrano più fresche di _____ (_these_).

4. Per favore mi dia un melone. Voglio _____ (_that one there_) sulla destra.

5. Se le arance sono dolci, prendo un chilogrammo di _____ (_those_).

6. _____ (_These_) arance non sono abbastanza dolci per me. Prendo _____ (_those_).

7. _____ (_These_) pomodori sono brutti. Vorrei _____ (_those_) vicino a te.

8. _____ (_These_) zucchini sono troppo grossi, preferisco _____ (_those_).

9. Da dove viene _____ (_that_) lettuga? _____ (_This_) viene dalla Spagna. _____ (_That_) viene dal Sud Italia.

10. Mi dà un sacchetto forte per favore? _____ (_This one here_) è rotto.

11. _____ (_This_) è tutto per oggi. Verrò di nuovo la prossima settimana.

Possessive pronouns

Possessive pronouns are used to replace a noun modified by a possessive adjective. They agree in gender and number with the noun they replace. They are preceded by the definite article or by a contraction (**al, alla, allo,** etc.).

il mio, la mia, i miei, le mie	*mine*
il tuo, la tua, i tuoi, le tue	*yours (familiar)*
il suo, la sua, i suoi, le sue	*his; hers; yours (formal)*
il nostro, la nostra, i nostri, le nostre	*ours*
il vostro, la vostra, i vostri, le vostre	*yours*
il loro, la loro, i loro, le loro	*theirs*

La mia casa è grande, **la tua** è piccola.	*My house is big, **yours** is small.*
La mia macchina è nel garage, dov'è **la tua**?	*My car is in the garage, where is **yours**?*

When a definite article and a preposition precede a possessive pronoun, (a definite article usually does), they form a contraction, but when the possessive pronoun follows the verb **essere**, a definite article is not used.

La piantina della città non è nella mia macchina. Dov'è? Lo sai? Sì, è **nella mia**.	*The map of the city is not in my car. Where is it? Do you know? Yes, it is **in mine**.*
Questo è **il mio** gatto.	*This is **my** cat.*
Questo gatto è **mio**.	*This cat is **mine**.*

The possessive pronouns always use definite articles even when referring to close family relatives in the second person singular (**tu**) form.

Mia moglie lavora, e **la tua**?	*My wife works, how about **yours**?*
La sua casa è vicina, e **la vostra**?	*His house is close, how about **yours**?*

Exercise 51

For each sentence give the correct possessive pronoun for the underlined words.

1. Questa è la mia casa, quella è la tua casa. _____

2. Stai parlando di tuo fratello o di mio fratello? _____

3. La mia macchina è nuova e bella; la tua macchina è vecchia. _____

4. Il suo cane è più vecchio del tuo cane. _____

5. I loro nonni sono più vecchi dei miei nonni. _____

6. Il mio vestito è azzurro. Di che colore è il tuo vestito? _____

7. Le mie scarpe sono nuove, e le tue scarpe _____ sono nuove?

8. Ho comprato le mie scarpe, e Maria ha comprato le sue scarpe? _____

9. Ho trovato le mie foto. Tu hai trovato le foto di Paolo? _____

10. Il mio anello è molto caro. L'anello di Maria è falso. _____

11. Tua madre è bella, ma la madre di Giovanni è più bella. _____

12. La mia festa è molto bella, ma la sua festa è noiosa. _____

Italian pronoun *ci*

The pronoun **ci** always refers to objects or places that have been previously mentioned. Usually it replaces the preposition **a** + noun, but it also replaces other prepositions such as **in**, **su**, or **da** + noun when **da** means *at* or *to*.

Chi va **in Italia** con loro?	*Who is going **to Italy with them?***
Ci andiamo noi.	*We will go **there**.*
Quando vai **dal dottore?**	*When will you go **to the doctor?***
Ci vado la prossima settimana.	*I will go **there** next week.*

The pronoun **ci** often means *to it* or *to them*, *in it*, *in them*, *on it*, *on them*, and *there* when the place is already known. These are often omitted in English sentences, as is shown in the following examples.

Andate in macelleria?	*Are you going to the butcher shop?*
Sì, **ci** vado oggi pomeriggio.	*Yes, I will go this afternoon.*

Ci is often used with the third person singular and plural conjugations of **essere** to express *there is*, or *there are*. **Ci** becomes **c'** before words starting with **e**.

C'è il sole.	***It is** sunny. (**There is** the sun.)*
C'era una volta...	*Once upon a time **there was** . . .*
Ci sono tanti bei fiori nei giardini.	***There are** many pretty flowers in the gardens.*

The pronoun **ci** may replace **a** + phrase or **a** + clause.

Perché credi **a quella ragazza?**	*Why do you believe **that girl?***
Ci credo perché è una persona sincera.	*I believe **her** because she is a sincere person.*

The pronoun **vi** is sometimes used instead of **ci** (**c'**). Although they are interchangeable, **vi** is not used as much as **ci**. However, **ci** cannot be used when a location is emphasized. **Lì** or **là** is used instead.

Dove hai messo le scarpe?	*Where did you put the shoes?*
Le ho messe **lì** (**là**).	*I put them **there**.*

The pronoun **ci** follows the same rules of placement as direct and indirect object pronouns.

Ci vado domani.	*I will go (**there**) tomorrow.*
Vuoi andar**ci** anche tu?	*Do you want to go (**there**), too?*
Ci vorrei andare da solo.	*I would like to go (**there**) by myself.*

With single syllable commands the **c-** in **ci** is doubled.

Va**cci** da solo.	*Go (**there**) by yourself.*

Exercise 52

Answer the following questions using the pronoun **ci**.

1. Vai spesso in discoteca?

   Sì, _____.

2. Sei stato a Chicago?

   No, non _____.

3. Vai al cinema da solo?

   No, non _____.

4. Riesci a fare quello che devi fare?

   Sì, _____.

5. Quante volte al mese vai in palestra?

   _____ tre volte al mese.

6. Credi a Babbo Natale?

   Sì, _____.

7. Vorresti andare in Cina?

   Sì, _____.

8. Andate in montagna questa estate?

   No, non _____.

9. Vedi bene con questi occhiali?

   Sì, _____.

10. Vai spesso dalle tue amiche?

   Sì, _____.

Idiomatic expressions with *ci*

Ci is used in common idiomatic expressions and with some specific verbs. For example:

- **crederci,** *to believe in something*

Loro credevano in Babbo Natale, e **ci credono** ancora.	*They believed in Santa Claus, and they still **believe in him**.*

- **entrarci,** *to have to do with*

Questo non **c'entra** niente.	*This **has nothing to do with it**.*

- **esserci,** *to arrive* (*at a place* or *an understanding*)

Finalmente **ci siete**.	*Finally, you **are here**.*

- **metterci,** *to take time*

Ci metto mezz'ora per arrivare a casa dal lavoro.	*It takes me half an hour to get home from work.*

- **pensarci,** *to think about it*

Pensi ancora a quell'incidente? Non **pensarci** più.	*Are you still thinking about the accident? Don't **think about it** anymore.*

- **rifletterci** *to think something over*

Prima di fare le cose, **ci rifletto** molto.	*Before doing something, **I think about it** for a long time.*

- **sentirci,** *to be able to hear*

    Parlate forte, la nonna **non ci sente.**   *Speak loudly, Grandma **cannot hear.***

- **starci,** *to have room/space for*

    Ci stanno i regali in valigia?   *Do you **have room** in the suitcase for the presents?*

- **tenerci,** *to value*

    Gli italiani **ci tengono** alla famiglia.   *Italians **value** their family.*

- **vederci,** *to be able to see*

    Senza occhiali **non ci vedo** niente.   *I **cannot see** anything without glasses.*

- **volerci** *to be needed; to take time*

    Ci vogliono sei uova per fare la torta.   *Six eggs **are needed** to make the cake.*

Exercise 53

Fill in the blanks to answer the following questions using the pronoun **ci.**

1. Perché non rifletti prima di fare le cose? _____ ma sbaglio lo stesso.
2. Quanto tempo occorre per venire a scuola da casa tua? _____ mezz'ora.
3. Mi porti queste cose nella tua valigia? Se _____ le porto.
4. Puoi parlare più forte? Non _____ bene.
5. Hai sentito la novità? Sì, ma non _____.
6. Con chi vai al cinema? Vorrei _____ da solo.
7. Che tempo ha fatto oggi? _____ il sole.
8. Quanti giorni stai in Italia? _____ una settimana.
9. Quante ore ci vogliono per arrivare in Italia da New York? _____ otto ore.
10. Ci tieni molto alla moda? Sì, _____ moltissimo.

Italian pronoun *ne*

The pronoun **ne** refers to people, places, or things previously mentioned in a dialogue. It usually replaces **di** + noun and it means *some, any, of it, of them, from it, from him/her,* and *from there*. The pronoun **ne** is always expressed in Italian, but there may not always be an English equivalent.

Luigi compra **dei fiori**.	*Luigi buys some flowers.*
Luigi **ne** compra.	*Luigi buys **some of them**.*
Sai delle novità?	*Do you know any news?*
Non **ne** so nessuna.	*I don't know **any of it**.*

Ne may replace **da** + noun (a place) when it means *from there*.

Vieni da Roma? Sì, **ne** torno adesso.	*Are you coming from Rome?*
	*Yes, I am returning now (**from Rome**).*

Ne may also replace **di** + clause.

Avete bisogno **di** soldi?	*Do you need **some** money?*
Sì, **ne** abbiamo bisogno per il viaggio.	*Yes, we need **some** for the trip.*

Ne replaces nouns accompanied by a number, or an expression of quantity such as **molto** (*much*), **troppo** (*too much*), **un chilogrammo di** (*a kilogram of*), **un litro di** (*a liter of*), and so on. **Ne** means *of it* or *of them* in these expressions and is never omitted.

Quante macchine hai?	*How many cars do you have?*
Ne ho due.	*I have two **of them**.*

Hai mangiato le paste?	*Did you eat the pastries?*
Sì, **ne** ho mangiate tre.	*Yes, I ate three **of them**.*

Ne follows the same rules of placement as the direct and indirect object pronouns.

Luisa **ne** vuole due.	*Luisa wants two (**of them**).*
I ragazzi non **ne** hanno mangiato.	*The boys did not eat **any** (**of it**).*
Carla vuole mangiar**ne**.	*Carla wants to eat **some** (**of it/them**).*
Scrivi**ne** un paio!	*Write a couple (**of them**).*
Non **ne** scrivere più.	*Don't write anymore (**of them**).*
Non scriver**ne** più.	*Don't write anymore (**of them**).*
Ecco**ne** una.	*Here is one (**of them**).*

Ne is used to replace **di** + infinitive in expressions such as **avere bisogno di** (*to need*), **avere paura di** (*to be afraid of*), and **avere voglia di** (*to feel like*).

Hanno **voglia di** studiare?	*Do they feel like studying?*
No, non **ne** hanno voglia per niente.	*No, they don't feel like it, at all.*

With single-syllable informal commands, the **n-** in **ne** doubles.

Vanne a prendere una!	*Go get one (of them).*
Và a prende**rne** una!	*Go get one (of them).*

Ne contracts to **n'** before words starting with **e**.

Non ce **n'è** più.	*There isn't any more.*

In compound tenses **ne** usually agrees with the past participle only when it replaces a partitive noun. When **ne** is used with numbers, there is no agreement.

Ho comprato **delle pesche**.	*I bought some peaches.*
Ne ho comprate.	*I bought some (of them).*

Hai letto qualche buon libro questa estate?	*Have you read some good books this summer?*
Ne ho letti alcuni.	*I read a few (of them).*

Exercise 54

Answer each question replacing the partitive article with the pronoun **ne**. Use the words in parentheses to guide your answers.

1. Lei prepara della minestra?

   Sì, _____ due tipi diversi.

2. Vuole del pane? (1 kg.)

   Sì, _____.

3. Hai mangiato dei panini? (due)

   Sì, _____.

4. Avete delle macchine? (due)

   Sì, _____.

5. Abbiamo del burro?

   No, _____.

6. Luisa porta dei dolci?

   Sì, _____ due.

7. Devo comprare delle candele? (quattro)

   Sì, _____.

8. Compri dei fiori?

   Sì, _____ tanti.

9. Ti occorrono delle sedie? (quattro)

   Sì, _____.

10. Compri dei carciofi? (sei)

    Sì, _____.

11. Bevete dello spumante?

    Sì, _____ un po'.

12. Conosci delle lingue straniere? (tre)

    Sì, _____

Interrogative pronouns

Interrogative pronouns are used when asking questions. In Italian there is no special word order for asking a question and in spoken Italian it's the speaker's tone of voice that indicates if the speaker is asking something or not. Interrogative pronouns can be used in both direct and indirect questions and for those questions that express doubt. The following list shows the various interrogative pronouns:

Chi?	*Who?*	Refers to people only and is used only in the singular masculine or feminine forms
Di chi?	*Whose?*	Refers to people only
Che cosa?	*What?*	Generally used for things
Quale/quali?	*Which?*	Used for people and things
Quanto/quanti?	*How much?*	Used for people and things

Chi arriva domani?	*Who is arriving tomorrow?*
Di chi è questa palla?	*Whose ball is this?*
Che cosa facciamo domani?	*What are we going to do tomorrow?*
Quale gonna volete?	*Which skirt do you want?*
Quanto costa?	*How much does it cost?*

Exercise 55

Translate the following questions into Italian.

1. Who is getting married on Sunday?

_____?

2. Whose shoes are these?

_____?

3. What do you want me to do?

_____?

4. Which one is the good soccer player?

_____?

5. Which ones are the best students in class?

_____?

6. How much (wine) do you want?

_____?

7. How many (children) are there at the park?

_____?

8. Who are you waiting for?

_____?

9. Whose kids are these?

_____?

10. What should I do?

_____?

11. Who is the strongest?

_____?

12. Which ones are your parents?

_____?

Relative pronouns

Relative pronouns are the linking words used to introduce a relative clause (one that modifies a noun). They provide additional information about the preceding noun or pronoun. In English the relative pronouns are: *whom, whose, which,* and *that.* They can be omitted in English, but never in Italian. The Italian relative pronouns are **che** and **cui.**

Che (*that, which, who, whom*) can be used to replace either a person or a thing. **Che** does not have gender or number differentiation.

La signora **che** vedi è mia madre.	*The lady (**whom**) you see is my mother.*
La poesia **che** ho letto è molto romantica.	*The poetry (**that**) I read is very romantic.*

Che can be preceded by an article or by an articulated preposition.

Mi ha comprato un bel vestito, **il che** mi ha sorpresa.	*She bought me a dress, **which** surprised me.*

Cui (*which, whom, of which*) also does not have gender differentiation. It is often preceded by a preposition or an article.

La persona **di cui** ti parlo è mio fratello.	*The person **whom** I am talking to you about is my brother.*
Ho un calcolatore, **il cui** uso non è molto facile.	*I have a calculator, **which** is not too easy to use.*

Il quale, la quale, i quali, le quali (*that, which*) can be used in place of **che** and **cui. Quale** agrees with the noun it refers to and therefore avoids ambiguity. It can only be used as the subject of a sentence.

che	il quale, la quale, i quali, le quali
a cui	al quale, alla quale, ai quali, alle quali
con cui	con il quale, con la quale, con i quali, con le quali
da cui	dal quale, dalla quale, dai quali, dalle quali
di cui	del quale, della quale, dei quali, delle quali
per cui	per il quale, per la quale, per i quali, per le quali
su cui	sul quale, sulla quale, sui quali, sulle quali

La signora **che** lavora in banca è la mia amica.	*The lady **who** works at the bank is my friend.*
La signora **la quale** lavora in banca è la mia amica.	*The lady **who** works at the bank is my friend.*
La città **da cui** vengo è molto piccola, ma bella.	*The town I come **from** (**from which** I come) is small, but beautiful.*
La città **dalla quale** vengo è molta piccola, ma bella.	*The town I come **from** is small, but beautiful.*

Chi (*who*) does not have gender differentiation and is only used to refer to unspecified people in the masculine and feminine singular. It is commonly used in both spoken and written Italian.

Chi ama la natura ha un cuore gentile.	*One **who** loves nature has a kind heart.*
Chi non lavora non mangia.	*One **who** doesn't work doesn't eat.*

Exercise 56

In each sentence replace the relative pronoun **che** with the appropriate form of **quale**. For example:

È arrivato uno studente che/**il quale** viene dall'Africa e che/**il quale** non sa l'italiano.

1. La signora che/_____ era con me, è mia zia.

2. Ho telefonato ai miei amici che/_____ non sentivo da molto tempo.

3. Mi piacciono i film che/_____ produce Benigni.

4. Abbiamo letto un libro che/_____ ci è piaciuto molto.

5. Mi piacciono i libri che/_____ hanno molte illustrazioni.

6. Dov'è andata la ragazza che/_____ era con te al cinema?

7. Ho comprato una casa che/_____ ha molto spazio.

8. Le spese che/_____ hai fatto ieri erano molto costose.

9. Abbiamo risolto i problemi che/_____ erano molto difficili.

10. Mi piacciono molto le poesie che/_____ ha scritto Leopardi.

Exercise 57

Fill in the blanks with either **che** or **cui**.

1. I ragazzi _____ sono molto volonterosi passeranno bene gli esami.

2. La palla con _____ giocava il bambino è andata nella strada.

3. La penna con _____ scrivo a scuola è una penna nuova.

4. La palestra in _____ vado tutti i giorni è molto attrezzata.

5. Il professore di _____ ti ho parlato abita vicino a casa mia.

6. La cassiera del supermercato _____ mi ha fatto il conto è molto gentile.

7. La macchina _____ ho visto alla mostra è molto bella, ma anche molto cara.

8. L'aereo con _____ ho viaggiato è arrivato con molto ritardo.

9. La scuola _____ frequenti tu è molto famosa.

10. Le persone a _____ ho portato i fiori hanno un giardino meraviglioso.

11. Le amiche con _____ vado in vacanza sono molto allegre.

Relative pronouns with *piacere, servire, mancare*

As previously shown, relative pronouns in English are not always used the same way in Italian. There are sentences in English that show the subject of a relative clause as *who*, but the same sentence in Italian expresses that thought by using the indirect object *to whom*. The expressions **piacere a** (*to be pleasing to*), **servire a** (*to be necessary to, to need to*), and **mancare a** (*to be lacking in*) are used in these cases. **A cui** must be used with these verbs.

Sono gli amici **a cui** piace portare la merce dagli Stati Uniti.	*These are the friends **who** like to bring merchandise from the United States.*
È una famiglia **a cui** non manca niente.	*It is a family **who** lacks nothing.*
Questa è la ragazza **a cui** serve questo libro.	*This is the girl **who** needs this book.*

In Italian how to say *whose* depends on whether *whose* refers to the subject or the object of the sentence. If it refers to the subject, it may be expressed with a definite article + **cui** making it **il cui, la cui, i cui, le cui**, or it can be expressed by using **di** + **il quale** (**del quale**), **la quale** (**della quale**), **i quali** (**dei quali**), **le quali** (**delle quali**). Both forms are interchangeable, but when there is ambiguity the use of **del quale, della quale,** and so on is preferred.

Il mio amico, **la cui** macchina è in
vendita, è una persona molto attiva.

*My friend, **whose** car is for sale, is a very
active person.*

Il mio amico, la macchina **del quale** è
in vendita, è una persona molto
attiva.

*My friend, **whose** car is for sale, is a very
active person.*

When *whose* + noun is the object of the verb in a relative clause, **di cui** is placed before the verb.
The definite article and the noun follow it.

È la signora **di cui** conosco bene i figli.   *She is the lady **whose** kids I know well.*

When *whose* is used as an interrogative pronoun, **di chi** is used in the sentence.

Di chi sono queste scarpe?   ***Whose** shoes are these?*

Exercise 58

Fill in the blanks using the pronouns **cui** or **quale** (or both), preceded by the appropriate prepositions
or definite articles.

1. La casa che preferisco è quella _____ vivono i miei amici.

2. Il cappotto _____ mi hai parlato costa troppo.

3. Maria, _____ conosco la vita, sta scrivendo un libro.

4. La signora _____ parlate è mia zia.

5. I signori _____ parlate sono i miei zii.

6. Il professore _____ porto la mia relazione viene da Roma.

7. La nave _____ sono andata in Italia era molto moderna.

8. L'operaio, _____ abbiamo telefonato, può venire solo sabato
   pomeriggio.

9. Il dermatologo _____ sono andata mi ha dato una buona
   pomata.

10. La nonna, _____ ti ho mostrato le foto, era molto bella.

In Italian there are also relative pronouns phrases that are used to refer to specific people or objects
and these pronouns must agree in gender and number with the noun they refer to. **Tutto quello che**
and **tutto ciò che** (*everything, all that*) are such pronoun phrases. They are interchangeable. **Tutti quelli**

che (*all those who*) refers to a specific group of people. **Quello che, quella che, quelli che,** and **quelle che** (*whichever, those which*) are used to refer to specific people, or objects.

Quel ragazzo fa sempre **tutto quello che** vuole.	*That boy always does **everything that** he wants.*
Tutti quelli che fanno molto allenamento vinceranno.	***All those who** train a lot will win.*
Quale ti do? **Quello che** vuoi.	*Which one should I give you?* ***Whichever one** you want.*

Exercise 59

Fill in the blanks with the appropriate relative pronouns.

1. La Cina è il centro di _____ è progresso.

2. Io ho raccolto _____ era caduto.

3. Io ho raccolto _____ ciliege che erano mature.

4. Ho comprato le scarpe come _____ hai comprato tu.

5. Io ho ascoltato _____ canzoni che piacevano a mio padre.

6. Mi piace _____ è nuovo e moderno.

7. Io sono pronta ad aiutare _____ si trovano in difficoltà.

8. I genitori italiani fanno _____ vogliono i figli.

9. Quale vestito vuoi? _____ ho visto in vetrina ieri.

10. Ho scritto su una cartolina _____ ho fatto in Italia.

11. Non so _____ vuoi fare domenica.

12. _____ vanno in Italia, ritornano al loro paese molto entusiasti.

Indefinite pronouns

Indefinite pronouns are used to express an indefinite quantity or number of people or objects.

Ci sono **molte** persone allo stadio.	*There are **many** people in the stadium.*
Non ho visto **nessuno** fuori.	*I didn't see **anybody** outside.*

The following list shows some of the most commonly used indefinite pronouns:

alcuni, alcune; qualcuno	*some; any; a few*
chiunque	*anyone, anybody*
gli altri, le altre	*the others*
l'uno (-a)... l'altro (-a)	*the one . . . the other*
gli uni... gli altri, le une... le altre	*some . . . the others; either one*
molti, molte	*many*
molto, molta	*much*
nessuno, nessuna	*no one, nobody*
ognuno, ognuna	*each, everyone*
parecchi, parecchie	*a lot, several*
pochi, poche	*a little, few*
poco, poca	*a little*
qualcosa	*something; anything*
qualcuno	*someone, somebody*
tanti, tante	*many*
troppi, troppe	*too many*
troppo, troppa	*too much*
tutti, tutte	*everyone*
tutto, tutta	*everything*
un altro, un'altra	*another*
uno, una	*a/any person*

Uno(-a) is used only in the singular and refers exclusively to people. It is often used to generalize. **Uno** means *a person* or *any person*. In this case English uses the term *someone* or *one*. When used in the impersonal form, **uno** is always treated as masculine.

Quando **uno** viaggia, impara molte cose.	*When **one** travels, one learns a lot.*

Uno(-a) is also used to refer to a person who is of little importance to the speaker, or when very little or nothing at all is known about him/her.

Ho parlato con **una** che non conoscevo.	*I spoke with **someone** I didn't know.*
C'è **una** che ti vuole al telefono.	*There is **someone** who wants you on the telephone.*

Sometimes **uno** is accompanied by **altro** or **altra**. In this case it can be used in the masculine or feminine forms in both the singular or plural and the article is placed before it. When used this way it means *either one*.

Non mi piace né **l'uno** né **l'altro**.   *I don't like **either one**.*

Sia **gli uni** che **gli altri** sono colpevoli.   ***Either one** is guilty.*

Ognuno(-a) (*each, everyone*) is used only in the singular for people or objects and will always agree with the noun in gender. **Ognuno di noi/di voi/di loro** means *all* or *every one of*. It is used with a singular verb.

Ognuno dei miei fratelli ha sposato   ***Each one of my brothers** has married a*
donna bella e intelligente.   *beautiful and intelligent woman.*

Ognuno di loro deve darsi da fare e   ***Each one of them** has to get busy and finish*
finire i compiti.   *the homework.*

Exercise 60

Fill in the blanks with the appropriate indefinite pronouns.

1. Ho visto _____ al cinema che mi sembrava di conoscere.

2. Ho comprato le mele ma ne ho mangiata solo _____.

3. Se _____ non volesse guardare la televisione, potrebbe leggere?

4. Non ho comprato né _____ né l'altro.

5. L'una sembra intelligente, _____ sembra non capisca bene.

6. Dovranno parlare con _____

   e _____.

7. _____ dei ragazzi partecipa a uno sport competitivo.

8. _____ deve darsi da fare per finire il lavoro.

9. _____ di voi ascolta la musica.

10. _____ di noi decide del suo destino.

Qualcuno(-a) or **qualcheduno(-a)** (*someone, somebody; any, anybody*), is used only in the singular, even if it refers to plural nouns. It is used with people and less frequently with objects. When it refers to plural persons or things, **alcuni(-e)** and a plural verb can be used, but this construction is not as common.

Fuori c'è **qualcuno** che ha chiesto di te.　*Outside there is **someone** asking for you.*

Conosci **qualcuna** delle ragazze che　*Do you know **any** of the girls who came*
　sono venute alla festa?　　*to the party?*

Qualcuno is the pronoun equivalent to **qualche**. It is always singular even when it refers to plural nouns. **Qualcuno** can be followed by **di noi, di voi,** or **di loro,** but the verb used remains singular.

Qualcuno di noi verrà a prenderti.　***One of us (someone)** will come to pick you up.*

Qualcuna di voi ragazze vuole　*Would **one of you (someone)** girls like to*
　giocare al tennis?　　*play tennis?*

When **qualcuno** is followed by **altro(-a)**, the final vowel -o in the masculine form must be omitted (**qualcun altro**), but no apostrophe is needed. The apostrophe is only needed when the feminine form **altra** follows **qualcuno** (**qualcun'altra**).

Pietro non l'ha chiamato, **qualcun**　*Peter did not call him, **somebody else** did.*
　altro l'ha chiamato.

Chiunque (*anyone, whoever, no matter who*) is invariable and therefore is the same in both the feminine and masculine forms. It refers exclusively to people and is usually followed by a subjunctive verb.

Chiunque abbia detto queste cose, non　***Whoever** said those things, cannot be*
　può essere che un pazzo.　　*anything but crazy.*

Exercise 61

Fill in the blanks with the appropriate indefinite pronouns.

1. _____ mi ha chiamato ma non so chi sia.

2. Fa' venire _____ a pulire la casa.

3. _____ voi ha una penna?

4. Non andate voi, mandate _____.

5. Non so se c'è _____ in casa.

6. _____ mi voglia aiutare, sarà il benvenuto.

7. _____ pensi di saperne più del professore, si sbaglia.

8. _____ sia, non voglio vederlo.

9. Spero che venga _____ ad aiutarci.

10. Se _____ lo vede, ditegli che gli devo parlare.

Niente and **nulla** (*nothing, not anything*) are used only in the singular and refer exclusively to objects.

Non ho detto **niente**.	*I didn't say **anything**.*
Non ho visto **niente** (**nulla**).	*I didn't see **anything**.*

Note that the pronouns **niente** and **nulla** give origin to many expressions. For example:

buono a nulla/niente	*good for nothing*
cosa da niente	*nothing much*
cosa da nulla	*nothing much*
fare finta di niente/ di nulla	*to pretend nothing is happening, going on*
non fa niente	*it doesn't matter*
per niente/nulla	*not at all*

Non ti fidare di lui, è **un buono a niente**.	*Don't trust him, he is **good for nothing**.*
Non mi sono fatto molto male, è una **cosa da niente**.	*I didn't get hurt badly; it is **nothing much**.*
Quando i suoi genitori entrano nella sua camera, **fa finta di niente**.	*When his parents enter his room, **he pretends nothing is going on**.*

Nessuno(-a) (*no one, nobody, not any*) is used only in the singular form and refers to people and objects.

Nessuno ha capito la lezione.	*Nobody understood the lesson.*

Note that when **nessuno** precedes a verb, it is treated as a singular noun and has regular placement within the sentence. When **nessuno** follows the verb, however, **non** must be placed before the verb, creating a double negative. Though never used in English, double negatives are very common in Italian.

Nessuno lo vuole vedere.	*Nobody wants to see him.*
Non lo vuole vedere **nessuno**.	*Nobody wants to see him.*

Exercise 62

Translate the following sentences into Italian, using the appropriate indefinite pronouns.

1. Nobody called you.

_____.

2. I didn't receive any letter today.

_____.

3. None of our kids live near us.

_____.

4. I didn't hear anything.

_____.

5. Nobody wants to eat.

_____.

6. I don't like either one of them.

_____.

7. Promise not to say anything.

_____.

8. It doesn't matter. I will come back.

_____.

9. Nobody wants to eat at home.

_____.

10. None of us wants to go to the beach.

_____.

11. Nobody wants to see them.

_____.

Molto(-a) (*much*), poco(-a) (*a little*), troppo(-a) (*too much*), and parecchio(-a) (*a few*) are all used in the singular form and refer to people and objects.

Gli italiani ne mangiano **molta**.	*Italians eat a lot of it.*
Ce ne sono **parecchi** in classe.	*There are a few of them in class.*

Tutto(-a) and tutti(-e) are used in a general sense to mean *everything* and *everyone*. They agree in gender and number with the noun they refer to.

> So **tutto** di loro.   *I know **everything** about them.*
> Alla festa c'erano **tutti**.   ***Everyone** came to the party.*

Note that when a form of **tutto** is followed by a number (two, three, etc.), the word e (*and*) is always positioned between the pronoun and the number.

> Vengono alla festa **tutti e due**.   ***Both** will come to the party.*
> Le ho imparate a memoria **tutte e due**.   *I learned **both** by heart.*

When using **tutto(-a) quanto(-a)** (*every single one*), both words must agree with the noun they refer to.

> Vanno **tutti quanti** al cinema.   ***Every one of them** is going to the movie.*

Exercise 63

Translate the following sentences into Italian.

1. I have many things to do.

_____.

2. Do you speak Italian? No, just a little.

_____.

3. She doesn't have any beds.

_____.

4. They do not sleep a lot.

_____.

5. I know everything you want to teach me.

_____.

6. I like many houses.

_____.

7. In that store you will find everything.

_____.

8. This evening everybody was in class.

   _____.

9. Both of them had a new dress.

   _____.

10. Everyone will go to Italy this summer.

   _____.

Alcuno (*some, a few*) is mostly used in the plural and is used more with people than objects.

Alcuni non hanno votato.	*Some did not vote.*
Penso di comprarne **alcune**.	*I think I will buy a few of them.*

Note that in questions the pronoun **qualcuno** replaces **alcuno**.

Qualcuno ha spedito la lettera alla nonna?	*Did **someone** send the letter to the grandmother?*

You have already seen **qualcuno** with **altro**. But there are a few more indefinite pronouns that appear with **altro** such as: **nessun altro** (*no one else*), **qualcos'altro** (*something else*), **nient'altro** (*nothing else*). **Nessun altro** drops the final vowel, **qualcos'altro** and **nient'altro** also drop the final vowel but add an apostrophe.

Non c'è **nessun altro** nel corridoio.	*There is **no one else** in the hallway.*
Vorrei **qualcos'altro** da mangiare.	*I would like **something else** to eat.*
Non voglio **nient'altro**, grazie.	*I don't want **anything else**, thank you.*

Note that **altro** becomes **gli altri/le altre** after **tutti**(-e) to mean *all the others* or *everyone else*, but **il resto** not **altro** follows **tutto** to say *everything else*.

Tutti gli altri sono già partiti per le vacanze.	*Everyone else has already left for vacation.*
Quando c'è la salute, **tutto il resto** non è importante.	*As long as you have good health, **everything else** is unimportant.*

Exercise 64

Translate the following sentences into Italian using the appropriate indefinite pronouns.

1. Do you have many friends? No, only a few.

   _____.

2. Do you want a few postcards? Yes, I want a few of them.

   _____.

3. Each one of you (boys) needs to write a letter.

   _____.

4. Each one of them received a prize.

   _____.

5. Would you like to tell him something else?

   _____.

6. No, I don't have anything else to tell him.

   _____.

7. Who is still at the gym? Nobody else is left.

   _____.

8. Would you like something else to drink?

   _____.

9. No, thank you. I don't want anything else.

   _____.

4

Prepositions

Prepositions link a noun or a pronoun to other words in a sentence to express time, location, possession, cause, manner, or purpose. To know how and when to use prepositions correctly is not an easy task in any language, and Italian is no exception. This chapter deals with prepositions used with nouns and pronouns and their most common rules. Verbs followed by a preposition will be studied later in this book.

Prepositions have various meanings in different contexts and have a wide variety of uses, especially in Italian. There are eight simple or basic Italian prepositions. All of them except **per, tra,** and **fra** can form a word with a definite article, becoming compound prepositions.

The simple Italian prepositions are:

a	*to; in; at*
con	*with*
da	*from; by; at*
di	*of; from*
in	*in, into; at; to*
per	*for*
su	*on, onto*
tra/fra	*between; among*

A

The preposition **a** (*to; at; in*) is used to:

- express *at* in Italian sentences. Equivalent English sentences might use a different preposition in some of these cases

La nostra casa è **a** dieci minuti dalla scuola.	*Our house is ten minutes **from** school.*
Sono **a** casa tutto il giorno.	*I will be **at** home all day.*

Arriviamo **a** Firenze **alle** otto.	*We'll arrive **in** Florence **at** eight o'clock.*
Bologna è **a** settanta km. da Firenze.	*Bologna is seventy km. **from** Florence.*

- express *in* or *to* when used before the name of a city or a town

Sono **a** Bologna.	*I am **in** Bologna.*
Vado **a** Milano.	*I go **to** Milan.*

- express *in* or *on* when there is no emphasis on being "inside"

Questa sera non c'è niente **alla** televisione.	*This evening there is nothing **on** television.*

- express place, position, motion, and direction

accanto a	*next to, beside*
all'entrata	*at the door*
a nord di	*north of*
ai piedi di	*at the foot of*
a sinistra	*on the left*
attraverso	*across*

- accompany the following expressions

a buon mercato	*at a good price*
a causa	*because*
a forza di	*by, by means of*
a letto	*in bed*
a memoria	*by heart*
all'aperto	*in the open air, outdoors*
all'estero	*abroad*
almeno	*at least*
a mani vuote	*empty-handed*
a metà	*half, halfway*
a pagina	*on page*
a poco a poco	*little by little*
a prima vista	*at first sight*
al posto di	*instead of*
a terra	*on the ground*

Exercise 65

Translate the following sentences into Italian.

1. You (sing.) bought this television at a good price.

_____.

2. Will she be home tonight?

_____.

3. I arrived late because of the fog.

_____.

4. You (pl.) are having breakfast in bed.

_____.

5. I don't like to learn things by heart.

_____.

6. The lesson begins on page nine.

_____.

7. She ate all the food little by little.

_____.

8. He believes in love at first sight.

_____.

9. The vase fell on the ground and broke.

_____.

10. Put the sweater on instead of the jacket.

_____.

11 We like to eat outdoors.

_____.

12. We have lived abroad for four years.

_____.

The preposition **a** is also used to mean _by_ when describing a method of transportation or when using other common expressions, especially with the following:

ai ferri; **alla** griglia	_grilled_
andare **a** cavallo	_to go horseback riding_

andare **a** piedi	*to go **by** foot, to walk*
barca **a** vela	*sailboat*
fare **a** mano	*to make **by** hand*
imparare **a** memoria	*to learn **by** memory/by heart*
parlare **ad** alta voce	*to speak **with** a loud voice*
Vado **a** casa **a** piedi.	*I go home **by** foot.*
L'ha fatto **a** mano.	*He made it **by** hand.*

Exercise 66

Translate the following sentences into Italian using the preposition **a** as needed.

1. I like to walk in the woods.

_____.

2. I have never gone horseback riding.

_____.

3. My husband would like having a sailboat.

_____.

4. I love handmade items.

_____.

5. In school we had to learn everything by memory.

_____.

6. She doesn't know she speaks with a loud voice.

_____.

7. I like the meat grilled.

_____.

8. The church is too far to go there by foot.

_____.

9. At the library we cannot speak with a loud voice.

_____.

10. Grilled fish is very good.

_____.

In addition, the preposition **a** is used:

- with a verb of separation. In English it translates to the word *from*.

Qualcuno ha rubato la borsa **a** Giovanna.	*Someone stole the purse **from** Giovanna.*

- with expressions meaning *good-bye* or *until another time*

a domani	*see you tomorrow*
a lunedì, martedì, ecc.	*see you **on** Monday, Tuesday, etc.*
a presto	*see you soon*
a stasera	*see you tonight*
Ciao, **a** presto.	*Bye, I'll see you soon.*

- to express the time of the day, months, holidays

a marzo (*also* **in** marzo)	*in March*
a mezzogiorno	*at noon*
a mezzanotte	*at midnight*
a Natale, **a** Pasqua, ecc.	*at Christmas, **at** Easter, etc.*
Siamo andati in Africa **a** Natale.	*We went to Africa **for** Christmas.*
Mangiamo **a** mezzogiorno.	*We eat **at** noon.*

- to express future time and duration, meaning *until* or *to*

La banca è aperta dal lunedì **al** venerdì.	*The bank is open from Monday **to** Friday.*
Il negozio apre dalle otto **alle** diciannove.	*The store is open from eight **to** seven.*

- to express how many times something is repeated. In English it translates as *per*.

Fa la doccia quattro volte **alla** settimana.	*He takes a shower four times **per** week.*

- with description features

una camicetta **a** fiori	*a flowered blouse*
un gelato **al** limone	*a lemon ice cream*

Ieri ho mangiato un buon gelato **al** limone.	*Yesterday, I ate a good lemon ice cream.*
Abbiamo comprato una casa **a** due piani.	*We bought a two-story house.*

Note that when the word following the preposition **a** starts with the vowel *a*, **-d** is added to the preposition to make it easier to pronounce.

Lui è il primo **ad** arrivare.	*He is the first to arrive.*

Exercise 67

Translate the following sentences into Italian.

1. We'll go on a cruise in March.

_____.

2. I go to bed at midnight.

_____.

3. At noon we usually have lunch.

_____.

4. My family comes for Christmas and Easter.

_____.

5. I have to go. See you soon.

_____.

6. Bye, see you tomorrow.

_____.

7. He takes a shower twice a day.

_____.

8. I call her twice a week.

_____.

9. I work from eight until five.

_____.

10. I bought a nice flowery dress.

_____.

11. She only likes hazelnut ice cream.

_____.

12. The churches close at noon.

_____.

The preposition **a** is also used with the following expressions of time:

a partire da	_from . . . on_
a quest'ora	_at this hour_
a un tratto	_all of a sudden_
a volte	_at times_
allo stesso tempo	_at the same time_

Dove andate **a quest'ora?**   _Where are you going **at this hour**?_
A un tratto ha cominciato a piovere.   _**All of a sudden**, it started to rain._

Most adverbs or adjectives are followed by the preposition **a** before an infinitive.

abituato a	_used to_
attento a	_careful to_
bravo a	_good at_
disposto a	_willing to_
facile a	_easy to_
lento a	_slow to_
pronto a	_ready to_
solo a	_only (one) to_
ultimo a	_last (one) to_

Exercise 68

Fill in the blanks with the preposition **a** or **ad** as necessary.

1. Non sono abituata _____ andare _____ camminare.

2. Stai attento _____ non scivolare sul ghiaccio.

3. Lei è sempre disposta _____ aiutarci.

4. Loro sono molto lenti _____ imparare.

5. Noi siamo pronti _____ uscire di casa.

6. Sono la sola _____ parlare italiano in casa mia.

7. Voi siete gli ultimi _____ consegnare la domanda di lavoro.

8. Loro sono sempre pronti _____ parlare.

9. Lei è molto brava _____ cucinare.

10. Luisa mi ha detto che era disposta _____ venire _____ aiutarmi.

In

The Italian preposition **in** is often used:

- just as the English preposition *in*

  Milano è **in** Italia.   *Milan is **in** Italy.*
  Noi viviamo **in** Canada.   *We live **in** Canada.*

- to express *going to* or *being in* a place

  andare **in** Svizzera   *to go **to** Switzerland*
  andare **in** città   *to go downtown*
  andare **in** campagna   *to go **to** the country*

- to express *by* when talking about transportation

  andare **in** treno   *to go **by** train*
  andare **in** aereo   *to go **by** plane*
  andare **in** macchina   *to go **by** car*
  andare **in** bicicletta   *to go **by** bicycle*

- with expressions of time

  in marzo, **in** primavera/estate   *in March, **in** spring/summer*
  arrivare **in** anticipo/ritardo/orario   *to arrive early/late/on time*

Exercise 69

Translate the following sentences into Italian using the preposition **in**.

1. I like to go to Switzerland.

_____.

2. He enjoys living in the country.

_____.

3. He goes by train.

_____.

4. You (sing.) like to travel by airplane.

_____.

5. In March we'll go to South Africa.

_____.

6. They always travel in summer.

_____.

7. The train arrived on time.

_____.

8. She is always late.

_____.

9. I don't like to arrive late for dinner.

_____.

10. We love to see the flowering trees in spring.

_____.

The Italian preposition **in** is also used:

• when speaking about a time frame it takes to complete something

Ha letto il libro **in** un'ora.   _He read the book **in** one hour._

• with **entrare** (_to go in, enter_) and **salire** (_to go/come up_) and to express motion

Salgo **in** treno.   _I go **on** the train._
Entro **in** casa.   _I go **in** (enter) the house._

- to answer the question *where?*

Leggo **in** treno.	*I read on the train.*
Abito **in** Italia.	*I live in Italy.*
È **nella** buca della posta.	*It is in the mailbox.*
Telefono **in** Italia.	*I call Italy.*

- to express quantity

In quanti venite?	*How many of you will come?*
Veniamo **in** cinque.	*Five of us will come.*

- to express time, months, seasons, years, and centuries

Sono nata **in** luglio.	*I was born in July.*
Viaggio molto **in** estate.	*I travel a lot in summer.*

- to express colors and materials

Era dipinto **in** (di) verde.	*It was painted in green.*
Il palazzo reale è tutto **in** marmo.	*The royal palace is all in marble.*
La statua del Nettuno a Bologna è **in** bronzo.	*The statue of Neptune in Bologna is in bronze.*

Exercise 70

Translate the following sentences into Italian.

1. I made a cake in half an hour.

_____.

2. She finished her homework in fifteen minutes.

_____.

3. He went on the train with the suitcases.

_____.

4. They would like to live in Italy.

_____.

5. We went in the house to eat.

_____.

6. Every Sunday I call Italy.

_____.

7. The letter is in the mailbox.

_____.

8. You (sing.) read the lesson on the train.

_____.

9. Everybody reads the newspaper on the train.

_____.

There are many other common expressions using the preposition **in**, such as:

in contanti	*cash*
indietro	*backward*
in famiglia	*within the family*
in fretta	*in a hurry*
in mezzo a	*in the middle of*
in quanto a	*as far as*
in quattro e quattr'otto	*right away, in a jiffy*
in tempo	*in time*
invano	*in vain*

Exercise 71

Fill in the blanks with the expressions in parentheses.

1. Io pago solo _____ (*cash*).

2. Abbiamo cenato _____ (*within the family*).

3. Lucia è uscita _____ (*in a hurry*) senza salutare.

4. Il gatto va sempre _____ (*in the middle*) alla strada.

5. _____ (*As far*) alla traduzione, non è ancora finita.

6. _____ (*In a jiffy*) hanno cambiato casa.

7. Sono arrivata _____ (*in time*) per la fine della partita.

8. Paola ha fatto un passo _____ (*backward*) ed è caduta
   nell'acqua.

9. Ho telefonato _____ (*in vain*) perché nessuno ha risposto.

10. Loro non pagano mai _____ (*cash*).

11. Luisa arriva sempre _____ (*late*).

12. A voi piace stare _____ (*within the family*).

Da

The Italian preposition **da** means *from* in English. The following list shows some of the most common uses for **da** in Italian.

- When **da** expresses movement or origin, it translates as *from*, *by*, *to*, or *through a place*.

Vengo **da** Firenze.	*I come from Florence.*
Passo **da** te.	*I go by your house.*
Lui va **dal** dottore.	*He goes to the doctor.*
Lei esce **dalla** porta di dietro.	*She goes out through the backdoor.*

- **Da** expresses purpose, intentions, and scope.

Hai una bella gonna **da** sera.	*You have a very nice evening gown.*
Le compro una tazza **da** tè.	*I buy her a teacup.*

- **Da** is used *before* an infinitive and *after* **molto, poco, niente, troppo, qualcosa**, and **nulla**.

C'è troppo **da** mangiare.	*There is too much to eat.*
Abbiamo molto **da** fare.	*We have a lot to do.*
Non ho nulla **da** dirti.	*I have nothing to tell you.*
Lui vuole qualcosa **da** mangiare e **da** bere.	*He wants something to eat and to drink.*

Exercise 72

Translate the following sentences into Italian.

1. They come from Rome.

_____.

2. I have to go to the doctor.

_____.

3. She has an appointment at the dentist.

_____.

4. She has bought nice evening shoes.

_____.

5. Today there was a lot to do at the office.

_____.

6. He never has anything to tell.

_____.

7. At Christmas there is always too much to eat.

_____.

8. I would like something to drink.

_____.

9. We still have a little to do at home.

_____.

10. They are coming from the game.

_____.

Da has many more uses. For example, it appears in sentences:

- to express time and age

Non ci parliamo **da** dieci anni.	*We haven't talked to each other **for** ten years.*
La conosco **da** tanto tempo.	*I have known her **for** a long time.*

- after a noun or an adjective to describe the physical characteristics of a person. In English *with* is used, where Italian uses **da**.

È una ragazza **dai** capelli biondi.	*She is a girl **with** blond hair.*
Chi è quella ragazza **dagli** occhi verdi?	*Who is that girl **with** the green eyes?*

- after a noun to describe value, worth, price and cost of something

Ho mangiato un gelato **da** tre euro.	*I ate an ice cream that cost three euros.*
Ho bisogno di un francobollo **da** due euro.	*I need a two-euros stamp.*
una casa **da** poco; da pochi soldi	*a cheap house*

- to convey manners

> Si comporta **da** persona bene educata. *He behaves **like** a well-mannered person.*
> Questa è una casa **da** milionari. *This is a house **for** millionaires.*

- to express *as* when it is the equivalent of *when*

> **Da** bambina amavo le bambole. *As a child, I loved dolls.*
> **Da** giovane gli piaceva andare a ballare. *As a young person, he loved going dancing.*

Exercise 73

Translate the following sentences into Italian.

1. I have bought a cheap car.

_____.

2. Who is that young man with blue eyes?

_____?

3. As a child I cried a lot.

_____.

4. As a young person I played basketball.

_____.

5. It is a cheap house.

_____.

6. I would like three stamps worth one euro.

_____.

7. Who is that man with gray hair?

_____?

8. He behaves as a mature person.

_____.

9. She lives like a princess.

_____.

When the preposition **da** is used with the disjunctive pronouns **me**, **te**, **sé** (sing.), **noi**, **voi**, and **sé** (pl.), it means *by myself, by yourself, by himself/herself, by ourselves, by yourselves, by themselves.* The subject of the sentence and the disjunctive pronoun always refer to the same person.

Luisa ha finito di pulire tutto **da** sé.　*Luisa finished cleaning all **by** herself.*
Io ho finito i compiti tutti **da** me.　*I finished the homework all **by** myself.*

Da means *since* or *for* in time expressions when the verb of the sentence is in the present indicative or in the imperfect indicative tense.

Sono in America **da** molti anni.　*I have been in America **for** many years.*
La conosco **da** tanto tempo.　*I have known her **for** a long time.*

Exercise 74

Translate the following sentences into Italian.

1. You want to do everything by yourself.

_____.

2. He carries all the bags by himself.

_____.

3. They cut the grass all by themselves.

_____.

4. We eat all by ourselves.

_____.

5. He ate his dinner all by himself.

_____.

6. I have not seen her for a long time.

_____.

7. He hasn't been talking to me for a year.

_____.

8. We haven't seen a movie in a long time.

_____.

9. You (sing.) have been living in that house since you were a child.

_____.

10. I have not gone skiing in five years.

_____.

There are still more common expressions using the preposition **da**:

da dove?	*from where?*
da mattina a sera	*from morning to night*
dal mattino alla sera	*from morning to night*
da parte	*aside*
da un pezzo	*for some time, for a while*
da un lato	*on one hand, from one side, aside*

Exercise 75

Fill in the blanks with the required prepositional phrases in parentheses using **da**.

1. _____ (*From where*) viene tuo marito?

2. Mettiamo questi libri _____ (*aside*).

3. _____ (*On one hand*) mi piace viaggiare, dall'altro mi

   stanco molto.

4. Non li vediamo _____ (*for a while*).

5. Il cane abbaia _____ (*from morning to night*).

6. Quella ragazza non fa niente _____ (*from morning to night*).

7. Metti _____ (*aside*) le cose estive.

8. Cammino _____ (*for some time*).

9. Non so _____ (*from where*) vengano.

10. Devo andare _____ (*to the*) parrucchiera.

Di

The Italian preposition **di** conveys the meaning of possession, specification, and definition (*of*):

Questa è la casa **di** mia cugina.	*This is my cousin's house (the house of my cousin).*
Mia cugina è professoressa **di** matematica.	*My cousin is a math professor (professor of math).*
È una giacca **di** pelle.	*It is a leather jacket (jacket of leather).*

Di, like **da,** is used in many common expressions.

di andata e ritorno	*round-trip*
di... anni	*. . . years old*
d'autunno	*in the fall*
di buon appetito	*a good appetite*
di buona voglia	*willingly*
di che colore... ?	*what color . . .?*
d'estate	*in the summer*
di fretta	*in a rush*
di fronte	*opposite, across*
di giorno	*in the daytime*
di giorno in giorno	*from day to day*
d'improvviso	*suddenly*
di mala voglia	*unwillingly*
di male in peggio	*from bad to worse*
di moda	*in fashion*
di notte	*at night*
di nuovo	*again*
di ritardo	*late*
di sera	*in the evening*
di tanto in tanto	*now and then*

Io lavoro sempre **di notte.**	*I always work **at night.***
D'estate mi alzo sempre presto.	***In summer** I always get up early.*
Sono persone **di buon appetito.**	*These people have **a good appetite.***

Exercise 76

Fill in the blanks with the correct forms of the expressions in parentheses.

1. _____ (*Suddenly*), Luisa venne da noi.

2. Cantate _____ (*again*) la canzone!

3. Faceva tutto _____ (*unwillingly*).

4. _____ (*What color*) è la tua macchina?

5. È un signore _____ (*fifty years old*).

6. Va sempre in Italia _____ (*in the fall*).

7. Quelle scarpe non sono _____ (*in fashion*).

8. Voglio un biglietto _____ (round-trip).

9. Tutto va _____ (from bad to worse).

10. L'aereo arriva con due ore _____ (late).

11. _____ (Now and then) andiamo al cinema.

Di is also used:

- after **qualcosa** (something) and **niente** (nothing), when followed by an adjective

Ho visto **qualcosa di** interessante.	*I saw **something** interesting.*
Questo dolce non è **niente di** speciale.	*This cake is **nothing** special.*

- with adverbial expressions

essere **di** buon umore	*to be in a good mood*
essere **di** cattivo umore	*to be in a bad mood*
arrivare **di** corsa	*to come running*
vestire **di** bianco	*to dress in white*
bere **d'**un fiato	*to drink in one gulp*

- to express what something is made of or contains

un vestito **di** lana	*a woolen dress*
una catena **d'**oro	*a golden chain*
un bicchiere **d'**acqua	*a glass of water*

Exercise 77

Translate the following sentences into Italian.

1. This is my parents' house.

_____.

2. We are from Naples.

_____.

3. It's going from bad to worse.

_____.

4. I would like to do something interesting.

_____.

5. There is nothing interesting on TV.

_____.

6. My husband is always in a good mood.

_____.

7. He came in the house running.

_____.

8. The bride was not dressed in white.

_____.

9. He drank the beer in one gulp.

_____.

10. I lost my golden chain.

_____.

The following adjectives are always followed by the preposition **di** plus a verb infinitive.

ansioso di	*anxious to*
capace di	*capable of*
contento di	*happy with*
certo di	*certain of*
felice di	*happy to*
sicuro di	*sure of*
stanco di	*tired of*
triste di	*sad to*

Sono ansioso **di** vederli.	*I am anxious to see them.*
È felice **di** venire in America.	*He is happy to come to America.*

Di is also used in combination with a definite article to express the partitive *any, some,* or *(one) of the.*

Abbiamo mangiato **del** pesce buonissimo.	*We ate (**some**) very good fish.*
Giovanni è uno **dei** giocatore della squadra di football.	*Giovanni is **one of the** football players.*

Exercise 78

Translate the following sentences into Italian.

1. We were happy with our trip.

_____.

2. I am very happy to see you.

_____.

3. Are you sure you know it?

_____?

4. At night it is still cold.

_____.

5. She is sad to see you go.

_____.

6. She is wearing a beautiful woolen dress.

_____.

7. I am going to the market to buy some fruit.

_____.

8. There are some flowers that have a beautiful fragrance.

_____.

9. In my class there are some men and some women.

_____.

10. I want to read some good books.

_____.

Exercise 79

Fill in the blanks with the appropriate forms of the prepositions **da** or **di** as necessary.

1. Compriamo la carne _____ macellaio.
2. Vorrei un bicchiere _____ acqua, per favore.
3. Questa è la bicicletta _____ Luisa.
4. Non vedo Maria _____ tanto tempo.
5. Ho ricevuto una lettera _____ Erica.

6. Le ho comprato un vestito _____ seta.

7. Il vestito viene _____ Italia.

8. È un film _____ ridere.

9. Compro due cartoline e due francobolli _____ cinquanta centesimi.

10. Ci piace camminare _____ mattina.

Su

The Italian preposition **su** is used to:

• express a location

| Ho messo il libro **sulla** scrivania. | *I put the book **on the** desk.* |

• express *by* or *near*

| Hanno la casa **sul** mare. | *They have a house **by the** sea.* |
| Lei abita in una città **sul** lago. | *She lives in a town **by the** lake.* |

• convey approximation

| Il prosciutto costa **sui** venti euro al chilogrammo. | *Prosciutto costs **around** twenty euros per kilogram.* |
| Un uomo **sulla** settantina. | *A man **about** seventy years old.* |

• to express *out of*

| Sei uomini **su** otto sono obesi. | *Six men **out of** eight are obese.* |
| Tre donne **su** quattro si tingono i capelli. | *Three women **out of** four dye their hair.* |

The following expressions using the preposition **su** are common in Italian:

dare su	*with a view on, to look onto*
Su!	*Come on!*
su e giù	*up and down*

Per

The Italian preposition **per** is used:

- to express intentions or destination

Ho comprato questo orologio **per** te.	*I bought this watch for you.*
I miei figli sono partiti **per** il mare.	*My kids left for the sea.*

- to convey *because of, out of, by means of,* or *for fear of*

Per il freddo, abbiamo acceso il riscaldamento.	*Because of the cold we turned on the heat.*
Per paura di non arrivare in tempo è partito presto.	*For fear of not arriving on time, he left early.*
Mandami la traduzione **per** via fax.	*Send me the translation by fax.*

- in mathematics

Due **per** due fanno quattro.	*Two times two makes four.*

Exercise 80

Translate the following sentences into Italian.

1. He doesn't have friends because of his shyness.

   _____.

2. She washes her hands all the time for fear of diseases.

   _____.

3. They don't eat for fear of getting fat.

   _____.

4. Because of the flu, Giacomo has not eaten for the last three days.

   _____.

5. Venice is known for its canals.

   _____.

6. Naples is known for its music.

_____.

7. Rome is important for its history.

_____.

8. I will communicate with you by phone.

_____.

9. This material is for the school.

_____.

10. We are going to the mountains to ski.

_____.

The following list shows some of the common Italian expressions using **per**:

per caso	*by chance*
per conto mio/tuo/ecc.	*as far as I am/you are/etc. concerned*
per esempio	*for example*
per favore	*please*
per lo meno	*at least*
per ora	*for the time being*
perciò	*therefore*
giorno per giorno	*day by day*

Exercise 81

Fill in the blanks using the prepositions in parentheses.

1. Avete visto le forbici _____ (*by chance*)?

2. _____ (*As far as*) nostro, sarebbe meglio andare in macchina.

3. _____ (*For example*), la parola "dentista" è maschile.

4. Vorrei un bicchiere d'acqua, _____ (*please*).

5. Ci sono _____ (*at least*) un centinaio di uccelli.

6. _____ (*For now*) non dire niente a nessuno.

7. Non hai studiato, _____ (*therefore*) sarai bocciato.

8. Si muove un po' _____ (*day by day*).

9. _____ (*Month by month*) si vede la differenza.

10. Questa casa vale _____ (*at least*) trecentomila dollari.

11. _____ (*As far as*) mio, non è stata una decisione molto saggia.

12. Hai visto i miei occhiali _____ (*by chance*)?

Con

The Italian preposition **con** is used to express *with* when it:

- conveys being or going *with* someone

Partono **con** noi.	*They are leaving **with** us.*
Marco ha un appuntamento **con** il dentista.	*Marco has an appointment **with** the dentist.*

- conveys description, manner, or means of

Mio fratello procede **con** molta cautela nel suo lavoro.	*My brother continues his job **with** great caution.*
Arrivano stasera **con** il treno.	*They will arrive tonight **with** the train.*

- means *despite* or *with*

Con tutto quello che mangia, è magro.	***Despite** all he eats, he is thin.*
Con il tempo umido, sento molti dolori.	***With** the damp weather, I have aches and pains.*

Tra and Fra

The prepositions **tra** and **fra** express position, time, and space and mean *between*, *in*, *within*, *among*, or *of*. Their meanings are the same, but their use is determined by phonetic sound more than by exact rules. So it is preferable to say **tra le fragole** rather than **fra le fragole** (*among the strawberries*); **fra Trento e Trieste** rather than **tra Trento e Trieste** (*between Trento and Trieste*).

Partiremo **tra** un'ora.   We'll leave *in an hour.*
È una discussione **fra** marito e   *It is a discussion **between** husband*
moglie.   *and wife.*

Exercise 82

Fill in the blanks using either the preposition **con** or **fra/tra**.

1. Io vado a casa _____ la mia macchina.

2. Io sono in vacanza _____ le mie amiche.

3. Io sono in vacanza _____ gli alberi.

4. _____ di noi c'è di mezzo il mare.

5. _____ questa pioggia, i fiori cresceranno in fretta.

6. _____ tutto quello che fai, lei non ti ringrazia mai.

7. La lezione comincia _____ dieci minuti.

8. _____ me e te non c'è comprensione.

9. Il gatto si è nascosto _____ i cespugli.

10. Ti ho riconosciuta _____ la folla.

Prepositions with geographical expressions

The preposition **a** is used to express *in* with names of cities. Most cities are feminine in Italian.

Ho trascorso un mese **a** Firenze.   *I spent a month **in** Florence.*

The preposition **in** means *in* when it is used with unmodified feminine names of countries, islands, states, continents, and provinces.

Io sono nata **in** Africa.   *I was born **in** Africa.*
Vorrei vivere **in** Arizona.   *I would like to live **in** Arizona.*

Remember that **in** + a definite article is used with modified feminine geographical names or with masculine geographical names, modified or not.

nell'Italia settentrionale	*in northern Italy*
negli Stati Uniti	*in the United States*
nel Canada	*in Canada*

The preposition **di** is used before the name of a person's city of origin.

Io sono **di** Bologna.	*I am from Bologna.*

Di + definite article is used with names of countries, states, or provinces.

del Canada	*from Canada*
del New Jersey	*from New Jersey*
della Lombardia	*from Lombardy*

The following list shows the names of some countries and regions that will be used in the next exercise.

l'Argentina	*Argentina*
l'Asia	*Asia*
l'Australia	*Australia*
il Brasile	*Brazil*
il Canada	*Canada*
la Cina	*China*
l'Europa	*Europe*
la Francia	*France*
la Germania	*Germany*
il Giappone	*Japan*
l'Inghilterra	*England*
il Messico	*Mexico*
i Paesi Bassi	*Netherlands*
la Russia	*Russia*
la Spagna	*Spain*
gli Stati Uniti	*United States*
la Svizzera	*Switzerland*

Exercise 83

Fill in the blanks with the prepositions and geographical nouns in parentheses.

1. Vorrei andare _____ (*to Germany*).

2. Viviamo _____(*in the United States*).

3. In futuro voglio andare _____ (*in Argentina*).

4. Giovanni è _____ (*from Canada*).

5. Milano è la capitale _____(*of Lombardy*).

6. Genova è _____ (*in Italy*).

7. _____ (*In Japan*) ci sono molte isole.

8. _____ (*In the Netherlands*) ci sono molti fiori.

9. I canguri vivono _____ (*in Australia*).

10. Le montagne _____ (*in Switzerland*) sono coperte di neve.

Di may omit the final -i and add an apostrophe before words that begin with a vowel: **d'inverno** (*in winter*), **d'oro** (*golden*).

Da omits the final -a before a vowel only when **da** is part of an idiom: **d'ora in poi** (*from now on*); **fin d'allora** (*since that time*).

The preposition **a** before words that begin with an **a** may change to **ad** to ease the pronunciation: **Vado ad Ancona** (*I go to Ancona*). Italian today, however, mostly uses just **a**, which is the most correct form.

The compound forms for **con** and **per** + the definite article, are not used anymore, except for **col** and **coi**, which are occasionally found in written language. The forms used today are: **con lo, con la, con gli, con le**, and so on and **per il, per la, per i, per le**, and so on.

Prepositions before infinitives

In Italian the infinitive is the only verb form that may follow a preposition.

Giovanni ha imparato **a guidare.**   *Giovanni has learned how **to drive.***
Luigi aveva appena finito **di mangiare.**   *Luigi had just finished **eating**.*

Some verbs are always followed by the preposition **a** before an infinitive. The best way to learn them is through study and memorization. Here is a list of just a few of them:

abituarsi a	*to get used to*
aiutare a	*to help to*
andare a	*to go to*
arrivare a	*to arrive at; to succeed in*
cominciare a	*to begin to*
continuare a	*to continue to*
imparare a	*to learn to*
incoraggiare a	*to encourage to*
insegnare a	*to teach to*
invitare a	*to invite to*
mandare a	*to send to*
mettersi a	*to begin to*
prepararsi a	*to prepare to*
provare a	*to try to*
riuscire a	*to succeed in*
servire a	*to serve in*
uscire a	*to go out to*

Exercise 84

Translate the following sentences into Italian.

1. Pietro is learning to drive.

_____.

2. Italian women go shopping for food every day.

_____.

3. The dog enjoys swimming in the lake.

_____.

4. Silvia hesitates speaking in front of people.

_____.

5. I will send him to learn Spanish.

_____.

6. She goes out to buy the newspaper.

_____.

7. Marco is learning to read.

_____.

8. We do not give up going on vacation.

_____ .

9. They will try calling us via satellite.

_____ .

10. He does not succeed opening the door.

_____ .

The following verbs are always followed by the preposition **di** before an infinitive. Again, these must be studied and memorized.

accettare di	_to accept_
accontentarsi di	_to be satisfied_
avere bisogno di	_to need to_
avere fretta di	_to be in a hurry to_
avere paura di	_to be afraid to_
cercare di	_to try to_
chiedere di	_to ask to_
credere di	_to believe in_
decidere di	_to decide to_
dimenticare di	_to forget to_
dire di	_to say, tell to_
domandare di	_to ask to_
finire di	_to finish_
meravigliarsi di	_to be surprised about_
pensare di	_to think; plan to_
permettere di	_to allow to_
pregare di	_to beg to_
preoccuparsi di	_to worry about_
proibire di	_to forbid to_
promettere di	_to promise to_
ricordarsi di	_to remember to_
ringraziare di	_to thank for_
sapere di	_to know about_
smettere di	_to stop_
sognare di	_to dream about_
sperare di	_to hope to_
valere la pena di	_to be worth it_

Exercise 85

Translate the following sentences into Italian.

1. Don't forget to call your mother.

   _____.

2. I promised to take her to the zoo.

   _____.

3. He should stop smoking.

   _____.

4. Try to arrive on time.

   _____.

5. She hopes to meet him at the park.

   _____.

6. They begged me to go visit them.

   _____.

7. He promised me he would study during the summer.

   _____.

8. I dream of having a house near Lake Como.

   _____.

9. She tries to learn the poetry by heart.

   _____.

10. My father prohibited me from going to the party.

   _____.

Exercise 86

Rewrite the following sentences inserting either the preposition **a** or **di** in the blanks.

1. Maria finisce _____ leggere la rivista.

   _____.

2. Giovanna continua _____ pulire la casa.

   _____.

3. Pietro comincia _____ suonare il violino.

   _____.

4. Noi cerchiamo _____ telefonare ai nostri nonni.

_____.

5. Lei promette _____ portare sua figlia al cinema.

_____.

6. Voglio mettermi _____ imparare lo spagnolo.

_____.

7. Loro si divertono _____ cantare mentre lavorano.

_____.

8. Voglio imparare _____ sciare.

_____.

9. Lei mi aiuta _____ fare le valige.

_____.

10. Loro si preparano _____ andare al campeggio.

_____.

The following prepositions showing ongoing action or action that is not yet complete are commonly used before an infinitive. The equivalent of this construction in English is when an **-ing** ending is used at the end of a verb.

al	*on, upon*
con il (col)	*with the*
da	*to, as to*
dopo	*after*
invece di	*instead of*
oltre a	*to, in order to*
prima di	*before*
senza	*without*

Prima di mangiare, bisogna lavarsi le mani.	*Before eating, you have to wash your hands.*
È partito **senza salutare**.	*He left **without saying** good-bye.*

The preposition **da** + infinitive may be used after a noun to describe the purpose of that noun.

una macchina **da cucire**	*a **sewing** machine*
carta **da scrivere**	***writing** paper*

The preposition **da** is also used after **qualcosa, niente, molto, altro,** and **poco** after an infinitive.

Hai **qualcosa da fare?**	*Do you have something to do?*
Ho **molto da fare.**	*I have a lot to do.*
Abbiamo **poco da fare.**	*We have little to do.*

The preposition **per** + infinitive expresses *to* or *in order to.*

Lavoriamo **per vivere.**	*We work to live.*

The construction **stare per** + infinitive is used for the expression *to be about to.*

Stava per uscire quando ho chiamato.	*He was about to go out when I called.*
Chiamalo, **sta per partire.**	*Call him, he is about to leave.*

To express *after having done something*, the preposition **dopo** (*after*) is followed by either **essere** or **avere** and then the past participle of the verb showing the action. For example, **avere dormito,** *to have slept* or **essere arrivato,** *to have arrived.*

Dopo aver cenato, abbiamo mangiato il gelato.	*After having eaten, we ate ice cream.*
Maria è partita **dopo essere rimasta** due mesi da me.	*Maria left after having stayed two months with me.*

Exercise 87

Fill in the blanks with the prepositions in parentheses.

1. Maria parla sempre _____ (*without*) riflettere.

2. Lucia lavora _____ (*in order to*) andare in Italia.

3. I bambini fanno la merenda _____ (*before*) andare a giocare.

4. La mamma cucina _____ (*without*) avere le ricette.

5. Pietro guarda la televisione _____ (*instead of*) pulire la sua camera.

6. Leggiamo i libri italiani _____ (*in order to*) imparare nuovi vocaboli.

7. Giorgio sorride _____ (*upon*) vedere i suoi amici.

8. Tutto si dimentica _____ (*with*) il passare del tempo.

9. Il padre dà la colpa al figlio _____ (*without*) ascoltare la sua spiegazione.

10. Parlano _____ (*before*) pensare a quello che dicono.

11. Luigi lavora tutta l'estate _____ (*in order to*) pagarsi l'università.

Some infinitives stand on their own without needing the assistance of a preposition after them. An example of the more commonly used ones are:

amare	*to love*
ascoltare	*to listen*
bastare	*to be enough*
camminare	*to walk*
desiderare	*to wish, desire*
dovere	*to have to, must*
fare	*to do; make*
guardare	*to watch*
piacere	*to be pleased, like*
potere	*to be able to*
preferire	*to prefer*
pulire	*to clean*
sapere	*to know*
sentire	*to hear*
stare	*to stay*
uscire	*to go out*
vedere	*to see*
volere	*to want*

Exercise 88

Translate the following sentences into Italian.

1. It is necessary to clean everything.

   _____.

2. You (sing.) have to stay home today.

   _____.

3. They can't go out without permission.

   _____.

4. She knows how to cook very well.

_____.

5. He prefers to speak English.

_____.

6. You (pl.) like to walk.

_____.

7. We don't like to walk.

_____.

8. It is necessary to study.

_____.

9. It is necessary to turn off the cellular phone.

_____.

10. I wish to eat cherries.

_____.

Adjectives and adverbs followed by a preposition

Most adjectives are followed by the preposition **a** before an infinitive.

abituato(-a) a	*used to*
attento(-a) a	*careful to*
disposto(-a) a	*willing to*
lento(-a) a	*slow to*
primo(-a) a	*first to*
pronto(-a) a	*ready to*
solo(-a) a	*only one to*
ultimo(-a) a	*last one to*

There are some adjectives, however, that are followed by the preposition **di** before an infinitive.

ansioso(-a) di	*anxious to*
capace di	*capable of*
contento(-a) di	*glad to*
certo(-a) di	*sure to/of*

felice di	*happy to*
incapace di	*incapable of*
sicuro(-a) di	*sure to/of*
stanco(-a) di	*tired of*
triste di	*sad to*

Exercise 89

Fill in the blanks with the appropriate preposition **a** or **di**.

1. Non sono abituati _____ chiudere la porta.

2. È disposta _____ viaggiare in seconda classe.

3. Luigi è lento _____ capire la lezione.

4. Siamo capaci _____ aprire la porta.

5. Sono stanco _____ dirti di studiare.

6. Pietro è felice _____ vederti.

7. Sono i soli _____ venire a trovarci.

8. Siamo certi _____ vederli a scuola.

9. Sono contenta _____ averti conosciuta.

10. Pietro è il primo _____ arrivare in ufficio la mattina.

Prepositional contractions

Before concluding this chapter on prepositions, let's review prepositional contractions. Contractions are discussed briefly in Chapter 2 and it is important to know them well.

Five of the most commonly used prepositions combine with the definite articles to form simple words. These prepositions are: **a** (*to; at*), **da** (*from; by*), **di** (*of; about; from*), **in** (*in; into*), and **su** (*on*). The combined prepositions follow the same rules as the definite articles.

a + il = al	Luigi va **al** cinema.	*Luigi goes **to the** movies.*
da + lo = dallo	I tifosi tornano **dallo** stadio.	*The fans return **from the** stadium.*
di + la = della	La casa **della** nonna è vecchia.	*Grandma's house (the house **of** the Grandma) is old.*
in + il = nel	I ragazzi giocano **nel** parco.	*The children play **in the** park.*
su + il = sul	Il bicchiere è **sul** tavolo.	*The glass is **on the** table.*

The following table shows the most common prepositional contractions.

	+ *il*	+ *lo*	+ *l'*	+ *i*	+ *gli*	+ *la*	+ *l'*	+ *le*
a	al	allo	all'	ai	agli	alla	all'	alle
da	dal	dallo	dall'	dai	dagli	dalla	dall'	dalle
di	del	dello	dell'	dei	degli	della	dell'	delle
in	nel	nello	nell'	nei	negli	nella	nell'	nelle
su	sul	sullo	sull'	sui	sugli	sulla	sull'	sulle

The preposition **con** can also contract with the masculine definite articles **il** and **i**. For example:

Luigi parla **con il** professore.   *Luigi speaks **with the** professor.*

Or:

Luigi parla **col** professore.   *Luigi speaks **with the** professor.*
Marisa parla **con i** professori.   *Marisa speaks **with the** professors.*

Or:

Marisa parla **coi** professori.   *Marisa speaks **with the** professors.*

A definite article is usually omitted when **in** appears before **casa**, **chiesa**, **città**, **cucina**, **banca**, and **biblioteca**, unless the noun is modified by another word or expression.

Maria va **in** chiesa.   *Maria goes **to** church.*

But:

Maria va **nella** chiesa di San Giovanni.   *Maria goes **to** Saint John's Church.*
Vado **in** banca.   *I go **to** the bank.*

But:

Vado **nella** banca d'Italia.   *I go **to the** Bank of Italy.*

Note that when contracting **di** or **in** with a definite article, **di** becomes **de** and **in** becomes **ne**.

In compound prepositions or prepositions consisting of more than one word, only the preposition (**a**, **da**, **di**, etc.) is combined with the definite article.

vicino a	Lo stadio è **vicino alla** piazza.	*The stadium is **near the square**.*
lontano da	L'ospedale è **lontano dal** centro.	*The hospital is **far from the** downtown area.*
davanti a	La scuola è **davanti al** museo.	*The school is **in front of the** museum.*

Exercise 90

Fill in the blanks with the appropriate prepositions or contractions using the prepositions in parentheses.

1. Luigi è _____ (in) Bar Stella.
2. Carlo è_____ (a) stadio _____
   (con) amici.
3. Maria torna _____ (da) lavoro
   _____ (a) otto.
4. Pietro è _____ (a) stazione.
5. Gian Piero è _____ (a) casa.
6. Il teatro è vicino _____ (a) museo.
7. Aspettiamo i nostri amici davanti _____ (a) cinema.
8. I ragazzi studiano sempre _____ (in) biblioteca.
9. Io non ho le chiavi _____ (di) camera.
10. Noi usciamo _____ (da) albergo
    _____ (a) tre.
11. Quella signora parla sempre _____ (di) stesse cose.
12. Non conosco il nome _____ (di) professore.

When the preposition **di** is combined with a definite article (**del, dello, della, dell'**, or **dei, degli, delle**), it expresses the English equivalent of *some* or *any*.

Exercise 91

Fill in the blanks with the appropriate forms of **di** + the definite article.

1. Conosco _____ studentesse americane.
2. Compro _____ caramelle per i bambini.
3. Desidero bere _____ vino.

4. Devo comprare _____ frutta.

5. Io ordino _____ insalata mista.

6. Giovanni porta _____ spumante italiano.

7. Loro hanno _____ begli alberghi a Rimini.

8. Vedo _____ bei ragazzi.

9. Vedo _____ belle ragazze.

10. Abbiamo _____ amici negli Stati Uniti.

5

Adjectives

In Italian there are many different types of adjectives: descriptive, demonstrative, possessive, indefinite, interogative. Whatever type, all adjectives agree in gender and number with the noun or pronoun they modify. This chapter will discuss adjectives and their uses in depth.

Descriptive adjectives

Descriptive adjectives describe a noun or a pronoun, adding information about it to the sentence.

una **bella** casa	*a **beautiful** house*
una **buona** cena	*a **good** dinner*
la macchina **nuova**	*the **new** car*

Ho letto un libro **interessante**.	*I read an **interesting** book.*
A Maria piacciono i vestiti **eleganti**.	*Maria likes **elegant** dresses.*

Adjectives are not always necessary, but they are important, because by using an adjective, more effective relevant nuances can be expressed. A car can be described as: **un'auto bella** (*beautiful*), **rossa** (*red*), **nuova** (*new*), **comoda** (*comfortable*), **veloce** (*fast*), **moderna** (*modern*), **scattante** (*sprinty/zippy*), and so on. There is no limit to the number of descriptive adjectives that can be used. For example:

- Color: **rosso** (*red*), **verde** (*green*), **giallognolo** (*yellowish*), **violaceo** (*purplish*)
- Shape: **rotondo** (*round*), **quadrato** (*square*), **triangolare** (*triangular*)
- Look: **robusto** (*sturdy*), **esile** (*thin*), **solido** (*solid*), **delicato** (*delicate*)
- Dimension: **largo** (*broad, large*), **stretto** (*tight, narrow*), **lungo** (*long*), **corto** (*short*), **grande** (*big*), **alto** (*tall*), **spazioso** (*spacious*)
- Time: **invernale** (*winter, wintry*), **estivo** (*summer*), **diurno** (*daytime*), **notturno** (*nighttime*), **pomeridiano** (*afternoon*), **quotidiano** (*daily*)

- Physical sensations: **caldo** (*warm*), **freddo** (*cold*), **dolce** (*sweet*), **aspro** (*sour*), **morbido** (*soft*), **ruvido** (*rough, coarse*)
- Feelings: **felice** (*happy*), **triste** (*sad*), **ansioso** (*anxious*), **calmo** (*calm*), **nervoso** (*nervous*), **malinconico** (*melancholic*), **studioso** (*studious*), **generoso** (*generous*), **giovane** (*young*)

Exercise 92

Fill in the blanks with the adjectives in parentheses.

1. La casa è _____ (*new*).

2. La minestra è _____ (*warm*).

3. I grattacieli sono edifici _____ (*modern*).

4. Il pane in Italia è_____ (*delicious*).

5. Le mele sono _____ (*red*).

6. Gli studenti sono _____ (*studious*).

7. Carlo e Pietro sono _____ (*tall*).

8. La mia amica è _____ (*generous*).

9. Il cane è un animale _____ (*domestic*).

10. Gli zii di Mario sono _____ (*young*).

11. La scuola è molto _____ (*spacious*).

12. Mia zia è _____ (*thin*).

Gender and number of adjectives

Italian adjectives are a variable part of speech changing in gender and number according to the noun or pronoun modified.

libro **nuovo**	*new book*	libri **nuovi**	*new books*
casa **nuova**	*new house*	case **nuove**	*new houses*

Adjectives ending in **-o** in the masculine singular form, change the **-o** to **-a** in the feminine singular. The **-o** changes to **-i** in the masculine plural and to **-e** in the feminine plural.

masculine singular	feminine singular	masculine plural	feminine plural	
bravo	brava	bravi	brave	*good*
famoso	famosa	famosi	famose	*famous*

Il **bravo** ragazzo	*the **good** boy*
La **brava** ragazza	*the **good** girl*
I **bravi** ragazzi	*the **good** boys*
Le **brave** ragazze	*the **good** girls*

The following table shows some common Italian adjectives and demonstrates the various adjective endings:

masculine singular	feminine singular	masculine plural	feminine plural	
allegro	allegra	allegri	allegre	*cheerful*
alto	alta	alti	alte	*tall, high*
basso	bassa	bassi	basse	*short*
buono	buona	buoni	buone	*good*
cattivo	cattiva	cattivi	cattive	*bad*
delizioso	deliziosa	deliziosi	deliziose	*delicious*
largo	larga	larghi	larghe	*broad, large*
magnifico	magnifica	magnifici	magnifiche	*magnificent*
moderno	moderna	moderni	moderne	*modern*
piatto	piatta	piatti	piatte	*flat*
povero	povera	poveri	povere	*poor*
ricco	ricca	ricchi	ricche	*rich*
timido	timida	timidi	timide	*shy*
umido	umida	umidi	umide	*humid, damp*
vecchio	vecchia	vecchi	vecchie	*old*
vuoto	vuota	vuoti	vuote	*empty*

Exercise 93

Fill in the blanks with the adjectives in parentheses.

1. I ragazzi sono _____ (*cheerful*).

2. È un uomo molto _____ (*greedy*).

3. Marco è _____ (*short*) e Adriana è _____ (*tall*).

4. Il cane è un animale _____ (loyal).

5. Questo dolce è _____ (delicious).

6. Queste paste sono _____ (delicious).

7. Il tramonto era _____ (magnificent).

8. La sua casa è _____ (modern), ma quella di Giovanni è

   _____ (old).

9. Il Michigan è uno stato _____ (flat).

10. L'Africa è un continente _____ (poor).

Most adjectives ending in -e have one form used for both the masculine and feminine singular. Adjectives ending in -e in the singular form, change to -i in the plural forms of the masculine and the feminine.

masculine singular	feminine singular	masculine plural	feminine plural	
elegante	elegante	eleganti	eleganti	*elegant*

uomo elegante	*elegant man*
donna elegante	*elegant woman*
uomini eleganti	*elegant men*
donne eleganti	*elegant women*

The following list gives some common Italian adjectives with an -e ending:

acre	*acrid, sour*
celebre	*famous*
eccellente	*excellent*
efficace	*effective*
elegante	*elegant*
facile	*easy*
felice	*happy*
forte	*strong*
grande	*big, large*
importante	*important*
intelligente	*intelligent*
interessante	*interesting*
semplice	*simple*
triste	*sad*

umile	*humble*			
veloce	*fast*			
vivace	*lively*			

Here is a summary of the forms of Italian adjectives:

masculine singular	feminine singular	masculine plural	feminine plural	
-o	-a	-i	-e	
-e	-e	-i	-i	
alto	alta	alti	alte	*tall*
intelligente	intelligente	intelligenti	intelligenti	*smart*

Adjectives ending in **-one** in the masculine singular, change to **-ona** in the feminine singular. In the plural forms they change to **-oni** and **-one** respectively. For example: **chiacchierone, chiacchierona, chiacchieroni,** and **chiacchierone** (*talkative*) or **giocherellone, giocherellona, giocherelloni,** and **giocherellone** (*playful*).

masculine singular	feminine singular	
bambino chiacchier**one**	bambina chiacchier**ona**	*talkative baby*

masculine plural	feminine plural	
bambini chiacchier**oni**	bambine chiacchier**one**	*talkative babies*

Exercise 94

Fill in the blanks with the adjectives in parentheses.

1. La ragazza è _____ (*intelligent*).

2. Mio padre è un uomo molto _____ (*important*).

3. I nostri amici sono _____ (*sad*) perché noi partiamo.

4. Il mio fidanzato mi scrive lettere _____ (*interesting*).

5. I gelati italiani sono _____ (*excellent*).

6. Quella signora è sempre molto _____ (*elegant*).

7. L'atleta è _____ (*strong*).

8. Questi documenti sono _____ (*important*).

9. Il signor Lolli è un uomo _____ (*humble*).

10. In estate il giardino è _____ (*green*).

11. Gli sciatori sono _____ (*fast*).

12. Mio figlio è _____ (*sad*).

Irregular adjectives

Some Italian adjectives are irregular in their treatment of endings. For example, **ottimista** (*optimistic*) and **egoista** (*selfish*) end in -a in both the masculine and feminine singular forms. The plural forms, however, are treated as regular adjective endings in that masculine plural forms take an -i ending and feminine plural takes an -e ending.

masculine singular	feminine singular	masculine plural	feminine plural	
-a	-a	-i	-e	
ottimista	ottimista	ottimisti	ottimiste	*optimistic*

Following are some common adjectives ending in -a:

comunista	*communist*
idiota	*idiotic*
ipocrita	*hypocritical*
pessimista	*pessimist*
terrorista	*terrorist*
vietnamita	*Vietnamese*

Exercise 95

Change the following phrases to the plural.

1. il vino forte _____

2. il negozio nuovo _____

3. il bambino vivace _____

4. il cane intelligente _____

5. la signora elegante _____

6. lo studente studioso _____

7. l'uomo famoso _____

8. l'animale notturno _____

9. il vestito estivo _____

10. la strada stretta _____

Adjectives ending in **-io**, use an **-i** ending to form the masculine plural: **vecchio, vecchi** (*old*). The feminine forms follow the pattern for regular adjectives: **-ia** for singular and **-ie** for plural (**vecchia, vecchie**). Exceptions to this rule are the adjectives stressing the **-i** syllable followed by **-o**, such as **natìo** (*native*). In this case the **-i** is retained and another **-i** is added to the ending, so the plural looks like this: **natìi**, not **nati**.

il nostro paese **natìo**	our **native** country
i nostri paesi **natìi**	our **native** countries
la nostra terra **natìa**	our **native** land
le nostre terre **natìe**	our **native** lands

Masculine adjectives ending in **-co** and **-go** and feminine adjectives ending in **-ca** and **-ga** in the singular form, usually add an **-h** in the plural to maintain the hard sound of the singular form.

masculine singular	masculine plural	feminine singular	feminine plural	
antico	antichi	antica	antiche	*antique, ancient*
bianco	bianchi	bianca	bianche	*white*
poco	pochi	poca	poche	*a little*
sciocco	sciocchi	sciocca	sciocche	*silly*
stanco	stanchi	stanca	stanche	*tired*
largo	larghi	larga	larghe	*broad, wide*
lungo	lunghi	lunga	lunghe	*long*

A few exceptions to this rule are: greco, greci, greca, greche (*Greek*); amico, amici, amica, amiche (*friendly*); and nemico, nemici, nemica, nemiche (*enemy, hostile*).

If adjectives end in **-ico** and have more than two syllables with the stress on a syllable other than the **-i**, the masculine plural is formed by using **-ci**. The feminine plural keeps the hard sound by using **-h** in the plural.

masculine singular	masculine plural	feminine singular	feminine plural	
atomico	atomici	atomica	atomiche	*atomic*
comico	comici	comica	comiche	*comical*
magico	magici	magica	magiche	*magic*

masculine singular	masculine plural	feminine singular	feminine plural	
poetico	poetici	poetica	poetiche	*poetic*
politico	politici	politica	politiche	*political*

Of course, there are exceptions to this rule. For example: **carico, carichi, carica, cariche** (*loaded*) and **ubriaco, ubriachi, ubriaca, ubriache** (*drunk*).

Adjectives ending in **-cio, -cia, -gio, -gia** in the singular, drop the **-i** in the plural.

masculine singular	masculine plural	feminine singular	feminine plural	
grigio	grigi	grigia	grige (grigie)	*gray*
saggio	saggi	saggia	sagge	*wise*
fradicio	fradici	fradicia	fradice	*soaking wet*
lercio	lerci	lercia	lerce	*dirty*

Exercise 96

Translate the following sentences into Italian.

1. Today the sky is gray.

_____.

2. He is a poetic writer.

_____.

3. The sweater is large.

_____.

4. I like a magic world.

_____.

5. Boys and girls are often silly.

_____.

6. At the end of the week everybody is tired.

_____.

7. My grandfather is very wise.

_____.

8. Old people are usually very wise.

_____.

9. In summer I like to wear white dresses.

_____.

10. The road is very wide.

_____.

11. This vase is antique.

_____.

12. The children are not tired.

_____.

Some Italian adjectives do not make a change at all. These are adjectives:

- ending in **-i**

pari	_even_
dispari	_odd_

- expressing colors that are also noun words

rosa	_pink_
viola	_violet_
ciclamino	_cyclamen_

- of color descriptions

rosa pallido	_light pink_
verde pastello	_pastel green_
giallo limone	_lemon yellow_
verde scuro	_dark green_

- of foreign origin

blu	_blue_
chic	_chic_

- formed by **anti** + a noun

antinebbia	_antifog_
antifurto	_antirobbery_
antiruggine	_antirust_

Exercise 97

Fill in the blanks with the adjectives in parentheses.

1. Otto è un numero _____ (*even*).

2. Cinque e sette sono numeri _____ (*odd*).

3. Il mio colore preferito è il _____ (*cyclamen*).

4. La sfumatura del _____ (*pastel green*) è molto di moda.

5. In inverno bisogna avere i fari _____ (*antifog*).

6. È prudente avere la sirena _____ (*antirobbery*) in casa.

7. Le macchine oggi hanno la vernice _____ (*antirust*).

8. Il _____ (*pink*) e il _____ (*violet*) sono colori primaverili.

9. Ho dimenticato di mettere il dispositivo _____ (*antirobbery*) in macchina.

10. Il _____ (*dark green*) è usato molto in inverno.

Common irregular adjectives. Some of the most commonly used adjectives are irregular in their endings: **Bello, grande, buono,** and **santo** have several forms for both the singular and the plural depending on the initial letter of the noun they modify.

- **Bello** follows the rules for definite articles for masculine nouns beginning with **z, ps, gn, x,** and **s** + consonant and is shortened to **bell'** before masculine nouns starting with a vowel. **Begli** is the plural form for these masculine nouns.

bello spettacolo	*nice show*	**begli** spettacoli	*nice shows*
bell'uomo	*handsome man*	**begli** uomini	*handsome men*

Bel is used in front of all other masculine nouns. **Bei** is the plural form.

bel giardino	*beautiful garden*	**bei** giardini	*beautiful gardens*

Bella is used in front of all feminine singular nouns starting with a consonant. When the noun begins with a vowel, **bell'** is used. The plural form for all feminine nouns is **belle**.

bella casa	*beautiful house*	**belle** case	*beautiful houses*
bell'estate	*beautiful summer*	**belle** estati	*beautiful summers*

- **Grande** is usually used shortened to **grand'** before nouns starting with a vowel and to **gran** before consonants for both feminine and masculine nouns. **Grande** is used if the noun begins with **s** + consonant, **z**, **ps**, or **gn**. The plural **grandi** is used for both the masculine and the feminine forms.

un **gran** tenore	*a **great** tenor*
un **grande** scienziato	*a **great** scientist*
un **grand'**uomo	*a **great** man*
una **gran** donna	*a **great** woman*
una **grand'**esploratrice	*a **great** explorer* (feminine)

- **Buono** mirrors the rules for the indefinite article **uno**. It shortens to **buon** before all masculine nouns except those that start with **s** + consonant, **z**, **ps**, **gn**, and **x**. In these cases **buono** is used. **Buona** is used with all feminine singular nouns starting with a consonant. When a feminine noun begins with a vowel, **buon'** is used. Both the masculine and feminine forms in the plural are regular, using -i and -e endings (**buoni** and **buone**).

masculine and feminine singular		masculine and feminine plural	
un **buon** libro	*a **good** book*	i **buoni** libri	*the **good** books*
un **buon** uomo	*a **good** man*	i **buoni** uomini	*the **good** men*
un **buono** sport	*a **good** sport*	i **buoni** sport	*the **good** sports*
una **buona** torta	*a **good** cake*	le **buone** torte	*the **good** cakes*
una **buon'**amica	*a **good** friend*	le **buone** amiche	*the **good** friends*

- **Santo** (*holy, saint*) is treated as a regular adjective except when it precedes a proper noun and means *Saint*. **San** is used before all nouns starting with a consonant except those starting with **s** + consonant, in which case **santo** is used. **Santa** is used before all feminine nouns and becomes **Sant'** in front of proper nouns starting with a vowel.

masculine	feminine
San Pietro	**Santa** Maria
San Giovanni	**Sant'**Agnese

When using **santo** for *holy*, it almost always follows the noun. It also follows the rule for regular adjectives ending in -o.

Il **Santo** Vangelo	*the **holy** Gospel*
La Settimana **Santa**	*the **holy** week*
Lo Spirito **Santo**	*the **Holy** Spirit*

Exercise 98

Fill in the blanks with the correct forms of the adjectives in parentheses.

1. Sono stato in un _____ (buono) ristorante.

2. Lei ha comprato due _____ (bello) appartamenti.

3. Ho affittato due camere spaziose e _____ (bello).

4. Abbiamo visto un _____ (bello) tramonto.

5. Ho comprato una cassa di _____ (bello) uva bianca.

6. In Italia al mercato si compra della _____ (bello) e
   _____ (buono) frutta.

7. Leonardo era un _____ (grande) genio.

8. In questa città c'è un ospedale _____ (buono).

9. A Roma ci sono tante _____ (bello) piazze.

10. Finalmente ho trovato un _____ (buono) lavoro.

Positions of descriptive adjectives

Placement of the descriptive adjective in a sentence is very important to the meaning of the sentence. Usually, descriptive adjectives in Italian are placed after the noun they modify even when there are several of them.

una signora **elegante, distinta, giovanile**	*an elegant, distinct, youthful* lady
una porta **segreta**	*a secret* door

There are some short descriptive adjectives, however, that are used before nouns. For example:

alto	*tall*
bello	*handsome, nice*
bravo	*good*
brutto	*ugly*
buono	*good*
caro	*dear*
cattivo	*bad*
giovane	*young*
grande	*big*

piccolo	*small*
vecchio	*old*

But when these adjectives are modified by **molto** (*very*), **abbastanza** (*fairly*), **piuttosto** (*rather*), or **troppo** (*too much*), they, too, follow the noun.

una **bella** gita	*a **nice** trip/outing*
una gita **molto bella**	*a **very nice** trip/outing*
un **bravo** direttore	*a **good** director*
un direttore **abbastanza bravo**	*a **fairly good** director*
una **bella** ragazza	*a **beautiful** girl*
una ragazza **piuttosto bella**	*a **rather beautiful** girl*

There are some basic rules to follow for the placement of adjectives. For example, adjectives follow nouns:

- when they specify color, shape, material, nationality, religion, or political affiliation

il vestito **rosso**	*the **red** dress*
una scatola **quadrata**	*a **square** box*
i ragazzi **americani**	*the **American** boys*
il partito **repubblicano**	*the **Republican** party*

- when specifying a category

una scuola **secondaria**	*a **high** school*
la rivoluzione **americana**	*the **American** Revolution*

- when the adjectives stem from the present participle and end in **-ante** or **-ente** and when derived from regular past participles like -**ato**, -**uto**, or -**ito**

il ponte **tremante**	*the **shaking** bridge*
la casa **barcollante**	*the **unsteady** house*
il pavimento **bagnato**	*the **wet** floor*
la tavola **pulita**	*the **clean** table*

- when they have suffixes such as: **-ino**, **-etto**, **-otto**, and **-one**

un uccello piccol**ino**	*a **small** bird*
un ragazzo cicci**otto**	*a **chubby** boy*
una ragazza chiacchier**ona**	*a **talkative** girl*

- when the verbs **essere, sembrare, sentirsi,** or **diventare** are used

Sua figlia è **bella.**	*Her daughter is **beautiful.***
Tuo figlio è **diventato alto.**	*Your son has gotten **tall.***

Limiting adjectives, numerals, adjectives of quantity, possessive adjectives, and demonstrative adjectives usually precede the noun.

tre cravatte	*three ties*
meno pasta	*less pasta*

An example of some limiting adjectives that precede the noun are:

alcuni	*some, any*
altro	*other*
certo	*certain*
ogni	*each*
parecchio	*several*
primo	*first*
qualche	*some*
qualsiasi	*any*
tutto	*all, the whole, every*
ultimo	*last*

Exercise 99

Translate the following sentences into Italian.

1. We went on a nice trip.

_____.

2. She is a good teacher.

_____.

3. They studied the American Revolution.

_____.

4. She likes the red dress.

_____.

5. This book is easy to read.

_____.

6. He is my dear, old friend.

_____.

7. They have very young parents.

_____.

8. After the earthquake the roof is shaky.

_____.

9. I found a small bird in the garden.

_____.

10. The child is a little too chubby.

_____.

Sometimes an adjective's meaning will change depending on whether it is placed before or after the noun. Here are the most common adjectives that can change their meanings in this way:

un **alto** ufficiale	*a **high-ranking** officer*	un ragazzo **alto**	*a **tall** boy*
gli **antichi** romani	*the **ancient** Romans*	un orologio **antico**	*an **old** watch*
un **bel** libro	*an **interesting** book*	un libro **bello**	*a **beautiful** book*
una **brutta** sera	*a **bad** evening*	una sera **brutta**	*an **ugly** evening*
un **buon** amico	*a **good** friend*	un amico **buono**	*a friend who is a **good** person*
un **caro** amico	*a **dear** friend*	una stoffa **cara**	*an **expensive** material*
un **cattivo** ragazzo	*a **naughty** boy*	una persona **cattiva**	*a **vicious** person*
un **cattivo** amico	*a **bad** friend*	un amico **cattivo**	*a friend who is a **bad** person*
diversi giorni	*several days*	giorni **diversi**	***different** days*
un **grande** amico	*a **good** friend*	un amico **grande**	*a friend who is a **big** person*
un **grand'**uomo	*a **great** man*	un uomo **grande**	*a **large** man*
una **leggera** ferita	*a **slight** wound*	una borsa **leggera**	*a **light(weight)** purse*
il **massimo** silenzio	*the **utmost** silence*	la velocità **massima**	*the **maximum** speed*
un **nuovo** libro	*a **new** book*	un libro **nuovo**	*a **brand new** book*

le **povere** famiglie	*the **unfortunate** families*	le famiglie **povere**	*the **poor** families*
un **povero** uomo	*an **unfortunate** man*	un uomo **povero**	*a **poor** man*
una **semplice** domanda	***just** a question*	una domanda **semplice**	*a **simple** question*
una **sola** donna	*the **only** woman*	una donna **sola**	*a woman **alone***
l'**unica** occasione	*the **only** chance*	un'occasione **unica**	*a **unique** opportunity*
l'**unico** figlio	*the **only** son*	un figlio **unico**	*an **only** son*
varie volte	***several** times*	un paesaggio **vario**	*a **varied** landscape*
un **vecchio** amico	*a **long-standing** friend*	un amico **vecchio**	*an **old** (age) friend*
una **vera** notizia	*a **truly** important piece of news*	una notizia **vera**	*a news story that is **true***
una **vera** amica	*a **true** friend*	una pietra **vera**	*an **authentic** stone*

Exercise 100

Translate the following sentences into Italian.

1. She is my dear friend.

   _____.

2. There are numerous reasons to move.

   _____.

3. I live in a large house.

   _____.

4. I read several books last summer.

   _____.

5. I read different books this summer.

   _____.

6. In northern Italy there are some beautiful lakes.

   _____.

7. There is a tall wall around Lucca.

   _____.

8. He had slight wounds on his legs.

   _____.

9. You have a light purse.

_____.

10. In the room there was the utmost silence.

_____.

11. This is the only chance to see you.

_____.

12. You are a unique person.

_____.

Sometimes one adjective will precede the noun in a sentence and one or more adjectives will follow it, giving a special, descriptive emphasis to the sentence.

Loro hanno una **bella** casa **grande**.   *They have a **beautiful**, **big** house.*

In literary language and journalism, adjectives are often placed before the noun for emphasis. Two adjectives in the same position are joined by the conjunction e (*and*).

La **sanguinosa** e **tragica** esplosione   *The **bloody** and **tragic** explosion at the*
alla stazione di Bologna...   *station in Bologna . . .*

Exercise 101

Translate the following sentences into Italian.

1. Your beautiful, large house is by the lake.

_____.

2. I like to watch documentaries of elegant, luxurious places.

_____.

3. His death was tragic and sad.

_____.

4. Your son is thin.

_____.

5. That man is a very old friend of mine.

_____.

6. I would like to ask you just a question.

_____.

7. It is not important. It is a simple question.

_____.

8. We have a new problem. We lost the brand new book.

_____.

9. I like rings made of authentic stones.

_____.

10. They have a beautiful new house.

_____.

11. It is an insignificant and boring movie.

_____.

Adjectives of nationality

Most adjectives of nationality end in -o and are treated the same as other regular adjectives ending in -o. They have four forms (-o/-a/-i/-e) and always follow the noun they modify. The adjectives of nationality ending in -e, however, have only two forms: -e for the singular masculine and feminine, and -i for masculine and feminine plural. They, too, always follow the nouns they modify. Note that in Italian adjectives of nationality are not capitalized.

la signora **americana**	*the American lady*
le signore **americane**	*the American ladies*
il giornale **italiano**	*the Italian newspaper*
i giornali **italiani**	*the Italian newspapers*

Following are some of the adjectives of nationality that end in -o.

americano	*American*
argentino	*Argentinean*
australiano	*Australian*
brasiliano	*Brazilian*
greco	*Greek*
italiano	*Italian*
messicano	*Mexican*
russo	*Russian*
scandinavo	*Scandinavian*

spagnolo	*Spanish*
svizzero	*Swiss*
tedesco	*German*

There are many adjectives of nationality that end in **-e**. The following list shows some of these adjectives and how they are used:

canadese	*Canadian*
cinese	*Chinese*
francese	*French*
giapponese	*Japanese*
inglese	*English*
irlandese	*Irish*
norvegese	*Norwegian*
olandese	*Dutch*
scozzese	*Scottish*
svedese	*Swedish*

il ragazzo **svedese**	*the **Swedish** boy*
la macchina **inglese**	*the **English** car*
gli zii **portoghesi**	*the **Portuguese** uncles*
le famiglie **francesi**	*the **French** families*

Exercise 102

Fill in the blanks with the appropriate forms of the adjectives in parentheses.

1. Maria è _____ (*Spanish*).

2. Il professore è _____ (*English*).

3. I nostri amici sono _____ (*Swiss*).

4. Il marito di nostra nipote è _____ (*French*).

5. Il vino è _____ (*Australian*).

6. Le stoffe sono _____ (*Scottish*).

7. L'opera è _____ (*Italian*).

8. I turisti sono _____ (*Canadian*).

9. La signora è _____ (*Greek*).

10. I suoi antenati sono _____ (*Greek*).

Demonstrative adjectives

Demonstrative adjectives are used to pinpoint nouns. In English they are: *this/these*, *that/those*. In Italian they have four forms: masculine singular and plural and feminine singular and plural. They agree with the noun to which they refer and are used with it.

masculine	feminine	
questo	questa	*this*
questi	queste	*these*
quel, quello	quella	*that*
quell'	quell'	*that*
quei, quegli	quelle	*those*

Demonstrative adjectives precede the noun and agree in gender and number with the noun they modify.

Questo libro	*this book*	Questi studenti	*these students*
Quella ragazza	*that girl*	Quelle ragazze	*those girls*

Questo(-a/-e/-i) indicates someone or something close to the person who is speaking. It follows the rules of all adjectives ending in -o. In front of a vowel, **questo** and **questa**, become **quest'**.

Ho letto **questo** libro.	*I have read **this** book.*
Ho ascoltato **quest'** opera.	*I listened to **this** opera.*

Quello(-a/-e, **quei, quegli**) indicates someone or something distant from the person who is speaking. **Quello** and **quella** before a vowel become **quell'**.

Quell'aereo vola molto in alto.	***That** plane flies very high.*

Quello follows the same rules previously seen for the definite article and has the same forms as **bello**.

quello studente (**lo** studente)	*that student*
quegli studenti (**gli** studenti)	*those students*
quel bambino (**il** bambino)	*that child*
quei bambini (**i** bambini)	*those children*

Demonstrative adjectives are repeated before each noun.

> Andate per **questo** sentiero e per *Go by **this** path and by **that** road.*
> **quella** strada.

For emphasis and to avoid ambiguity between *this* and *that*, or *these* and *those*, **qui**, **qua** (*here*) or **lì**, **là** (*there*) follow the noun.

> Devo scegliere fra **questo** vestito **qui** *I have to choose between **this** dress **here***
> e **quel** vestito **lì**. *and **that** dress **there**.*

The feminine form **questa** becomes **sta** in some compound words. For example:

stamattina	*this morning*
stasera	*this evening*
stanotte	*tonight* (*this night*)
stavolta	*this time*

Exercise 103

Translate the following sentences into Italian.

1. This young man is my brother.

_____.

2. That house is old.

_____.

3. In that photo you can see my family.

_____.

4. That book is very interesting.

_____.

5. Those students came from far away.

_____.

6. That student is extremely intelligent.

_____.

7. Those people work a lot.

_____.

8. Who is this man in the photograph?

_____?

9. These apples are very expensive.

_____.

10. I want to buy those two grapefruits.

_____.

In Italian **questo** and **quello** are not used in expressions equivalent to the English sentence *This is where . . .* Italian uses: **È qui/qua che...** (*It is here where . . ., This is where . . .*), or **È lì/là che...** (*It is there where . . .*) instead.

È qui che compro le scarpe tutti gli anni.	*This is where I buy shoes every year.*
È qui che dobbiamo comprare il biglietto?	*Is this where we need to buy the ticket?*
È là che ho comprato la casa.	*It is there where I bought my house.*

Possessive adjectives

Possessive adjectives indicate one's possession of something. They agree in gender and number with the noun they modify. The definite article usually precedes the possessive adjective and both are repeated before each noun: **La mia** casa, **il mio** giardino. (*My house, my garden.*) The possessive adjectives are as follows:

masculine singular	feminine singular	masculine plural	feminine plural	
il mio	la mia	i miei	le mie	*my*
il tuo	la tua	i tuoi	le tue	*your* (familiar)
il suo	la sua	i suoi	le sue	*his; her; its; your* (formal)
il nostro	la nostra	i nostri	le nostre	*our*
il vostro	la vostra	i vostri	le vostre	*your* (plural)
il loro	la loro	i loro	le loro	*their; your* (formal)

The definite article is not used with possessive adjectives before certain nouns of close family members in the singular form or when they are unmodified. The definite article is used with those nouns that are variations of the basic forms, such as with: **babbo** (*dad*), **mamma** (*mom*), **sorellina** (*little sister*), **nonnino** (*small, dear grandfather*), and so on.

Mio fratello e **mia** sorella sono in Italia.	*My brother and **my** sister are in Italy.*
I loro zii e i **loro** nonni arrivano domani.	***Their** uncles and **their** grandparents will arrive tomorrow.*

A definite article is used when the family name is modified by another adjective or includes a suffix.

il mio caro zio	***my dear** uncle*
il mio fratellino	***my little** brother*

A definite article (not a possessive adjective) is used with parts of the body and with articles of clothing when the possessor of such items is obvious. The possession in these cases is expressed with a reflexive verb or an indirect object pronoun.

Mi sono rotto **il** piede.	*I broke **my** foot.*
Non so dove ho messo **la** giacca.	*I don't know where I put **my** jacket.*

A definite article is not used with the possessive adjective when the adjective comes after the noun in an expression or in exclamations.

A **mio** parere...	*In **my** opinion . . .*
Dio **mio**!	*My God!*
Cara **mia**!	*My dear!*
Mamma **mia**!	*Oh **my**! (idiomatic)*

Exercise 104

Write the appropriate possessive adjective for each sentence on the line provided.

1. Roberto dov'è (il tuo, la tua, i tuoi) orologio? _____

2. (Suo, Sua, Sue) sorella è molto alta. _____

3. (Il nostro, La nostra, I nostri) casa è grande. _____

4. Dove abitano (i loro, il loro, le loro) genitori? _____

5. Hai chiamato (il tuo, la tua, tuoi) babbo? _____

6. (Il tuo, La tua, Le tue) lettere non sono arrivate. _____

7. Sono italiani (i tuoi, le tue, il tuo) amici? _____

8. Pietro gioca con (il suo, la sua, i suoi) cani. _____

9. (Il tuo, I tuoi, La tua) giardino è molto bello. _____

10. Ci sono molti fiori nel (tua, tuo, tuoi) giardino. _____

Exercise 105

Change the following sentences to the plural and then translate them into English.

1. Mio fratello suona la chitarra.

_____.

_____.

2. Sua sorella suona il violino.

_____.

_____.

3. La tua chiave è sulla tavola.

_____.

_____.

4. Nostro zio abita a Firenze.

_____.

_____.

5. Ho perso il mio libro.

_____.

_____.

6. Il vostro amico è americano.

_____.

_____.

7. La nostra mamma cucina molto bene.

_____.

_____.

8. A che ora arriva nostra sorella?

_____?

_____?

9. La mia macchina è nuova.

_____.

_____.

10. Il tuo orologio è elegante.

_____.

_____.

Expressions such as *a friend of mine* use the pronoun *mine* in English, but in Italian are expressed by the possessive adjective *mio* and its various forms.

un **mio** amico	*a friend of **mine***
quei **miei** amici	*those friends of **mine***
due **miei** amici	*two of **my** friends (two friends of **mine**)*
una **mia** collega	*a colleague of **mine***

Sometimes the demonstrative adjectives **questo(-a/-e/-i)** and **quello(-a)**, or **quei** and **quelle** precede the possessive adjective in a sentence. In this case the demonstrative adjective always agrees with the possessive adjective. Other times, numbers or indefinite adjectives are placed before a possessive adjective.

Questa tua macchina è molto veloce.	*This car of yours is very fast.*
Quel tuo amico non mi piace affatto.	*I don't like **that** friend **of yours** at all.*
Due tuoi amici sono venuti a casa mia.	*Two of **your** friends came to my house.*
Viene con **alcuni suoi** parenti.	*He will come with **some of his** relatives.*

Il suo and **la sua** both express *his, her,* or *its.* They refer to singular objects owned by one person, male or female. They agree with the noun they modify and not with the possessor.

la sua sorella	*her sister, his sister*

If there is ambiguity and it is not clear whose possession is indicated, **di lui** or **di lei** (*of his* or *of hers*) are added and the definite article is omitted.

Sua sorella (La sorella **di lui**) arriva domani.	*His sister will arrive tomorrow.*

I suoi and **le sue** (*his* and *hers*) refer to plural objects or people with one possessor.

i suoi libri	*his books*
i suoi libri	*her books*

| le **sue** sorelle | *his* sisters |
| le **sue** sorelle | *her* sisters |

Il/la/i/le loro (*their*) can indicate one or more object, and the possessor is always more than one.

| il **loro** cane | *their* dog |
| i **loro** cani | *their* dogs |

Exercise 106

Translate the following sentences into Italian.

1. An old friend of mine called me last night.

_____.

2. Their friends are busy.

_____.

3. His brothers are tall.

_____.

4. Their grandparents are very nice.

_____.

5. My two sisters are in Italy for a month.

_____.

6. Their watches are slow.

_____.

7. Their watches are very expensive.

_____.

8. His book is new.

_____.

9. His books are new.

_____.

10. A colleague of mine has lost his job.

_____.

When a definite article + a possessive adjective is preceded by a preposition, the preposition and the article contract.

La fermata dell'autobus è vicino **alla mia** scuola.   *The bus stop is near (**to**) **my** school.*

La mia casa è lontana **dalla mia** scuola.   *My house is far **from my** school.*

Exercise 107

Rewrite the sentences below replacing the underlined words with the appropriate forms of the possessive adjectives.

1. Non ho mai visto la macchina nuova di Lia.

   _____.

2. La casa di Cecilia è molto grande.

   _____.

3. La casa di Roberto ha un grande giardino.

   _____.

4. L'appartamento dei signori Marconi è in una bella zona.

   _____.

5. I parenti di Marco vivono lontano.

   _____.

6. Le amiche di Roberto e Dario sono molto carine.

   _____.

7. Hanno dimenticato i libri di Edoardo.

   _____.

8. Hanno venduto la macchina di Maria.

   _____.

9. La ragazza di Giovanni non è molto bella.

   _____.

10. L'appartamento di Daniela è al terzo piano.

    _____.

The *'s* or *s'* in English possessive words is expressed in Italian by using **di** or **quello(-a/-i/-e) di**.

La madre **di Dario** sta male.

Il gatto **dei vicini** miagola sempre.

Hanno rubato le mie chiavi e anche **quelle di mia** figlia.

Dario's mother is sick.

The neighbors' cat always meows.

They have stolen my keys and my daughter's as well.

Indefinite adjectives

Indefinite adjectives refer to people, objects, and animals that cannot be defined. The indefinite adjectives in English are: *someone, something, every, all, some, any,* and so on. In Italian they are:

alcuno(**-a/-i/-e**)	*some*
altro(**-a/-i/-e**)	*other*
ogni	*each, every*
molto(**-a/-i/-e**)	*a lot, much, many*
poco(**-a/-chi/-che**)	*a little, a few*
qualche	*some*
troppo(**-a/-i/-e**)	*too much, too many*
tutto(**-a/-i/-e**)	*all, the whole*

Ogni (*each, every*) is always used with a singular noun.

Lia mi chiama **ogni** giorno.

Ogni studente dovrebbe studiare.

Ogni casa in America ha il giardino.

Lia calls me every day.

Every student should study.

Every house in America has a garden.

Qualche (*some, any, a few*) has several different meanings. It is always used with a singular noun although its meaning is mostly plural.

Maria ha **qualche** vestito nuovo.

Ho perso **qualche** ora dormendo.

Maria has a few new dresses.

I lost a few hours sleeping.

Tutto(-a), or **tutti(-e)** in the plural, means *all* (*the*) or *the whole*. As an adjective it is followed by a definite article and a noun. It agrees in gender and number with the noun it modifies.

Ho pulito **tutto il giorno**.	*I cleaned **all day** long.*
Tutti i bambini devono imparare a nuotare.	***All children** have to learn how to swim.*
Hanno finito **tutta la pizza**.	*They have finished **the whole pizza**.*

Tanto (*a lot of*), **molto** (*many, a lot of; much*), **parecchio** (*lots, lots of*), **troppo** (*too many; too much*), **poco** (*a little*), and their equivalent plurals are used both as pronouns and as adjectives. As adjectives they agree in gender and number with the noun they modify.

Ho comprato **molto** pane.	*I have bought **a lot of** bread.*
Voi avete **parecchio** tempo.	*You have **lots of** time.*
Tanti bambini non hanno **molti** giocattoli.	***A lot of** children don't have **many** toys.*
Ci sono **troppe** persone in chiesa.	*There are **too many** people in church.*

Qualche and **alcuni**(-e), both mean *some* and are interchangeable. **Alcuni**(-e) used in this sense is always plural, followed by a plural noun, and **qualche** is always singular, followed by a singular noun.

Ecco **alcuni** fiori.	*Here are **some** flowers.*
C'era **qualche** svendita ieri.	*There were **some** sales yesterday.*

A form of **altro**(-a) or **altri**(-e) (*other*) is usually preceded by a definite or indefinite article.

Visitate anche **l'altro** museo.	*Visit **the other** museum, too.*
Vogliamo visitare **un altro** museo.	*We want to visit **another** museum.*

Exercise 108

Fill in the blanks with the appropriate forms of the indefinite adjectives in parentheses.

1. _____ (*Some*) strade erano bloccate per un incidente.

2. Abbiamo aiutato _____ (*some*) persona anziana.

3. _____ (*Every*) uomo guarda lo sport alla televisione.

4. _____ (*Some*) uomini guardano lo sport alla televisione.

5. _____ (*All*) gli uomini guardano lo sport alla televisione.

6. _____ (*Some*) macchine erano coperte di neve.

7. Le _____ (*other*) case sono molto grandi.

8. _____ (*Every*) casa nella mia città è bella.

9. A Roma ci sono _____ (*many*) macchine.

10. L'Italia ha _____ (*too many*) chiese.

11. Ci sono _____ (*many*) campi da tennis e _____ (*a few*) piscine.

Color adjectives

When adjectives of color end in **-o**, they have the regular four forms (**-o/-a/-i/-e**); if they end in **-e** they have two forms (**-e/-i**); if they end in **-a**, or **-u**, they remain the same in the singular, plural, masculine and feminine forms.

arancione	*orange*
bianco	*white*
blu	*blue*
giallo	*yellow*
grigio	*gray*
marrone	*brown*
nero	*black*
rosa	*pink*
rosso	*red*
verde	*green*
viola	*purple*

Exercise 109

Translate the following sentences into Italian.

1. Brides wear white dresses.

_____.

2. My favorite color is red.

_____.

3. Sunflowers are yellow.

_____.

4. I bought him a pink shirt.

_____.

5. The sky is blue.

_____.

6. I like pink roses.

_____.

7. Some singers don't like purple.

_____.

8. Tibetans wear orange robes.

_____.

9. In Switzerland there are many gray buildings.

_____.

10. My husband likes green grass.

_____.

Interrogative adjectives

Interrogative adjectives are used to introduce a question. They are always placed before a noun and are never followed by a definite article.

Quale (*Which?* or *What?*) has two forms only: **quale** in the masculine and feminine singular and **quali** in the plural.

Quale macchina usi?	*Which car will you use?*
Quali verdure preferisci?	*Which vegetables do you prefer?*

The interrogative adjective **quanto** has the four regular adjective forms. The two singular forms **quanto** and **quanta** mean *how much*, and the two plural forms **quanti** and **quante** mean *how many*.

Quanto pane devo comprare?	*How much bread should I buy?*
Quanti soldati sono andati a combattere?	*How many soldiers went to fight?*
Quanta pasta devo cuocere?	*How much pasta should I cook?*
Quante piante hai comprato?	*How many plants did you buy?*

Che (*What?* or *Which?*) is invariable and used only in the singular.

Che ora è?	**What** *time is it?*
Che giorno è oggi?	**What** *day is today?*

Exercise 110

Fill in the blanks with the appropriate interrogative adjectives.

1. _____ cravatta preferisce tuo marito?

2. _____ sedie occorrono?

3. _____ giornali italiani leggete?

4. _____ ore sono?

5. _____ treno prendi?

6. _____ studenti ci sono in classe?

7. _____ frutta preferisci?

8. _____ chili di frutta devo comprare?

9. _____ vestito preferisci?

10. _____ gattini ha tuo figlio?

11. _____ animali preferisci?

12. _____ tipo di persona è?

6

Adverbs

An adverb modifies a verb, an adjective, or another adverb in a sentence, expressing manner, to what degree, or how a specific action is done.

Lei parla **bene** l'italiano.   *She speaks Italian **well.***
Il gelato era **molto** delizioso.   *The ice cream was **very** delicious.*

Many adverbs in Italian ending in **-o** are formed by adding **-mente** to the feminine singular form of an adjective. The following list of commonly used adverbs demonstrates how this is done:

adjectives		adverbs	
certo, certa	*certain*	certa**mente**	*certainly*
fortunato, fortunata	*fortunate*	fortunata**mente**	*fortunately*
lento, lenta	*slow*	lenta**mente**	*slowly*
moderato, moderata	*moderate*	moderata**mente**	*moderately*
provvisorio, provvisoria	*temporary*	provvisoria**mente**	*temporarily*
silenzioso, silenziosa	*silent*	silenziosa**mente**	*silently*
sincero, sincera	*sincere*	sincera**mente**	*sincerely*

There are some exceptions, however.

altro	*other*	altrimenti	*otherwise*
leggero	*light*	leggermente	*lightly*
violento	*violent*	violentemente	*violently*

Adjectives ending in **-e**, also form the adverb by adding **-mente**. When the adjective ends in **-le** or **-re** preceded by a vowel, the final **-e** is dropped before the suffix **-mente** is added. If there is a consonant before **-le** or **-re**, the final **-e** of the adjective is retained.

adjectives		adverbs	
cordiale	*cordial*	cordial**mente**	*cordially*
dolce	*sweet*	dolcemente	*sweetly*
facile	*easy*	facil**mente**	*easily*

folle	*mad*	folle**mente**	*madly*
frequente	*frequent*	frequente**mente**	*frequently*
gentile	*kind, gentle*	genti**lmente**	*sweetly*
regolare	*regular*	regola**rmente**	*regularly*

Some adverbs have forms that differ from the adjectives all together.

adjectives		**adverbs**	
buono	*good*	bene	*well*
cattivo	*bad*	male	*bad*
migliore	*better*	meglio	*better*
peggiore	*worse*	peggio	*worse*

Exercise 111

Translate the following sentences into Italian using an adjective or an adverb as required.

1. I will certainly go to the game next week.

_____.

2. The men were walking slowly.

_____.

3. The men were very slow.

_____.

4. The crowd was silent.

_____.

5. Fortunately I was at home.

_____.

6. It was a delicious dessert.

_____.

7. We go to the movies frequently.

_____.

8. Many Italians are kind.

_____.

9. I kindly asked her to sit down.

_____.

10. He is madly in love with her.

_____.

Some adverbs have the same forms as the adjectives. For example:

abbastanza	*enough; quite*
affatto	*at all*
assai	*very much*
così	*this way; so*
meno	*less*
molto	*much, a lot*
poco	*some, a little*
quasi	*almost*
tanto	*so, so much; a lot*
troppo	*too much*

adjectives

Gina ha **abbastanza** pane.
  *Gina has **enough** bread.*
Ho **troppi** vestiti.
  *I have **too many** dresses.*
Ha **tanto** spazio.
  *He has **a lot** of space.*
Mangiano **tante** castagne.
  *They eat **many** chestnuts.*

adverbs

Ne ho **abbastanza**.
  *I have **enough** of it.*
È **troppo** stanco.
  *He is **too** tired.*
Sono **tanto** gentili.
  *They are **very** kind.*
Le castagne costano **tanto**.
  *Chestnuts cost **a lot**.*

Exercise 112

Fill in each blank with the appropriate adverb or adjective in parentheses.

1. Giovanna è _____ (*very*) stanca.

2. Maria ha _____ (*many*) amiche.

3. Questa casa mi piace _____ (*a lot*).

4. Il libro è _____ (*very*) interessante.

5. Edoardo gioca _____ (*well*) a calcio.

6. Linda ama _____ (*a lot*) i gatti.

7. Enrico è _____ (*too*) silenzioso.

8. Sto _____ (*quite*) bene.

9. Siamo _____ (*almost*) arrivati.

10. Hanno una casa _____ (*very*) grande.

11. Non pensa _____ (*at all*).

12. Parlano _____ (*slowly*).

In certain Italian expressions there are some common adjectives that are used as adverbs in the masculine singular.

caro	costare **caro**	*to cost **dearly***
chiaro	parlare **chiaro**	*to speak **honestly** or **clearly***
diritto	andare **diritto**	*to go **straight***
forte	parlare **forte**	*to speak **loudly***
piano	parlare **piano**	*to speak **slowly** or **softly***
sodo	lavorare **sodo**	*to work **hard***
veloce	camminare **veloce**	*to walk **fast***

Exercise 113

Translate the following sentences into Italian.

1. In church everybody speaks softly.

_____.

2. The trip to Australia costs dearly.

_____.

3. People at the market speak loudly.

_____.

4. He drives fast.

_____.

5. I worked hard all day on Saturday.

_____.

6. I told him to go slowly.

_____.

7. They asked me to speak slowly.

_____.

8. He needs to go straight.

_____.

9. I cannot walk fast.

_____.

10. Gina has spent enough.

_____.

11. Your friends are very kind.

_____.

12. They speak kindly.

_____.

13. Your friend is too tired.

_____.

14. Don't walk so fast!

_____!

The following lists show many of the most commonly used adverbs in various categories. They are just as common in Italian as they are in English.

adverbs of time

adesso	*now*
allora	*then*
ancora	*yet*
appena	*as soon as*
domani	*tomorrow*
dopo	*after*
fino a	*until*
finora	*until now*
frequentemente	*frequently*
già	*already*
ieri	*yesterday*
mai	*never*
oggi	*today*
ogni tanto	*every once in a while*
ora	*now*

ormai	*by now*
poi	*next, then*
presto	*soon; quickly*
raramente	*rarely*
sempre	*always*
spesso	*often*
tardi	*late*

adverbs of location

dappertutto	*everywhere*
davanti	*in front*
dietro	*behind*
dove	*where*
fuori	*out*
giù	*down*
indietro	*behind*
lì, là	*there*
lontano	*far*
ovunque	*wherever*
sotto	*under, underneath*
su	*up*
vicino	*near*

Still more commonly used adverbs are:

anche	*also*
ancora	*still*
appena	*as soon as*
apposta	*on purpose*
benchè	*even if*
certo	*exactly; for sure*
come	*how*
così	*thus, so*
forse	*maybe*
infatti	*in fact*
infine	*at last*
inoltre	*besides*
insieme	*together*

insomma	*all in all*
intanto	*meanwhile*
neanche	*not even*
nemmeno	*not even*
piuttosto	*rather*
pressappoco	*about; approximately*
proprio	*really, exactly*
pure	*also*
quasi	*almost*
soprattutto	*especially, above all*

Exercise 114

Translate the following sentences into Italian.

1. Now I eat, then I will study.

_____.

2. As soon as I get home I will go to sleep.

_____.

3. Today I have a lot to do.

_____.

4. I rarely see them.

_____.

5. She is always in front of her house.

_____.

6. The children are playing outside.

_____.

7. It is cold everywhere.

_____.

8. I like to stay underneath the blankets.

_____.

9. Now I go to bed.

_____.

10. Carla has already gone to bed.

_____.

Sometimes instead of adding the suffix -**mente** to create an adverb, Italian can say the same thing by using the preposition **con** + a noun or by using the expressions **in modo** or **in una maniera** + an adjective.

Domani la vedrò **certamente**.	*Tomorrow I will **certainly** see her.*
Domani la vedrò **con certezza**.	*Tomorrow I will see her **with certainty**.*
Roberta si comporta **in modo strano**.	*Roberta behaves **strangely**.*
Roberta si comporta **in una maniera strana**.	*Roberta behaves **in a strange manner**.*

Italian often uses adverbial expressions with the prepositions **a**, **da**, **di**, and **in**. For example:

a distanza	*from a distance*
a lungo	*at length*
da lontano	*from a distance*
da vicino	*close up*
di certo	*certainly*
di nuovo	*again*
di recente	*recently*
di sicuro	*certainly*
di solito	*usually*
in alto	*up*
in basso	*down*
in breve	*briefly*
in generale	*generally*
in mezzo	*in the middle*
in orario	*on time*
in ritardo	*late*

Exercise 115

Translate the following sentences into Italian.

1. I want to go back to see the movie again.

_____.

2. I will certainly write her.

_____.

3. I saw her recently.

_____.

4. Tell me briefly what you are doing.

_____.

5. I beg you to arrive on time.

_____.

6. Roberta is always late.

_____.

7. Let me look at you close up.

_____.

8. He looked at her at length.

_____.

9. From a distance, the painting looks real.

_____.

10. They always do it on purpose.

_____.

Positions of the adverbs

In Italian adverbs usually follow the verb they modify, but usually precede adjectives in a sentence.

Carlo parla **bene** l'italiano.	_Carlo speaks Italian **well**._
Questa sera ho mangiato **troppo**.	_Tonight I ate **too much**._

But adverbs of time (**oggi, presto, tardi**, etc.) and adverbs expressing certainty or doubt usually precede the verb.

Oggi andiamo in chiesa.	_**Today** we'll go to church._

An adverb generally precedes a direct object noun.

Marco chiude **sempre** la porta con chiave quando entra in casa.	_Marco **always** locks the door when he goes in the house._

Adverbs of location are often placed before the direct object noun when considered part of the verb's meaning. Otherwise, their position within a sentence is flexible.

Devi **mandare via** i bambini.	*You have to **send away** the children.*
Devo **mandare indietro** il pacco.	*I have to **send back** the package.*
Non posso **andare avanti** così.	*I cannot **go on** like this.*

In compound tenses the position of an adverb varies. Adverbs of time, manner, and place follow the past participle. Some adverbs like **affatto** (*at all*), **ancora** (*still, yet*), **appena** (*as soon as; just*), **già** (*already*), **mai** (*never*), and **sempre** (*always*) can also be placed between the auxiliary and the past participle.

Siamo **appena** arrivati.	*We have **just** arrived.*
Siamo arrivati **appena** in tempo prima che la banca chiudesse.	*We arrived **just** in time before the bank closed.*
Non gli ho **ancora** parlato.	*I have not **yet** spoken to him.*
Non ti ho vista **mai** vestita bene.	*I have **never** seen you well dressed.*

Exercise 116

Fill in the blanks with the adverbs in parentheses.

1. Lei parla _____ (*well*) l'italiano.

2. I ragazzi hanno studiato _____ (*a lot*).

3. _____ (*Yesterday*) ho spedito le cartoline alle mie nipoti.

4. Marco chiude _____ (*always*) le finestre alla sera.

5. _____ (*Tomorrow*) andremo in chiesa.

6. Lei non può _____ (*go on*) da sola.

7. I suoi genitori sono _____ (*just*) arrivati in America.

8. Non sono stata _____ (*at all*) male in macchina.

9. Paolo ha _____ (*just*) fatto la doccia.

10. Sono _____ (*just*) arrivati e hanno _____ (*already*) chiamato i figli.

11. Lei ha portato il bambino al mare _____ (*during*) l'estate.

12. _____ (*Today*) abbiamo dormito _____ (*too much*).

Special uses of specific adverbs

Sempre usually means *always*. It is placed after the verb; in compound sentences it is placed before the past participle. (This will be discussed later in this book.)

Studio **sempre** la sera.	I *always study in the evening.*
Studierò **sempre** la sera.	I *will always study in the evening.*
Studiavo **sempre** la domenica.	I *always used to study on Sunday.*
Ho **sempre** studiato con le mie amiche.	I *always studied with my friends.*

In Italian there are many ways to say *late* or *early*: **in ritardo** (*late*), **con un ritardo di** (*with a delay of*), **tardi** (*late*), **presto** (*early*), **in anticipo** (*in advance*), **con un anticipo di** (*early*). **In ritardo** is used when a timetable is implied, but when the meaning is more general, the use of **tardi** is preferred.

Il treno arriva **in ritardo**.	The train arrives **late**.
Il treno parte **con** dieci minuti **di** ritardo.	The train departs **with ten minutes' delay**.
È **tardi** per uscire a pranzo.	It is **late** to go out to lunch.
È **presto** per cenare.	It is **early** to eat dinner.
È **tardi**.	It is **late**.
È **presto**.	It is **early**.

Ancora (*again*), **già** (*already*), and the word **più** of **non... più** (*not . . . anymore*) are usually placed after the verb they modify. In compound tenses they are placed between the auxiliary and the past participle.

Lo chiamo **ancora**.	I *will call him **again**.*
L'hai **già** chiamato?	Have you **already** called him?

Ancora translates as *still*, *again*, or *more*.

È **ancora** buio.	It is **still** dark.
Hai **ancora** voglia di andare al cinema?	Do you **still** want to go to the movies?
La chiamerò **ancora** domani.	I *will call her **again** tomorrow.*
Ci sono **ancora** due paste.	There are two **more** pastries.

Sometimes **ancora** is replaced by **di nuovo, un'altra volta,** or with a verb with the prefix of **ri-**.

Vuoi ascoltare **di nuovo** il CD?   *Do you want to listen to the CD again?*
Sì, voglio **riascoltarlo**.   *Yes, I want to listen to it again.*

Exercise 117

Fill in the blanks with the adverbs given in parentheses.

1. Marco è _____ (*still*) a casa.

2. Giovanni non aiuta _____ (*never*) sua moglie.

3. Marco e sua moglie andavano _____ (*always*) in chiesa.

4. Il treno è _____ (*late*).

5. È _____ (*late*), dobbiamo andare a casa.

6. Noi ci alziamo molto _____ (*early*) alla mattina.

7. Io telefono _____ (*always*) a mia mamma.

8. Carla è _____ (*already*) arrivata all'aeroporto.

9. Vado _____ (*always*) al cinema con le mie amiche.

10. Non la chiamo _____ (*anymore*) perché non risponde
    _____ (*never*).

11. Rimango a letto perché è _____ (*still*) buio.

12. Hai _____ (*already*) fatto il letto?

There are some rules to follow for adverbs. Some adverbs:

- express doubt and possibility and usually are placed before the verb in a sentence

forse	*maybe*
magari	*possibly*
probabilmente	*probably*

- express opinions

economicamente	*economically*
francamente	*frankly*
ovviamente	*obviously*
sinceramente	*sincerely*

• emphasize an adjective and are usually placed after the verb in a sentence

addirittura	*even*
anche	*even*
assolutamente	*absolutely*
davvero	*really*
persino/perfino	*even*
proprio	*really*
veramente	*really*

Note that **davvero, proprio,** and **veramente** are interchangeable, as are **addirittura, anche,** and **persino/perfino.**

Exercise 118

Fill in the blanks with the adverbs in parentheses.

1. Maria e Giovanni _____ (*maybe*) vengono con noi.

2. Maria e Giovanni _____ (*probably*) vengono con noi.

3. _____ (*Frankly*) il film non mi è piaciuto affatto.

4. Non è _____ (*economically*) possibile comperare una casa in California.

5. Non c'era _____ (*absolutely*) nessuno nel parco.

6. Siamo stati _____ (*really*) bene con loro.

7. Fa _____ (*really*) caldo.

8. Quel film è _____ (*certainly*) deprimente.

9. È _____ (*absolutely*) impossibile viaggiare in questi giorni.

10. _____ (*Maybe*) puoi rimanere a dormire a casa mia.

11. Mi piacerebbe _____ (*really*) saper sciare.

12. I ladri hanno _____ (*even*) rotto le serrature.

13. Quando vengono i miei genitori, _____ (*possibly*) faremo un bel pranzo assieme.

7

Comparative and Superlative Forms of Adjectives and Adverbs

Comparatives are classified in three ways: comparatives of equality, majority (or superiority), and minority (or inferiority). The last two types are also referred to as comparatives of inequality.

Comparatives of equality

In English a comparative of equality is used when the two adjectives being compared have equal characteristics. In this case, *as . . . as* is used in the sentence (*She is as tall as her sister.*). Italian uses **così... come** or **tanto... quanto** (Lei è *così* alta *come* sua sorella.). These phrases are interchangeable.

Luisa è **così** studiosa **come** Alberto.	*Luisa is as studious as Alberto.*
Luisa è **tanto** studiosa **quanto** Alberto.	*Luisa is as studious as Alberto.*
Questa musica è **così** bella **come** quella che abbiamo sentito ieri.	*This music is as nice as the music we heard yesterday.*
Questa musica è **tanto** bella **quanto** quella che abbiamo ascoltato ieri.	*This music is as nice as the music we listened to yesterday.*

The comparative of equality with nouns is expressed with **tanto... quanto** (*as much . . . as, as many . . . as*). In this case **tanto** must agree with the noun it modifies. **Quanto** does not change when followed by a pronoun. When a comparison of equality is made with adjectives, **tanto** and **quanto** do not change.

Noi mangiamo **tanta** pasta **quanto** voi.	*We eat as **much** pasta as you.*
Questo lago ha **tanti** pesci **quanto** quello.	*This lake has as **many** fish as that one.*

But:

Quella ragazza è **tanto** bella **quanto** intelligente.	*That girl is as beautiful as she is intelligent.*

Così and **quanto** are optional when they do not modify the word that follows them.

Tu studi **così come** me.	*You study as much as I do.*
Tu studi **come** me.	*You study as I do.*
Antonio mangia **tanto quanto** un leone.	*Antonio eats as much as a lion.*
Antonio mangia **come** un leone.	*Antonio eats as much as a lion.*

Tanto... quanto (*as . . . as*) and **così... come** (*as . . . as*) do not change before adjectives or adverbs but *do* change when followed by nouns.

Quella ragazza è **tanto** bella **quanto** gentile.	*That girl is as beautiful as she is kind.*
Quella ragazza parla **così** gentilmente **come** correttamente.	*That girl speaks as kindly as she does correctly.*
Abbiamo **tante** videocassette **quanti** CD.	*We have as many videos as CDs.*

There is no agreement when a definite article or a demonstrative adjective precedes the noun.

Mi piacciono **tanto** i film **quanto** i libri.	*I like movies as much as books.*
Mi piacciono **tanto** queste scarpe **quanto** quelle in vetrina.	*I like these shoes as much as those in the window.*

Exercise 119

Fill in the blanks with the missing comparison words.

1. Maria è così brava _____ Stefano.

2. Maria è tanto brava _____ Stefano.

3. Questa spiaggia non è così bella _____ quella di Sarasota in Florida.

4. Questo ristorante è tanto buono _____ quello vicino a casa tua.

5. Ho mangiato tanto bene oggi _____ ieri.

6. Questo negozio non ha tanti articoli _____ l'altro.

7. Lui mangia _____ verdure quanto frutta.

8. Carla mangia _____ pesce quanto carne.

9. Noi abbiamo _____ libri quanto Maria.

10. Questa casa non è così bella _____ quella che avevo prima.

Comparatives of majority

The comparative of majority is expressed by using **più... di** or **più... che** (*more . . . than, -er . . . than*).

Più... di is used when two different objects or subjects are compared, and before numbers. **Di** in this expression follows the same rules as **di** + definite article.

Il calcio è **più** interessante **del** nuoto.	*Soccer is **more** interesting **than** swimming.*
Le case americane sono **più** grandi **delle** case italiane.	*American homes are bigger **than** Italian homes.*
Ci sono **più di** quaranta oche nel laghetto.	*There are **more than** forty geese in the pond.*

Più... che is used when the comparison being made is between two aspects of the same subject or when comparing two adjectives, adverbs, nouns, pronouns, or infinitives that depend on the same verb, and with comparisons followed by a preposition.

Agli italiani piace **più** bere il cappuccino **che** il tè.	*Italians like to drink cappuccino **more than** tea.*
È **più** bello viaggiare **che** riposare.	*It is nicer to travel **than** to rest.*
Sono **più** belli **che** interessanti.	*They are **more beautiful than** interesting.*

Exercise 120

Fill in the blanks with the appropriate words for the comparative of majority, inserting the definite articles as necessary.

1. Il calcio è _____ divertente _____ baseball.

2. Le strade americane sono _____ larghe _____ strade italiane.

3. Gli europei guidano _____ velocemente _____ americani.

4. È _____ interessante leggere _____ guardare la televisione.

5. Alla mia famiglia piacciono _____ gli spaghetti

   _____ bistecche.

6. Maria è_____ elegante _____ Elisabetta.

7. Luca è _____ alto _____ Marco.

8. Luigi è _____ interessato allo sport _____ allo studio.

9. Giovanni e Luisa sono _____ studiosi _____ Carlo e

   Maria.

10. Le case americane sono _____ spaziose _____ case

    europee.

11. La vita nelle grandi città è _____ stressante _____

    vita nei paesi.

12. I giornali italiani sono _____ interessanti _____

    giornali americani.

Comparatives of minority

Comparatives of minority are used in the same way as comparatives of majority, but with the comparison words **meno... di** or **meno... che** (*less than*).

Gli italiani bevono **meno** caffè **degli** americani.	*Italians drink **less** coffee **than** Americans.*
Ci sono **meno di** dieci bambini nel parco.	*There are **less than** ten children at the park.*

Exercise 121

Fill in the blanks with the appropriate words for the comparative of minority, inserting the definite articles as necessary.

1. Michela è _____ elegante _____

   Elisabetta.

2. La vita nei paesi è _____ stressante

   _____ nelle città.

3. Luigi è _____ alto _____ Luca.

4. Io ho _____ fame _____ sete.

5. Agli italiani piace _____ la birra

    _____ il vino.

6. In questa classe ci sono _____ bambine

    _____ bambini.

7. Io leggo _____ libri _____

    riviste.

8. Noi andiamo _____ al cinema

    _____ al teatro.

9. Voi avete _____ soldi _____

    vostri amici.

10. Le case costano _____ appartamenti in centro.

Exercise 122

Fill in the blanks with the correct words for the comparisons of equality, minority, and majority in parentheses, inserting the definite articles where necessary.

1. Vedo _____ bambini _____ adulti. (*more . . . than*)

2. Nel lago ci sono _____ oche _____ anatre.

    (*less . . . than*)

3. C'è _____ acqua nel Po _____ nel Reno.

    (*more . . . than*)

4. I fiumi nell'Amazzonia sono _____ lunghi _____

    quelli in Africa. (*more . . . than*)

5. Lui è _____ intelligente _____ studioso. (*as . . . as*)

6. Il gelato italiano è _____ buono _____ quello

    svizzero. (*as . . . as*)

7. La sua casa è _____ luminosa _____ mia.

    (*less . . . than*)

8. La sua casa è _____ bella _____ grande.

    (*less . . . than*)

9. Il ristorante è _____ buono _____ elegante.

   (*as much . . . as*)

10. Il ristorante è _____ elegante _____ buono.

    (*more . . . than*)

Regular and irregular forms of comparatives between common adjectives

There are some Italian adjectives with both regular and irregular forms of the comparative.

adjective		comparative form	
buono	*good*	più buono *or* migliore	*better*
cattivo	*bad*	più cattivo *or* peggiore	*worse*
grande	*big, old*	più grande *or* maggiore	*bigger; older*
piccolo	*small, young*	più piccolo *or* minore	*smaller; younger*

The expressions **più grande di** (*bigger than*) and **più piccolo di** (*smaller than*) are generally used when referring to size, but are also used when speaking about age. **Maggiore** and **minore** are only used with age.

Carlo è **più grande di** Pietro.	*Carlo is **bigger than** Pietro.*
Carlo è **il maggiore dei** due fratelli.	*Carlo is **the older of the** two brothers.*

Usually the regular and irregular forms of the comparative of these adjectives are interchangeable. Also, **migliore** (*better*), **peggiore** (*worse*), **maggiore** (*bigger*), and **minore** (*smaller*) are already a form of the comparative and therefore never follow **più** (*more*) or **meno** (*less*).

Il formaggio francese è **più buono di** quello olandese.	*French cheese is **better than** that of the Dutch.*
Il formaggio francese è **migliore di** quello olandese.	*French cheese is **better than** that of the Dutch.*
Il **migliore** film che abbia visto è «Via col Vento».	*The **best** movie I have ever seen is Gone with the Wind.*
Suo fratello **maggiore** si chiama Giovanni.	*His **older** brother's name is Giovanni.*

Exercise 123

Fill in the blanks with the irregular comparatives in parentheses.

1. Questo formaggio è _____ (*better*) di quello.

2. Il gelato italiano è _____ (*better*) di quello americano.

3. Questo ragazzo è _____ (*bigger*) di quello.

4. Questa ragazza è _____ (*older*) di sua sorella.

5. La sua casa è _____ (*smaller*) della tua.

6. Luisa è la _____ (*older*) delle due sorelle.

7. Il _____ (*older*) dei due fratelli va all'università.

8. La _____ (*younger*) delle due sorelle è ancora al liceo.

9. Il primo libro di Harry Potter è _____ (*better*) degli altri.

10. Il mio cane è _____ (*smaller*) del tuo.

Superlative of adjectives

The superlative in English ends in *-est* (*smallest, biggest*) or it uses the word *most* before the adjective (*most intelligent*). There are two forms of the superlative in Italian: relative superlative and absolute superlative. Superlative adjectives in Italian agree in gender and number with the noun they modify.

The relative superlative is one of the easiest grammatical rules in Italian. It is formed by using the definite article + noun + superlative + **di** + the object being compared. In Italian the word **di** is used where in English the word *in* is used.

<table>
<tr><td>Tu sei lo studente più intelligente della classe.</td><td>You are the most intelligent student in the class.</td></tr>
</table>

Exercise 124

Fill in the blanks with the appropriate forms of the relative superlatives in parentheses.

1. Le strade americane sono _____ (*biggest*) del mondo.

2. Lei è la ragazza _____ (*prettiest*) della classe.

3. Giovanni è il tennista _____ (*best*) della classe.

4. Giuseppina ha avuto la vita _____ (*most difficult*) della famiglia.

5. Questo libro è il _____ (*most interesting*) che ho letto.

6. La storia che hai scritto è la _____ (*most interesting*) della classe.

7. Questo è il film _____ (*silliest*) che abbia mai visto.

8. Il ragazzo è il _____ (*most studious*) della classe.

9. Lei ha la casa _____ (*most beautiful*) di tutte.

10. Il treno che viaggia _____ (*slowest*) di tutti è l'accelerato.

The absolute superlative is the equivalent of the English phrase using *very* + an adjective, or of an adjective + *-est*, or of saying *the most, the least*. In Italian this is expressed by dropping the final vowel of an adjective and adding **-issimo(-a/-i/-e)**. The new word always agrees with the noun it modifies.

molto pane	*a lot of bread*
mol**tissimo** pane	***very much*** *bread*

The following table shows how this is done with some common Italian adjectives:

bello(-a/-i/-e)	*beautiful*	bel**lissimo**(-a/-i/-e)	*very beautiful*
ricco(-a/-chi/-che)	*rich*	ric**chissimo**(-a/-e/-i)	*very rich*
simpatico(-a/-i/-e)	*pleasant, nice*	simpati**cissimo**(-a/-i/-e)	*very pleasant*

Il Lago di Como è bellissimo.	*Lake Como is very beautiful.*

The absolute superlative is also formed by placing **molto** (*very*), **tanto** (*very, a lot*), **assai** (*very much*), or the prefixes **super** (*super*), **ultra** (*ultra*), or **stra** (*very*) before an adjective.

L'Africa è **tanto** lontana.	*Africa is **very** far.*
Quella casa è **stravecchia**.	*That house is **very** old.*

Sometimes special expressions are used to exaggerate the meaning of adjectives. These expressions follow no rules, however, and take time before one can easily use them. For example:

bagnato fradicio	*soaking wet*
stanco morto	*dead tired*
ricco sfondato	*filthy rich*
innamorato cotto	*madly in love*

Quando il cane è venuto in casa era **bagnato fradicio**.		*When the dog came inside it was soaking wet.*	
Ritorna dal lavoro **stanco morto**.		*He returns from work dead tired.*	

The following tables review the various forms of the comparative and superlative:

adjective		**comparative**	
buono	*good*	più buono *or* migliore	*better*
cattivo	*bad*	più cattivo *or* peggiore	*worse*
grande	*big*	più grande *or* maggiore	*bigger, older*
piccolo	*small*	più piccolo *or* minore	*smaller, younger*

relative superlative		**absolute superlative**	
il migliore	*the best*	buonissimo(-a/-i/-e) *or* ottimo(-a/-i/-e)	*very good*
il peggiore	*the worst*	cattivissimo(-a/-i/-e) *or* pessimo(-a/-i/-e)	*very bad*
il maggiore	*the biggest*	grandissimo(-a/-i/-e) *or* massimo(-a/-i/-e)	*very big*
il minore	*the smallest*	piccolissimo(-a/-i/-e) *or* minimo(-a/-i/-e)	*very small*

Il più (*the most*), **il meno** (*the least*), **migliore** (*better*), and **peggiore** (*worse*) generally precede the noun they modify. **Maggiore** (*bigger, older*) and **minore** (*smaller, younger*) generally follow the noun. The superlatives **ottimo, pessimo, massimo,** and **minimo** do not need to be preceded by **il più** or **il meno**.

Questo dolce è **ottimo**.		*This cake is **very good**.*	
Il cibo in quel ristorante è **pessimo**.		*The food in that restaurant is **very bad**.*	
Questa è la **minima** cosa da fare.		*This is a **very small** thing to do.*	

Exercise 125

Translate the following sentences into Italian using the appropriate forms of the absolute superlative.

1. Soccer is a very important sport in Italy.

_____.

2. Pascoli is a very famous Italian poet.

_____.

3. Mt. Everest is very tall.

_____.

4. The American supermarkets are very large.

_____.

5. Italian coffee is very strong.

_____.

6. Maria is very intelligent.

_____.

7. The Coliseum in Rome is very large.

_____.

8. The airplane flies very fast.

_____.

9. My friend (f.) writes very many letters.

_____.

10. Lavender is very fragrant.

_____.

There is no superlative for adjectives that already express an absolute superlative quality, as with:

colossale	*colossal*
divino	*divine*
eccellente	*excellent*
enorme	*enormous*
eterno	*eternal*
immenso	*immense*
infinito	*infinite*
meraviglioso	*wonderful, marvelous*

There are some adjectives that are irregular in the superlative. The following list gives a few examples.

adjective		**superlative**	
acre	*sour*	acerrimo	*very sour*
celebre	*famous*	celeberrimo	*very famous*

aspro	*sour*	asperrimo, asprissimo	*very sour*
salubre	*healthy*	saluberrimo	*very healthy*

The superlative forms of these adjectives are rarely used. The more common method is to precede them with the words **molto: molto aspro** (*very sour*) or **assai: assai celebre** (*very famous*).

Ho mangiato un limone **molto aspro**.	*I ate a **very sour** lemon.*
Quell'attrice è **assai celebre**.	*That actress is **very famous**.*

Exercise 126

Fill in the blanks with the superlative adjectives in parentheses.

1. Il Grand Canyon è _____ (*immense*).

2. «Ben Hur» è un film _____ (*colossal*).

3. La sua pagella aveva voti _____ (*excellent*).

4. I parchi americani sono _____ (*wonderful*).

5. L'universo è _____ (*infinite*).

6. La voce di Pavarotti è _____ (*divine*).

7. Le piramidi d'Egitto sono _____ (*enormous*).

8. I limoni sono _____ (*very sour*).

9. La vita non è _____ (*eternal*).

10. I monaci del Tibet fanno una vita _____ (*very healthy*).

There are some very common comparative and superlative expressions in both English and Italian:

- **alla meglio**   *as good/well as possible*

Si va **alla meglio**.	*We are **as well as possible**.*

- **di meglio in meglio**   *better and better*

La vita va **di meglio in meglio**.	*Life is going **better and better**.*

- **fare a meno di** *to do without*

    Non posso **fare a meno di** frutta.   *I can't **do without** fruit.*

- **fare del suo meglio**   *to do one's best*

    Lei fa sempre del **suo meglio**.   *She always **does her best**.*

- **meno male**   *thank goodness*

    Meno male che sei arrivato presto.   ***Thank goodness**, you arrived early.*

- **meno... meno**   *the less . . . the less*

    Meno si scrive, **meno** si vuole scrivere.   *The less one writes, **the less** one wants to write.*

- **per lo meno**   *at least*

    Ci sono **per lo meno** venti persone.   *There are **at least** twenty people.*

- **più o meno**   *more or less*

    Ha **più o meno** venti anni.   *She is **more or less** twenty years old.*

- **più... più**   *the more . . . the more*

    Più si mangia, **più** si vuole mangiare.   *The more one eats, **the more** one wants to eat.*

Comparative and superlative of adverbs

Like adjectives, adverbs also have comparative and superlative forms. Some are regular and some are not. The adverbs **bene** (*well*), **male** (*bad*), **molto** (*much*), and **poco** (*a little*) have irregular forms in the comparative and relative superlative, but they are regular in the absolute superlative.

adverb		comparative	
bene	*well*	meglio	*better*
male	*bad*	peggio	*worse*

molto	*much*	più, di più	*more*
poco	*a little*	meno di meno	*less*

relative superlative		**absolute superlative**	
il meglio	*the best*	benissimo	*very well*
il peggio	*the worst*	malissimo	*very bad*
il più	*the most*	moltissimo	*very much*
il meno	*the least*	pochissimo	*very little*

Ieri stavo **bene**.	*Yesterday I was **well**.*
Oggi sto **meglio** di ieri.	*Today I feel **better** than yesterday.*
Domani starò **benissimo**.	*Tomorrow I will feel **very well**.*

Exercise 127

Fill in the blanks with the correct forms of the adverbs in parentheses.

1. Erica legge _____ (*well*).

2. Erica quest'anno legge _____ (*better*).

3. Oggi Luisa sta _____ (*worse*) di ieri.

4. Non ho _____ (*much*) interesse ad andare al mercato.

5. Mi piace _____ (*very much*) la musica.

6. Lucia non ha pulito _____ (*well*) la casa.

7. Le scriviamo _____ (*very little*).

8. Ho mangiato _____ (*very little*).

9. Scrive _____ (*worse*) delle galline.

10. In questa casa mi trovo _____ (*well*).

11. La Grande Muraglia della Cina è _____ (*immense*).

12. Gli studenti leggono sempre _____ (*worse*).

Comparative forms of regular adverbs

Regular adverbs (those ending in **-mente**) form the comparative by adding **più** or **meno** before the adverb and form the superlative by adding **il più** or **il meno** before the adverb.

I treni vecchi viaggiano **meno** rapidamente di quelli moderni.	*The old trains don't travel as fast as the modern ones. (The old trains travel **less** rapidly than the modern ones.)*
Voglio arrivare **il più** rapidamente possibile.	*I want to arrive as **quickly** as possible.*

The absolute comparative of regular adverbs is formed by adding -**mente** to the feminine superlative adjective: rapid**issima** (*very rapid*) becomes rapidissima**mente** (*very rapidly*). Adverbs not ending in -**mente** form the absolute superlative by dropping the final vowel of the adverb and adding -**issimo**: presto (*early*), prest**issimo** (*very early*).

Mio zio si alza sempre **prestissimo**.	*My uncle always gets up **very early**.*
Gli italiani parlano **rapidissimamente**.	*Italians speak **very fast**.*

When **più** is used for the comparative and superlative of an adverb, the preposition **di** follows the adverb. When the comparison is made between two adverbs, **che** is used.

Pietro legge più rapidamente **di** tutti.	*Peter reads faster **than** everybody.*
Pietro legge più rapidamente **che** correttamente.	*Peter reads faster **than** he does correctly.*

Il is the only definite article used with superlative adverbs. Often **il** is dropped unless **possibile** is used.

Carlo studia **il più** rapidamente **possibile**.	*Carlo studies as **fast as** possible.*
Carlo studia **più** diligentemente **di** suo fratello.	*Carlo studies **more** diligently **than** his brother.*

Exercise 128

Fill in the blanks with the correct forms of the adverbs in parentheses.

1. Il nonno cammina _____ (*slowly*).

2. Il nonno cammina _____ (*slower*) della nonna.

3. Il Polo Nord è _____ (*extremely*) freddo.

4. Il malato oggi sta _____ (*very bad*).

5. _____ (*Strangely*) oggi mi sono alzata presto.

6. Mi ha guardato _____ (*very strangely*).

7. Le macchine oggi viaggiano _____ (*faster*) di quelle di

   un tempo.

8. Il mio amico mi ha trattata _____ (*very, very coldly*).

9. Ieri sono andata a letto _____ (*very, very late*).

10. Il padre di Carlo era _____ (*very strangely*) di buon umore.

11. I ragazzi a scuola fanno _____ (*their best*).

12. Il cinese non si impara _____ (*easily*).

13. Il giapponese si impara _____ (*more easily*) del cinese.

14. I bambini non ascoltano _____ (*attentively*) la maestra.

15. Gina parla _____ (*correctly*) ma scrive

    _____ (*uncorrectly*).

8

Present Tense

A verb expresses a physical or mental action or state, such as walking, talking, thinking, eating, sleeping, or being. All Italian verbs have four moods: the *infinitive* is the unconjugated verb expressing the action itself, with no reference to time or person. This is the form found in a dictionary. The *indicative* expresses something as a fact. It is the most commonly used mood. The *imperative* is the command form, used to give orders. The *subjunctive* expresses possibility, hope, feelings, and wishes and is almost always preceded by **che**, such as **Lui vuole che io dorma** (*He wants me to sleep*).

Familiar and formal forms

In Italian there are four ways to express the pronoun *you*. When addressing a relative, child, or close friend, the pronoun **tu** (*you*, sing.) is used. **Tu** is referred to as the familiar singular form. The plural of **tu** is **voi** (*you*, pl.). **Voi** is used when addressing more than one relative, child, or close friend.

When addressing a stranger, an older person, or someone you do not know well, the pronoun **Lei** (*you*, formal sing.) is used. In writing the pronoun Lei is always capitalized. The plural of **Lei** is **Loro** and this, too, is capitalized in writing. One usually must wait for permission before using the familiar **tu** form with someone. However, today, in modern Italy, the less formal address is fairly well accepted among young people.

Italian verbs come in three types and have first, second, and third person singular conjugations and first, second, and third person plural conjugations. The three different categories of Italian verbs are:

- Verbs ending in **-are**, such as **parlare** (*to speak*)
- Verbs ending in **-ere**, such as **vedere** (*to see*)
- Verbs ending in **-ire**, such as **dormire** (*to sleep*)

It is not necessary to use subject pronouns before every verb conjugation in Italian, since the ending for each conjugation is different, making it obvious who is doing the action. When there is ambiguity, the pronoun is required.

Present indicative tense

The present indicative expresses a fact, tells what usually happens, what is happening now, and general truths. In addition, the Italian present tense is often used to refer to the immediate future and also refers to the past, which is called the historic present. The present tense of Italian verbs is formed by adding various present tense endings to the root of a verb. The root is obtained by dropping the -are, -ere, -ire endings of the infinitives.

present tense of regular verbs

	-are *parlare* to speak, talk	-ere *vedere* to see	-ire *dormire* to sleep	-ire *finire* to finish
io	parlo	vedo	dormo	finisco
tu	parli	vedi	dormi	finisci
lui/lei/Lei	parla	vede	dorme	finisce
noi	parliamo	vediamo	dormiamo	finiamo
voi	parlate	vedete	dormite	finite
loro/Loro	parlano	vedono	dormono	finiscono

Verbs ending in *-are*

The first category of verbs are those ending in -are. Most are regular in their endings except for **stare** (*to stay*), **dare** (*to give*), **andare** (*to go*), **fare** (*to make; do*).

Regular endings for the -are verbs are:

io (*I*)	-o	noi (*we*)	-iamo
tu (*you*, fam. sing.)	-i	voi (*you*, fam. pl.)	-ate
lui (*he*)	-a	loro (*they*, m. or f.)	-ano
lei (*she*)	-a		
Lei (*you*, form. sing.)	-a	Loro (*you*, form. pl.)	-ano

To conjugate the regular -are verb **parlare**, find the root of the verb by dropping the -are ending. Then add the endings from the previous table for each of the subjects. The complete conjugation looks like this:

io parlo	*I speak*		noi parl**iamo**	*we speak*
tu parl**i**	*you speak* (fam. sing.)		voi parl**ate**	*you speak*
lui parl**a**	*he speaks*		loro parl**ano**	*they speak*
lei parl**a**	*she speaks*			
Lei parl**a**	*you speak* (form., m. or f.)		Loro parl**ano**	*you speak* (form. pl.)

Some common **-are** verbs in Italian are:

abitare	*to live*
aiutare	*to help*
arrivare	*to arrive*
ascoltare	*to listen to*
aspettare	*to wait for*
ballare	*to dance*
camminare	*to walk*
cantare	*to sing*
cenare	*to have supper*
cominciare	*to start*
dimenticare	*to forget*
domandare	*to ask*
giocare	*to play*
imparare	*to learn*
lavare	*to wash*
lavorare	*to work*
pagare	*to pay*
pranzare	*to have lunch*
provare	*to try*
raccontare	*to narrate; tell*
rallentare	*to slow down*
regalare	*to give a gift*
ricordare	*to remember*
riposare	*to rest*
ritornare	*to return*
studiare	*to study*
suonare	*to play (an instrument)*
trovare	*to find*
viaggiare	*to travel*
volare	*to fly*

Exercise 129

Fill in the blanks with the appropriate present tense forms of the verbs in parentheses.

1. Io _____ (ballare) con i miei amici.

2. Tu _____ (cantare) con il coro della scuola.

3. Lui _____ (giocare) con la palla nuova.

4. Lei _____ (lavorare) tutto il giorno.

5. Noi _____ (cominciare) a guardare la corsa delle bambine.

6. Voi _____ (aiutare) le vostre compagne di scuola.

7. Loro _____ (aspettare) l'autobus tutte le mattine.

8. Io e Giovanna _____ (riposare) tutti i giorni.

9. Loro _____ (viaggiare) sempre.

10. Kyria _____ (suonare) il flauto.

11. Voi _____ (provare) ad andare in bicicletta.

12. Lei _____ (pagare) il conto.

As mentioned, there are four important irregular -are verbs. What makes them irregular is that their conjugated endings are different from the regular -are verb endings. The four irregular verbs are **stare**, **dare**, **fare**, and **andare**, and their complete conjugations in the present tense are as follows:

stare		*dare*	
io **sto**	*I stay*	io **do**	*I give*
tu **stai**	*you stay*	tu **dai**	*you give*
lui **sta**	*he stays*	lui **dà**	*he gives*
lei **sta**	*she stays*	lei **dà**	*she gives*
noi **stiamo**	*we stay*	noi **diamo**	*we give*
voi **state**	*you stay*	voi **date**	*you give*
loro **stanno**	*they stay*	loro **danno**	*they give*

fare		*andare*	
io **faccio**	*I make; I do*	io **vado**	*I go*
tu **fai**	*you make; you do*	tu **vai**	*you go*
lui **fa**	*he makes; he does*	lui **va**	*he goes*
lei **fa**	*she makes; she does*	lei **va**	*she goes*
noi **facciamo**	*we make; we do*	noi **andiamo**	*we go*

| voi **fate** | *you make; you do* | voi **andate** | *you go* |
| loro **fanno** | *they make; they do* | loro **vanno** | *they go* |

There are some **-are** verbs that are considered regular, but do have some spelling irregularities:

- Verbs ending in **-care**, like **cercare** (*to look for*) and **toccare** (*to touch*), or those ending in **-gare**, like **pagare** (*to pay*), add an **h** before adding the verb endings starting with **-i** (**tu** and **noi**) in order to maintain the same hard -c and -g sound of the root of the verb.

io cerco	*I look for*
tu cerchi	*you look for*
lui/lei cerca	*he/she looks for*
noi cerchiamo	*we look for*
voi cercate	*you look for*
loro cercano	*they look for*

- Verbs ending in **-ciare** or **-giare**, like **cominciare** (*to begin*), **mangiare** (*to eat*), and **viaggiare** (*to travel*), omit the **-i** before the **tu** and the **noi** endings.

io mangio	*I eat*
tu mangi (not mangii)	*you eat*
lui/lei mangia	*he/she eats*
noi mangiamo (not mangiiamo)	*we eat*
voi mangiate	*you eat*
loro mangiano	*they eat*

- Other verbs ending in **-iare** like **studiare** (*to study*) omit the **-i** before the **tu** and **noi** endings of the present tense if the **-i** is not in the accented syllable.

io studio	*I study*
tu studi (not studii)	*you study*
lui/lei studia	*he/she studies*
noi studiamo (not studiiamo)	*we study*
voi studiate	*you study*
loro studiano	*they study*

An exception to this is with the verb **avviare** (*to start*).

| io avvio | *I start* |
| tu avvii (not avvi) | *you start* |

lui/lei avvia	*he/she starts*
noi avviamo	*we start*
voi avviate	*you start*
loro avviano	*they start*

Some of the common Italian verbs ending in **-ciare, -giare, -chiare, -ghiare, -care,** and **-gare** are:

assaggiare	*to taste*
attaccare	*to attack*
cominciare	*to start*
indagare	*to investigate*
invecchiare	*to age*
noleggiare	*to rent*
parcheggiare	*to park*
passeggiare	*to stroll*
toccare	*to touch*
viaggiare	*to travel*

Exercise 130

Fill in the blanks with the conjugated forms of the verbs in parentheses.

1. Io _____ (stare) molto bene in Italia.

2. Tu _____ (dare) il dizionario agli studenti.

3. Lei _____ (fare) un buon dolce.

4. Noi _____ (andare) al cinema con i nostri amici.

5. Io _____ (cercare) sempre dei libri per i miei studenti.

6. Tu _____ (cercare) una parola nuova.

7. Lei _____ (pagare) il conto.

8. Noi _____ (pagare) un affitto molto alto.

9. Voi _____ (cominciare) a lavorare alle otto.

10. Tu _____ (mangiare) la pizza con molto gusto.

11. Noi _____ (cominciare) la scuola in settembre.

12. Tu _____ (studiare) molto.

Verbs ending in -*ere*

The second category of verbs are those ending in **-ere**. Some are regular, but many of them are irregular. The endings for **-ere** verbs are:

io (*I*)	**-o**	noi (*we*)	**-iamo**
tu (*you*, fam. sing.)	**-i**	voi (*you*, fam. pl.)	**-ete**
lui (*he*)	**-e**	loro (*they*, m. or f.)	**-ono**
lei (*she*)	**-e**		
Lei (*you*, form. sing.)	**-e**	Loro (*you*, form. pl.)	**-ono**

The complete present tense conjugation of the **-ere** verb **vedere** (*to see*) is:

io ved**o**	*I see*	noi ved**iamo**	*we see*
tu ved**i**	*you see* (fam. sing.)	voi ved**ete**	*you see*
lui ved**e**	*he sees*	loro ved**ono**	*they see*
lei ved**e**	*she sees*		
Lei ved**e**	*you see* (form. sing.)	Loro ved**ono**	*you see* (form. pl.)

The following verbs are some common **-ere** verbs in Italian:

accendere	*to turn on*
apprendere	*to learn*
attendere	*to wait for, attend*
chiedere	*to ask*
chiudere	*to close*
conoscere	*to know someone*
credere	*to believe*
crescere	*to grow*
includere	*to include*
insistere	*to insist*
leggere	*to read*
mettere	*to put*
perdere	*to lose*
permettere	*to allow*
piangere	*to cry*
prendere	*to take*
promettere	*to promise*

rispondere	to answer
scendere	to descend, go down; get off
scrivere	to write
vedere	to see
vivere	to live

Exercise 131

Fill in the blanks with the conjugated forms of the verbs in parentheses.

1. Io _____ (accendere) la luce perché è una giornata senza sole.

2. Tu _____ (attendere) la tua amica per molte ore.

3. Lui _____ (chiedere) a che ora aprono i musei.

4. Lei _____ (chiudere) sempre la finestra.

5. Noi _____ (conoscere) molte persone.

6. In primavera, i fiori _____ (crescere) in tutti i prati.

7. Voi _____ (insistere) per portarci al ristorante.

8. Loro _____ (leggere) solo libri di spionaggio.

9. Io _____ (mettere) in tasca la chiave della macchina.

10. Olga _____ (perdere) sempre tutto.

11. Io le _____ (permettere) di andare fuori di sera.

12. I bambini piccoli _____ (piangere) quando hanno fame e sonno.

As mentioned, with -ere conjugations there are many irregular verbs.

- Some -ere verbs change in pronunciation in the present tense, but the spelling of the root stays the same. For example, with verbs ending in -cere and -gere, as in vincere (to win) and leggere (to read), the pronunciation changes to a hard sound when the -o ending in the io and loro forms follows the -c or -g in the root of the verb. For example:

io vinco (pronounced veen-ko)	I win
tu vinci	you win
lui/lei vince	he/she wins
noi vinciamo	we win
voi vincete	you win
loro vincono (pronounced veen-ko-no)	they win

io leggo (pronounced le-*gh*o)	*I read*
tu leggi	*you read*
lui/lei legge	*he/she reads*
noi leggiamo	*we read*
voi leggete	*you read*
loro leggono (pronounced leg-*gh*o-no)	*they read*

- Some **-ere** verbs add a **-g** to the first person singular and third person plural such as: **rimanere** (*to remain*), **scegliere** (*to choose*), **spegnere** (*to turn off*), **togliere** (*to remove*), **valere** (*to be worth*).

    io rimango, loro rimangono
    io scelgo, loro scelgono
    io spengo, loro spengono
    io tolgo, loro tolgono
    io valgo, loro valgono

    It is only in the **io** and **loro** forms that these verbs change, however. The other endings remain the same as regular **-ere** verbs.

- Other **-ere** verbs like **tenere** (*to keep*) and **contenere** (*to contain*), add a **-g** in the first person singular and third person plural, and also add an **-i** to the root of the verb in the second and third person singular.

    tengo, tieni, tiene, teniamo, tenete, tengono
    contengo, contieni, contiene, conteniamo, contenete, contengono

- Other **-ere** verbs like **sedere** (*to sit*) and **parere** (*to seem*) make a vowel change in some of the root forms:

    siedo, siedi, siede, sediamo, sedete, siedono
    paio, pari, pare, pariamo, parete, paiono

- An **-ere** verb that has a conjugation all its own is **bere** (*to drink*). But realizing that it as a shortened version of the Latin verb *bevere*, it actually follows the regular conjugation for **-ere** verbs.

    bevo, bevi, beve, beviamo, bevete, bevono

Exercise 132

Translate the sentences into Italian using the conjugated forms of **-ere** verbs.

1. They remain at our house for three nights.

_____.

2. I choose my new book.

_____.

3. She turns off the light.

_____.

4. They turn off the motor.

_____.

5. He takes off his jacket.

_____.

6. You keep the door closed.

_____.

7. She keeps her jewelry in a safe.

_____.

8. This box contains hazardous material.

_____.

9. I sit down because I am tired.

_____.

10. The mother keeps the baby on her lap.

_____.

11. Giovanni chooses the flowers for his wife.

_____.

12. I remain in Italy for three weeks.

_____.

Modal verbs

Modal verbs are "helpers." They modify the meaning of the verbs that follow them, and indicate the attitude of the speaker. The modal verbs **dovere** (*to have to*), **potere** (*to be able to*), **sapere** (*to know* *how to*), and **volere** (*to want to*) are almost always used before an infinitive. Their conjugations look like this:

> devo/debbo, devi, deve, dobbiamo, dovete, devono/debbono
> posso, puoi, può, possiamo, potete, possono
> so, sai, sa, sappiamo, sapete, sanno
> voglio, vuoi, vuole, vogliamo, volete, vogliono

Sapere can be used as a modal verb or as a regular verb without a dependent infinitive.

Exercise 133

Translate the following sentences into Italian using the conjugated forms of the modal verbs.

1. I have to go to work.

_____.

2. He must study more.

_____.

3. I can make a cake for the children.

_____.

4. We can wait for you.

_____.

5. Can you (sing.) go to the movies with me? Yes, I can.

_____.

6. Do you (sing.) know how to go to the airport?

_____?

7. They know how to speak several languages.

_____.

8. I want to send a package to my grandchildren.

_____.

9. He wants to learn how to swim.

_____.

10. We have to go shopping today.

_____.

11. You (pl.) can wait for me here.

_____.

12. Do you (sing.) know if they want to go with us?

_____?

Verbs ending in -*ire*

The third category of verbs are those ending in **-ire**. There are two types of **-ire** verbs. One type follows the pattern of **dormire** (*to sleep*) and the other follows the pattern of **finire** (*to finish*). The present tense endings are the same for both types. The difference is that verbs like **finire** add **-isc-** before adding the endings in all forms except **noi** and **voi**. Verbs ending in **-ire** are conjugated with the following endings:

io (*I*)	**-o**	noi (*we*)	**-iamo**
tu (*you*, fam. sing.)	**-i**	voi (*you*, fam. pl.)	**-ite**
lui (*he*)	**-e**	loro (*they*, m. or f.)	**-ono**
lei (*she*)	**-e**		
Lei (*you*, form. sing.)	**-e**	Loro (*you*, form. pl.)	**-ono**

The complete present tense conjugations of **dormire** and **finire** look like this:

io dormo	*I sleep*	io finisco	*I finish*
tu dormi	*you sleep* (fam. sing.)	tu finisci	*you finish* (fam. sing.)
lui dorme	*he sleeps*	lui finisce	*he finishes*
lei dorme	*she sleeps*	lei finisce	*she finishes*
Lei dorme	*you sleep* (form. sing)	Lei finisce	*you finish* (form. sing.)
noi dorm**iamo**	*we sleep*	noi fin**iamo**	*we finish*
voi dorm**ite**	*you sleep* (fam. pl.)	voi fin**ite**	*you finish*
loro dorm**ono**	*they sleep*	loro fin**iscono**	*they finish*
Loro dorm**ono**	*you sleep* (form. pl.)	Loro fin**iscono**	*you finish* (form. pl.)

Some of the common **-ire** verbs that follow the pattern of **dormire** are:

aprire	*to open*
bollire	*to boil*
coprire	*to cover*
offrire	*to offer*

partire	to leave
scoprire	to discover; uncover
seguire	to follow
sentire	to hear, to listen
servire	to serve
vestire	to dress

Some of the common -ire verbs that follow the pattern of **finire** by adding the **-isc-** to the verb root are:

capire	to understand
costruire	to build
dimagrire	to lose weight
impedire	to prevent
ingrandire	to enlarge
preferire	to prefer
pulire	to clean
spedire	to send
ubbidire	to obey

Exercise 134

Fill in the blanks using the conjugated forms of the verbs in parentheses.

1. Io _____ (dormire) per molte ore.

2. Tu _____ (coprire) le piante quando fa freddo.

3. Lui _____ (partire) per Roma.

4. Carla _____ (aprire) la porta.

5. Maria _____ (offrire) una tazza di tè.

6. Maria e Carlo _____ (offrire) un bicchiere di vino ai loro amici.

7. Noi _____ (partire) domenica mattina.

8. Gli scalatori _____ (seguire) la guida.

9. Erica _____ (partire) per l'America.

10. Lara _____ (sentire) quello che le dice la sua maestra.

11. Loro _____ (scoprire) la verità.

12. I due nonni _____ (partire) molto malvolentieri.

Exercise 135

Fill in the blanks using the conjugated forms of the verbs in parentheses.

1. Io _____ (finire) il libro.

2. Luisa _____ (preferire) il caldo al freddo.

3. Lui non _____ (capire) bene l'italiano.

4. Franca _____ (costruire) una bellissima casa.

5. Cristina _____ (pulire) sempre la casa.

6. Roberto e Marco _____ (spedire) i pacchi dall'Italia.

7. Le bambine _____ (ubbidire) i loro genitori.

8. Noi _____ (preferire) andare al mare.

9. Voi _____ (finire) i compiti.

10. L'anno prossimo noi _____ (ingrandire) il garage.

11. L'acqua _____ (impedire) alla gente di entrare in casa.

12. Il professore _____ (capire) quando gli studenti non hanno studiato.

Exercise 136

Translate the following sentences into Italian.

1. I sleep.

_____.

2. He opens the door.

_____.

3. He builds a wall.

_____.

4. She offers me a cup of coffee.

_____.

5. We follow you.

_____.

6. You (fam. sing.) offer them a glass of water.

_____.

7. We open the store.

_____.

8. I prefer going by bus.

_____.

9. They prefer flying.

_____.

10. He doesn't understand Italian.

_____.

11. He cleans his desk.

_____.

12. They clean the floor.

_____.

There are some **-ire** verbs that can take either ending. They are:

applaudire	_to applaud_
assorbire	_to absorb_
inghiottire	_to swallow_
mentire	_to lie_
nutrire	_to nourish_
starnutire	_to sneeze_
tossire	_to cough_

There are also irregularities with **-ire** verbs that add **-g** in the first person singular and third person plural, and that add a vowel change in the second and third person singular. For example:

venire (_to come_): vengo, vieni, viene, veniamo, venite, vengono

intervenire (_to intervene_): intervengo, intervieni, interviene, interveniamo, intervenite, intervengono

Other irregularities of verbs ending in **-ire** are vowel changes in the stem as in:

apparire (_to appear_): appaio, appari, appare, appariamo, apparite, appaiono

morire (_to die_): muoio, muori, muore, moriamo, morite, muoiono

udire (_to hear_): odo, odi, ode, udiamo, udite, odono

The irregular -ire verb **dire** (*to say, to tell*) derives from the Latin **dicere**. This explains, then, the addition of the -c- in its conjugation:

> dico, dici, dice, diciamo, dite, dicono

Exercise 137

Fill in the blanks with the conjugated forms of the verbs in parentheses.

1. Il pubblico _____ (applaudire) il tenore.

2. La ragazza _____ (inghiottire) il pane.

3. Gli uccelli _____ (nutrire) i loro piccoli con il becco.

4. Noi ci _____ (nutrire) molto bene.

5. Quando abbiamo il raffreddore _____ (starnutire) spesso.

6. In inverno tutti _____ (tossire).

7. Le bambine _____ (venire) a casa da scuola alle 16,30.

8. La luna _____ (apparire) alla sera.

9. A volte _____ (io-morire) dalla stanchezza.

10. I pinguini _____ (morire) dal freddo.

11. La casa _____ (apparire) sulla collina.

12. Loro _____ (udire) la musica.

Special uses of the present tense

The present tense, not the future tense, is used when one wants to express definite intentions or plans in the future.

Ti telefono domani mattina.   *I will call you tomorrow morning.*

Da + present tense is used when referring to an action that has not yet been completed or has been interrupted. This corresponds to the English present perfect tense + *since* or *for*.

Sono in Italia **da** tre settimane.   *I have been in Italy for three weeks.*

Stare per + a verb infinitive expresses something that is about to happen.

Sta per nevicare.   *It is about to snow.*

Present continuous

In English the present continuous expresses an action taking place at the time of speaking. In Italian this can be expressed with the present tense of the verb showing the action taking place at the moment, or with the present tense of **stare** + the gerund of the verb. The gerund has two endings in Italian: **-ando** for **-are** verbs (**parlando**) and **-endo** for **-ere** and **-ire** verbs (**leggendo**).

The regular forms of gerunds are:

io sto ascolt**ando**	*I am listening*
tu stai guard**ando**	*you are watching*
lui/lei sta parl**ando**	*he/she is speaking*
noi stiamo ved**endo**	*we are seeing*
voi state dorm**endo**	*you are sleeping*
loro stanno fin**endo**	*they are finishing*

One can say:

Io **ascolto** la radio.	*I am listening to the radio.*
Io **sto ascoltando** la radio.	*I am listening to the radio.*

Exercise 138

Translate the following sentences into Italian.

1. I have been studying for an hour.

_____.

2. She is going out with him.

_____.

3. He has been writing a book.

_____.

4. The boy will sell the tickets for two hours.

_____.

5. I want to go out, but it is about to rain.

_____.

6. I am about to go to the dentist.

_____.

7. They are about to go to bed.

_____.

8. You (sing.) are listening to the opera.

_____.

9. I am going to bed.

_____.

10. She is cooking dinner.

_____.

11. We are closing the door.

_____.

12. The baby is sleeping.

_____.

Making a sentence negative

To make a positive sentence negative, place the word **non** immediately before the conjugated verb. The equivalent *do not* or *does not*, used in English for negative sentences, is not used in Italian.

Io **non** parlo l'italiano.	*I **don't** speak Italian.*
Noi **non** lavoriamo con tuo padre.	*We **don't** work with your father.*
Tu **non** canti bene.	*You **don't** sing well.*

Asking a question

To ask a question in Italian, place the verb (or subject and verb) at the beginning or end of a question that requires a yes or no answer. The tone of voice also lets a person know when a question is being asked.

Abiti ancora a Milano?	***Do you still live in Milan?***
Abitate ancora nella stessa casa?	***Do you still live in the same house?***

If the question requires a more involved answer, words such as **dove, come, quando, quanto, quale, chi, che,** or **che cosa** introduce the question. **Chi** (*who*) is always used with the third person singular. And all of these words are usually followed by a verb.

Dove vai?	***Where are you going?***
Come stanno i tuoi nonni?	***How are your grandparents?***
Quando ritornate a casa?	***When will you return home?***
Perché vai in Italia?	***Why are you going to Italy?***
Quale vuoi?	***Which one do you want?***

Quanto, quanti, quanta, and **quante** (*how much, how many*) are generally followed by a noun.

Quanto pane compri?	***How much bread will you buy?***
Quanti giornali leggi?	***How many newspapers do you read?***

To give a negative answer to a question, put **no** at the beginning of the sentence.

Vai a fare la spesa? **No,** non vado a fare la spesa.	*Are you going to do some shopping?* *No, I am not going to go shopping.*
Andate a votare? **No,** non andiamo a votare.	*Are you going to vote? No, we are not going to vote.*

Exercise 139

Translate the following questions into Italian.

1. Do you (sing.) study in Italy?

_____?

2. Does she go to church every Sunday?

_____?

3. Does he work far away?

_____?

4. Do we go to Italy next summer?

_____?

5. Do you (pl.) like to eat at the restaurant?

_____?

6. Where is the museum?

_____?

7. How do you (pl.) go to school?

_____?

8. When will you (sing.) pick up the girls from school?

_____?

9. Where does your husband work?

_____?

10. Who is calling you (sing.)?

_____?

11. When does he come home from work?

_____?

12. Which one do you (sing.) like?

_____?

13. How many boats does he have?

_____?

Exercise 140

Change the following positive sentences into the negative.

1. Io vado a Roma.

_____.

2. Tu scrivi molto bene.

_____.

3. Lei studia molto.

_____.

4. Lui vuole una macchina nuova.

_____.

5. Noi abbiamo bisogno di un computer nuovo.

_____.

6. Voi parlate al telefono.

_____.

7. I miei amici mi chiamano tutte le sere.

_____.

8. Voi partite domenica.

_____.

9. Loro aspettano i nonni.

_____.

10. Io arrivo in ritardo.

_____.

Give a negative answer to the questions below.

11. Vai al ristorante questa sera?

_____.

12. Vuoi chiamare tua sorella?

_____.

13. Ritornate a casa subito?

_____.

14. Giochi al tennis domani?

_____.

15. Ascolti le canzoni nuove?

_____.

16. Ti piace giocare a carte?

_____.

17. Vuoi vedere un film questa sera?

_____.

18. Vanno a scuola i tuoi figli?

_____.

19. Volete un caffè?

_____.

20. Hai bisogno di soldi?

_____.

Essere (to be) and *avere* (to have)

Essere and **avere** are the two most commonly used Italian verbs. They are both irregular in all their forms. Besides being used alone in the usual conjugations, they are also used to form the compound tenses.

Essere

Essere, unlike the other verbs discussed so far, cannot be conjugated using the root as its basis. It is best that you memorize all its forms.

io	**sono**	*I am*
tu	**sei**	*you are*
lui/lei	**è**	*he/she is*
Lei	**è**	*you are*
noi	**siamo**	*we are*
voi	**siete**	*you are*
loro	**sono**	*they are*

The **io** and **loro** forms have the same spelling: **sono.** This is seldom confusing since the correct meaning is obvious from the context of the sentence.

Essere is used to express:

- colors that describe things

  La neve è bianca.   *The snow **is** white.*

- date and time

  Oggi è il 4 luglio.   *Today **is** the 4th of July.*

- location

  Io **sono** in casa.   *I **am** at home.*

- mood

    Carla è molto buona.   *Carla **is** very good.*

- nationality

    Giovanni è italiano.   *Giovanni **is** Italian.*

- personal traits

    Lei è una persona intelligente.   *She **is** an intelligent person.*

- physical characteristics

    Lei è una donna attraente.   *She **is** an attractive woman.*

- physical status

    Loro **sono** vecchi.   *They **are** old.*

- profession

    Tu **sei** studentessa.   *You **are** a student.*

- conditions

    La sua faccia è sporca.   *His face **is** dirty.*

Exercise 141

Fill in the blanks with the correct forms of **essere**.

1. Io _____ felice.
2. Tu _____ in casa.
3. Lui _____ dal dottore.
4. Lei _____ molto bella.
5. Noi _____ al cinema.

6. Voi _____ intelligenti.

7. Loro _____ alti.

8. La mia casa _____ in collina.

9. La vita _____ bella.

10. Tu e Carlo _____ vicino alla finestra.

11. Io e Maria _____ a scuola tutti i lunedì.

12. Luisa e Antonio _____ a Las Vegas.

13. Tu _____ alto.

Exercise 142

Translate the following sentences into Italian.

1. She is my aunt.

_____.

2. Carlo is very handsome.

_____.

3. Tomorrow is Saturday and we are at home.

_____.

4. At what time is the concert?

_____?

5. Paola's father is a doctor.

_____.

6. We are Italians.

_____.

7. My parents are happy.

_____.

8. They are very tired.

_____.

9. The sky is blue.

_____.

10. She is very elegant.

_____.

Avere

Avere is also best memorized in all its forms. The present tense conjugation of **avere** is:

io	**ho**	*I have*
tu	**hai**	*you have*
lui/lei	**ha**	*he/she has*
Lei	**ha**	*you have*
noi	**abbiamo**	*we have*
voi	**avete**	*you have*
loro	**hanno**	*they have*

The **h** in **ho**, **hai**, **ha**, and **hanno** is never pronounced. It is used to differentiate between the verb form and other words with the same pronunciation but different meaning, as in: **ho** (*I have*) and **o** (*or*) or **ha** (*he/she has*) and **a** (*at; to*).

Sometimes when in English *to be* is used, in Italian **avere** (*to have*) is used. For example, in English *to be* is used when telling or asking one's age (*How old are you? How old is she?*), but in Italian **avere** is the verb used. In Italian people say, "How many years do you/does he or she *have?*

Quanti anni **hai**?	*How old are you? (How many years do you have?)*

Avere is used in many idiomatic expressions in Italian. The following is a list of some of the most common idiomatic expressions using **avere**:

avere bisogno (di)	*to need*
avere caldo	*to be warm*
avere fame	*to be hungry*
avere freddo	*to be cold*
avere fretta	*to be in a hurry*
avere paura (di)	*to be afraid (of)*
avere pazienza	*to be patient*
avere ragione	*to be right*
avere sete	*to be thirsty*
avere sonno	*to be sleepy*
avere torto	*to be wrong*
avere vergogna	*to be ashamed*
avere voglia (di)	*to feel like (to want to)*

Exercise 143

Translate the following sentences into Italian.

1. I need to go to the library.

_____.

2. You (sing.) are cold.

_____.

3. I am in a hurry. I have to take the bus.

_____.

4. Children are afraid of the dark.

_____.

5. In summer we are always thirsty.

_____.

6. She is afraid of speaking in front of people.

_____.

7. I feel like having an ice cream.

_____.

8. How old is your mother?

_____?

9. She is eighty-eight years old.

_____.

10. I am not patient.

_____.

11. I am going to bed. I am very sleepy.

_____.

12. You are right. It is cold outside!

_____!

Exercise 144

Fill in the blanks with the appropriate forms of **avere** or **essere** as necessary.

1. La signora Bianchi _____ di Roma.

2. Il cane _____ quattordici anni.

3. Io _____ una macchina nuova.

4. Loro _____ sempre ragione.

5. Loro _____ molto contenti di venire in America.

6. Non (io) _____ voglia di andare a fare la spesa.

7. Noi _____ tutti molto stanchi alla sera.

8. Voi _____ un giardino molto bello.

9. Lei _____ paura dei topi.

10. Lui _____ sempre fretta.

C'è, ci sono; com'è, come sono

C'è (a contraction of ci è) and ci sono correspond to the English *there is* and *there are*.

C'è molta gente al museo.	*There are many people at the museum.*
Ci sono tanti bambini al parco.	*There are many children at the park.*

The expressions com'è and come sono (*how is* and *how are*) are used to find out information about people, objects, or places.

Exercise 145

Fill in the blanks with c'è, ci sono, com'è, or come sono as appropriate.

1. _____ molti soldati nel campo di battaglia.

2. _____ molta gente al cinema.

3. _____ la tua casa?

4. _____ le lezioni di italiano?

5. Non so se _____ ancora tempo per andare alla partita.

6. Se _____ pochi atleti non si può giocare.

7. _____ molti spettatori allo stadio.

8. _____ bella la primavera!

9. _____ grandi i tuoi figli!

10. Oggi _____ la nebbia.

11. Nei laghi americani _____ molti pesci.

12. In America _____ molti aeroporti enormi.

Piacere

The verb **piacere** (*to like, to be pleasing to*) is an irregular verb but a very commonly used one. **Piacere** is not an easy verb to use and takes practice and patience. Its present tense conjugation is as follows:

io	piaccio (a)	*I am pleasing to*
tu	piaci (a)	*you are pleasing to*
lui/lei/Lei	piace (a)	*he is/she is/you are pleasing to*
noi	piacciamo (a)	*we are pleasing to*
voi	piacete (a)	*you are pleasing to*
loro	piacciono (a)	*they are pleasing to*

The third person singular conjugation **piace** is often used with indirect object pronouns to say that one likes something and is followed by a singular noun or an infinitive verb. To say *I like that book* in Italian, you are really saying *That book is pleasing to me*: **Mi piace quel libro** or **A me piace quel libro.**

Le piace **il libro.**	*She likes **the book**.*
Le piace **leggere.**	*She likes **to read**.*

The third person plural conjugation **piacciono** is also used with indirect object pronouns and is followed by a plural noun. It is never followed by an infinitive.

Le piacciono **le rose.**	*She likes **roses**.*

Piacere is usually used in either the third person singular or the third person plural, but it is possible to use it in the first and second person conjugations also:

Io piaccio a Roberto.	*Roberto likes me. (I am pleasing to Roberto.)*
Voi piacete a tutti.	*Everybody likes you. (You are pleasing to everyone.)*

With **piacere** you can use either unstressed or stressed pronouns. They are positioned within a sentence before **piacere**. When the subject is not expressed, only the stressed pronouns can be used.

unstressed pronouns	stressed pronouns	
mi	a me	*to me*
ti	a te	*to you*
gli	a lui	*to him*
le	a lei	*to her*
Le	a Lei	*to you*
ci	a noi	*to us*
vi	a voi	*to you*
gli	a loro	*to them*

Mi piace la pasta.   *I like pasta.*
Mi piacciono le paste.   *I like pastries.*

A me piace la pasta.   *I like pasta.*
A me piacciono le paste.   *I like pastries.*

Mi piace andare al cinema.   *I like to go to the movies.*
A me, no.   *I don't.*

Ti piace l'italiano?   *Do you like Italian?*
A te, sì.   *You do.*

Exercise 146

Translate the following sentences into Italian.

1. I like fish.

_____.

2. You (sing.) like to go to the beach.

_____.

3. He likes to work with the computer.

_____.

4. She likes to work with children.

_____.

5. We like to travel.

_____.

6. You (pl.) like to visit friends.

_____.

7. They like to cook.

_____.

8. Luisa likes to talk.

_____.

9. Carlo likes to play soccer.

_____.

10. Giovanni and Maria like to visit their grandchildren.

_____.

11. Giovanni and Maria like children.

_____.

12. I like to travel by airplane.

_____.

There are other verbs similar to **piacere** that also require frequent use of the indirect object pronouns. They are:

accadere	*to happen*
affascinare	*to fascinate, be fascinated by*
apparire	*to appear*
bastare	*to be enough, sufficient*
bisognare	*to be necessary*
dispiacere	*to be sorry*
dolere	*to suffer*
importare	*to matter, be important*
interessare	*to interest*
mancare	*to miss*
occorrere	*to be necessary, needed*
rimanere	*to remain*
rincrescere	*to regret*
sembrare	*to seem*
servire	*to be of use*
succedere	*to happen*

Apparire (*to appear*), **dolere** (*to suffer*), and **rimanere** (*to remain*) are irregular in the present tense. The complete conjugations of these three verbs look like this:

	apparire	*dolere*	*rimanere*
io	appaio	dolgo	rimango
tu	appari	duoli	rimani
lui/lei/Lei	appare	duole	rimane
noi	appaiamo	dogliamo	rimaniamo
voi	apparite	dolete	rimanete
loro	appaiono	dolgono	rimangono

Like **piacere**, these verbs are usually used in the third person singular and the third person plural.

La sua bellezza **mi affascina**.	*Her beauty **fascinates me**.*
Mi sembra un film molto interessante.	*It **seems to me** like a very interesting movie.*
Ti sembrano belle quelle scarpe?	*Do those shoes **seem nice to you**?*
Non mi importa se vengono o no.	*It **doesn't matter to me** if they come or not.*

Exercise 147

Fill in the blanks with the appropriate forms of **piacere**.

1. A mia moglie _____ gli alberghi di lusso.

2. Ai miei figli _____ la piscina e le discoteche.

3. Gli _____ molto camminare in montagna.

4. Vi _____ le castagne?

5. Ci _____ leggere.

6. A noi _____ il prosciutto.

7. Vi _____ il pesce?

8. A noi _____ il pesce.

9. Gli _____ le passeggiate in riva al mare.

10. A loro _____ andare in barca.

11. Ti _____ la macchina.

12. Ti _____ le macchine italiane.

Exercise 148

Fill in the blanks with the conjugated forms of the verbs in parentheses.

1. Che cosa _____ (accadere) nel mondo oggi?

2. Le _____ (servire) una penna colorata.

3. Vi _____ (servire) due caffè con latte.

4. Ci _____ (dispiacere) di non poter venire.

5. Ti _____ (convenire) comperare il biglietto in Italia.

6. Ci _____ (sembrare) difficile capire il cinese.

7. Ti _____ (bastare) questa carta?

8. Gli _____ (toccare) andare a prendere i bambini.

9. Gli _____ (succedere) sempre dei guai.

10. Mi _____ (sembrare) una persona educata.

11. Gli _____ (interessare) molto la politica.

12. Vi _____ (rincrescere) rimandare il viaggio.

Exercise 149

Translate the following sentences into Italian.

1. Marco, do you like the new boss? Yes, I like him very much.

_____.

2. Signora, do you like the flowers? Yes, I like them a lot.

_____.

3. Luisa, do you like going to the gym? Yes, I like it.

_____.

4. Luisa, do you like going to the gym? No, I don't like it.

_____.

5. Elena, do you like to read? Yes, I like it.

_____.

6. Elena and Franco, do you like the new course? No, we don't like it.

_____.

7. Elena and Franco, do you like the beach? No, we don't like it.

_____.

8. We like to ski, you (pl.) don't.

_____.

9. Do you (pl.) like green beans? Yes, we do, but Carlo doesn't.

_____.

10. He likes ice cream, we don't. He likes coffee, I like cappuccino.

_____.

Sapere and *conoscere*

Both **sapere** and **conoscere** mean *to know*, but they are used in different ways. **Sapere** is an irregular verb in the present tense and **conoscere** is regular. They are conjugated as follows:

	sapere	*conoscere*
io	so	conosco
tu	sai	conosci
lui/lei/Lei	sa	conosce
noi	sappiamo	conosciamo
voi	sapete	conoscete
loro	sanno	conoscono

Sapere means *to know something*: facts or information. If followed by an infinitive, it means *to know how to do something.*

Luigi **sa** tante lingue.	*Luigi **knows** many languages.*
Luisa **sa** il mio numero di telefono.	*Luisa **knows** my telephone number.*
Franca non **sa** guidare la macchina.	*Franca doesn't **know** how to drive the car.*

Conoscere states familiarity with places, objects, and people. It is used to express *knowing someone* or *being familiar with something*. **Conoscere** is also used with familiarity of a location.

| **Conosciamo** molto bene i signori Gerli. | *We **know** the Gerlis quite well.* |
| **Conosco** bene Firenze. | *I **know** Florence well.* |

Exercise 150

Translate the following sentences into Italian using the conjugated forms of **sapere** or **conoscere**.

1. I don't know many people.

_____.

2. You (sing.) know how to play the piano.

_____.

3. You (pl.) know the Italian operas.

_____.

4. He knows my telephone number.

_____.

5. She knows many good stores.

_____.

6. We know many things.

_____.

7. My brother knows Arabic.

_____.

8. My brother knows many Arabs.

_____.

9. You (pl.) know where the museum is.

_____.

10. You (pl.) do not know the Indian museum.

_____.

11. They know how to paint.

_____.

12. They know the name of that painter.

_____.

9

The Imperative

The imperative tense is used for giving commands and orders. It can be used in both the informal and the formal way of addressing people. First, let's take a look at the familiar imperative. The forms of the familiar imperative of regular verbs are the same as for the present indicative, except in the **tu** form of **-are** verbs. These change the final **-i** of the present indicative to **-a**: **Parla bene!** (*Speak well!*) Note that in Italian an exclamation mark always follows the imperative.

The following shows conjugation of the familiar imperative forms for the **-are**, **-ere**, and **-ire** regular verbs.

	parlare **to speak**	*scrivere* **to write**	*sentire* **to hear**	*finire* **to finish**
tu	Parla!	Scrivi!	Senti!	Finisci!
noi	Parliamo!	Scriviamo!	Sentiamo!	Finiamo!
voi	Parlate!	Scrivete!	Sentite!	Finite!

The **noi** form of the imperative is the same as the **noi** form of the present tense. It corresponds to the English *let's* + verb.

Scriviamo una lettera ai nostri amici!   ***Let's write** a letter to our friends!*

In the negative, **non** appears before the verb: **Non parlate!** (*Do not speak!*) The negative imperative of the **tu** form uses the infinitive of the verb. The **non** precedes the verb: **Non parlare!** (*Do not speak!*) The negative imperative for **noi** and **voi** forms places **non** before **noi** and **voi**.

	parlare	*scrivere*	*sentire*	*finire*
tu	Non Parlare!	Non scrivere!	Non sentire!	Non finire!
noi	Non parliamo!	Non scriviamo!	Non sentiamo!	Non finiamo!
voi	Non parlate!	Non scrivete!	Non sentite!	Non finite!

Non parlare al telefono!	***Don't speak** on the telephone!*
Non scrivete sui muri!	***Don't write** on the walls!*
Non finiamo la torta!	***Let's not finish** the cake!*

Irregular imperatives

There are some irregular verbs with the imperative. Some are only irregular when using the **tu** form, and some are irregular using both the **tu** and the **voi** forms.

infinitive		imperative	
andare	*to go*	tu va' *or* vai	*go*
avere	*to have*	tu abbi *and* voi abbiate	*have*
dare	*to give*	tu da' *or* dai	*give*
dire	*to say, tell*	tu dì *or* di'	*say*
essere	*to be*	tu sii *and* voi siate	*be*
stare	*to stay*	tu sta' *or* stai	*stay*

Formal forms of the imperative

Sometimes the imperative is used with the formal forms of *you*. To form the imperative for **Lei**, add **-i** to the stem of **-are** verbs and add **-ino** to the stem for the imperative with **Loro**. When using **Lei** with **-ere** verbs and both forms of **-ire** verbs, **-a** is added to the verb stem. Add **-ano** when using **Loro**.

	parlare	*scrivere*	*sentire*	*finire*
Lei	parli	scriva	senta	finisca
Loro	parlino	scrivano	sentano	finiscano

Singular:

Signora, **parli** con il direttore!   *Ma'am, **speak** with the manager!*
Finisca il suo lavoro!   ***Finish** your work!*

Plural:

Signore, **parlino** con il direttore!   *Ladies, **speak** with the manager!*
Finiscano il lavoro!   ***Finish** the job!*

Many common Italian verbs have irregular command forms for the formal singular and plural.

		singular	plural	
andare	*to go*	Lei vada	Loro vadano	*go*
bere	*to drink*	Lei beva	Loro bevano	*drink*
dare	*to give*	Lei dia	Loro diano	*give*
dire	*to say, tell*	Lei dica	Loro dicano	*say, tell*
fare	*to do; make*	Lei faccia	Loro facciano	*do; make*
stare	*to stay*	Lei stia	Loro stiano	*stay*
venire	*to come*	Lei venga	Loro vengano	*come*

Formal negative imperatives

To use the formal negative of the imperative, place **non** before the imperative form of the verb.

Non parli! (**Lei**)   *Do not speak!*
Non vengano! (**Loro**)   *Do not come!*

When using object pronouns and reflexive pronouns, they *always* precede the **Lei** and **Loro** imperative verb forms.

Mi scriva presto !   ***Write to me** soon!*
Si vestano in fretta!   ***Get dressed** in a hurry!*

Exercise 151

Translate the following commands into Italian using the informal and the formal forms of the imperative as indicated.

	informal	formal
1. Speak! (sing.)	_____!	_____!
2. Speak! (pl.)	_____!	_____!
3. Walk! (sing.)	_____!	_____!
4. Sing! (sing.)	_____!	_____!
5. Sing! (pl.)	_____!	_____!

6. Eat! (sing.) _____! _____!

7. Go! (sing.) _____! _____!

8. Drink! (sing.) _____! _____!

9. Drink! (pl.) _____! _____!

10. Think! (sing.) _____! _____!

Verbs that add an **-h** (for example, **pagare**) in the present tense do so also in the imperative.

Paga il conto!   *Pay the bill!* (informal)

Paghi il conto!   *Pay the bill!* (formal)

10

Reflexive Verbs

Reflexive verbs express an action reflecting back to the subject. In other words, the subject and the object are the same within a sentence. Many verbs that are reflexive in English are also reflexive in Italian, but not all are reflexive in both languages. This chapter covers the simple tense with reflexive verbs. (Later in this book we will look at the compound tenses with reflexive verbs.)

Reflexive verbs are easy to recognize because they add the reflexive pronoun **si** (*oneself*) to the infinitive form of the verb. For example: **svegliarsi** (*to wake up*), **lavarsi** (to *wash oneself*), **sedersi** (*to sit down*), **divertirsi** (*to have fun*). Notice that the -e ending for the -**are**, -**ere**, and -**ire** infinitives is dropped before adding **si**.

When conjugating reflexive verbs, however, the reflexive pronoun *precedes* the indicative form of the verb. Reflexive verbs are conjugated the same as regular verbs but do not have the option of omitting the pronouns. Again, within a sentence the reflexive pronouns always precede the verb.

The reflexive pronouns are:

mi	*myself*
ti	*yourself*
si	*himself; herself; yourself* (form. sing.)
ci	*ourselves*
vi	*yourselves*
si	*themselves; yourselves* (form. pl.)

The complete present tense conjugation of reflexive verbs looks like this:

	svegliarsi **to wake up**	*sedersi* **to sit down**	*divertirsi* **to have fun**
mi	sveglio	siedo	diverto
ti	svegli	siedi	diverti
si	sveglia	siede	diverte
ci	svegliamo	sediamo	divertiamo
vi	svegliate	sedete	divertite
si	svegliano	siedono	divertono

Mi sveglio.	*I wake (**myself**) up.*
Ci sediamo.	*We sit (**ourselves**) down.*
Si divertono.	*They have fun.*

The following list gives an example of some commonly used Italian verbs that are reflexive. Some may also be reflexive in English, but not all are.

abituarsi	*to get used to*
addormentarsi	*to fall asleep*
alzarsi	*to get oneself up*
ammalarsi	*to get sick*
annoiarsi	*to get bored*
chiamarsi	*to call oneself*
dimenticarsi	*to forget*
divertirsi	*to have fun*
domandarsi	*to wonder*
farsi la barba	*to shave*
farsi il bagno	*to take a bath*
fermarsi	*to stop oneself*
girarsi	*to turn around*
lamentarsi	*to complain*
lavarsi	*to wash oneself*
meravigliarsi	*to be amazed*
mettersi	*to put on, wear*
mettersi a	*to begin to*
prepararsi	*to get ready*
presentarsi	*to introduce oneself*
ricordarsi	*to remember*
riposarsi	*to rest*
sedersi	*to sit down*
sentirsi	*to feel*
sposarsi	*to get married*
svegliarsi	*to wake up*
vergognarsi	*to be ashamed*
vestirsi	*to get dressed*

Note that in Italian the definite article is used with parts of the body instead of the possessive adjectives used in English.

Mi lavo **le mani.**   *I wash **my hands.** (I wash the hands.)*

Exercise 152

Translate the sentences into Italian using the conjugated forms of the reflexive verbs.

1. I get up early.

_____.

2. You have fun.

_____.

3. They get dressed in a hurry.

_____.

4. We get married this summer.

_____.

5. She stops in front of the museum.

_____.

6. He shaves every morning.

_____.

7. They fall asleep in class.

_____.

8. We wash our hands when we get home.

_____.

9. I get ready to go out to dinner.

_____.

10. They are bored.

_____.

11. I am amazed.

_____.

12. She doesn't remember anything.

_____.

13. I always forget to call her.

_____.

14. On Saturdays I wake up late.

_____.

Two verbs require special attention: **andarsene** (_to go away_) and **chiamarsi** (_to call oneself_). **Andarsene** is conjugated like any other reflexive verb with the addition of **ne** which follows the pronoun. In this case **ne** means _away_. The reflexive pronouns **mi, ti, si,** and so on are not used with **ne**; instead, **me, te,** and **se** are used. Observe how this verb is conjugated:

io	me ne vado	_I go away_
tu	te ne vai	_you go away_
lui/lei	se ne va	_he/she goes away_
Lei	se ne va	_you_ (form. sing.) _go away_
noi	ce ne andiamo	_we go away_
voi	ve ne andate	_you go away_
loro	se ne vanno	_they go away_

Me ne vado subito.   _I go (away) immediately._

Chiamarsi is used in Italian to ask or tell one's name.

Come **ti chiami?**   _What is your name?_
                         (_What **do you call yourself?**_)
Mi chiamo Carla.   _My **name** is Carla._ (**_I call myself_** _Carla._)

If the infinitive of a reflexive verb is preceded by the models **dovere, potere,** or **volere,** the reflexive pronoun may either precede the infinitive or be attached to the end of the infinitive.

Mi devo **lavare** le mani.   _I have **to wash my hands.**_
Devo **lavarmi** le mani.   _I have **to wash my hands.**_

Exercise 153

Translate the following sentences into Italian using the models and reflexive verbs in both methods as previously shown.

1. I want to get up early.

_____.

_____.

2. He wants to wake up early.

_____.

_____.

3. They want to take a bath.

_____.

_____.

4. You (sing.) must wash your face.

_____.

_____.

5. We must wake up early.

_____.

_____.

6. He wants to fall asleep.

_____.

_____.

7. She wants to have fun.

_____.

_____.

8. We want to get married this summer.

_____.

_____.

9. You (sing.) have to remember your passport.

_____.

_____.

10. I cannot forget my passport.

_____.

_____.

11. You (pl.) have to rest.

_____.

_____.

12. He can shave on the airplane.

_____.

_____.

13. I don't want to put my new shoes on.

_____.

_____.

11

Future Tense

Future tense expresses an action that will take place in the near or the distant future. Italian uses only one word to express the future, while English uses two words: *will* or *shall* + the infinitive of a verb. The future tense of regular verbs in Italian is formed by dropping the final -e of an infinitive and adding various future tense endings. Also, in -are verbs, the -a- of the infinitive changes to -e-. For example: **parlare** becomes **parler-** + a future tense ending. The endings for the -are, -ere, and -ire verbs in the future tense are shown in the following table.

	parlare	*scrivere*	*sentire*
io	parler**ò**	scriver**ò**	sentir**ò**
tu	parler**ai**	scriver**ai**	sentir**ai**
lui/lei/Lei	parler**à**	scriver**à**	sentir**à**
noi	parler**emo**	scriver**emo**	sentir**emo**
voi	parler**ete**	scriver**ete**	sentir**ete**
loro	parler**anno**	scriver**anno**	sentir**anno**

In Italian the future tense can be replaced by the present tense when the action will take place in the near future.

Domani **mangiamo** al ristorante.   *Tomorrow we will eat at the restaurant.*

The future tense is used if a dependent clause referring to an action taking place in the near future is introduced by **se** (*if*), **quando** (*when*), or **appena** (*as soon as*).

Dormiremo **se avremo** tempo.   *We will sleep if we will have time.*

Verbs like **pagare** (*to pay*) and **cercare** (*to look for*) add an **-h-** in the future tense to preserve the hard sound of the infinitive.

pagherò, pagherai, pagherà, pagheremo, pagherete, pagheranno
cercherò, cecherai, cercherà, cercheremo, cercherete, cercheranno

Verbs like **cominciare** (*to start*) and **mangiare** (*to eat*) drop the -i- before adding the future tense endings.

comincerò, comincerai, comincerà, cominceremo, comincerete, cominceranno

mangerò, mangerai, mangerà, mangeremo, mangerete, mangeranno

There are many other verbs that have irregular stems in the future tense, but the endings are the same for the irregular verbs as those used for regular verbs. Some irregular verbs in the future tense are as follows:

infinitive		future stem	conjugation
andare	*to go*	andr-	andrò, andrai, andrà, etc.
avere	*to have*	avr-	avrò, avrai, avrà, etc.
bere	*to drink*	berr-	berrò, berrai, berrà, etc.
dare	*to give*	dar-	darò, darai, darà, etc.
dovere	*to have to*	dovr-	dovrò, dovrai, dovrà, etc.
essere	*to be*	sar-	sarò, sarai, sarà, etc.
fare	*to make; do*	far-	farò, farai, farà, etc.
potere	*to be able to*	potr-	potrò, potrai, potrà, etc.
sapere	*to know*	sapr-	saprò, saprai, saprà, etc.
tenere	*to keep; hold*	terr-	terrò, terrai, terrà, etc.
vedere	*to see*	vedr-	vedrò, vedrai, vedrà, etc.
venire	*to come*	verr-	verrò, verrai, verrà, etc.
vivere	*to live*	vivr-	vivrò, vivrai, vivrà, etc.

Exercise 154

Translate the following sentences into Italian using the future tense.

1. I will drink only mineral water.

_____.

2. You (sing.) will go to church.

_____.

3. He will eat at his mother's house.

_____.

4. She will rest and will drink a cup of coffee.

_____.

5. I will visit my friends tomorrow.

_____.

6. We will talk to them.

_____.

7. You (pl.) will see Lake Como.

_____.

8. Luigi will wait for the train.

_____.

9. Carla will live in Italy.

_____.

10. You (sing.) will make her a cake for her birthday.

_____.

11. We will not sleep.

_____.

12. They will pay the bill.

_____.

Exercise 155

Fill in the blanks with the future tense conjugations of the verbs in parentheses.

Io (1.) _____ (essere) molto contenta quando (2.) _____
(arrivare) la primavera. Io (3.) _____ (andare) a fare delle lunghe passeggiate
nel bosco e (4.) _____ (raccogliere) tanti bei fiori. (5.) _____
(Respirare) aria fresca e pura e (6.) _____ (camminare) sul sentiero asfaltato
e non mi (7.) _____ (sporcare) le scarpe anche se il terreno
(8.) _____ (essere) bagnato. (9.) _____ (Chiedere) ad
alcune mie amiche se (10.) _____ (loro volere) andare nel bosco con me per
ammirare la natura e per fare un esercizio sano. Vedrò che cosa mi (11.) _____
(loro-rispondere). Anche se nessuna di loro (12.) _____ (venire) con me io ci
(13.) _____ (andare) lo stesso.

Present Perfect Tense

The present perfect tense is used to describe actions and events that happened in the recent past. The verb is often preceded by or followed by time expressions like: **ieri** (*yesterday*), **domenica scorsa** (*last Sunday*), **l'anno scorso** (*last year*), **un anno fa** (*a year ago*), or **un'ora fa** (*an hour ago*).

The present perfect tense is formed by using the present tense conjugation of **avere** or **essere** + the past participle of the verb showing the action. The majority of Italian verbs use **avere** in the present perfect. When **avere** is used, the past participle doesn't agree in gender and number with the subject. The present perfect tense for verbs of motion or states of being is formed by using **essere**. The past participle, when **essere** is used, must agree in gender and number with the subject. There are exceptions, however, that will be discussed later in this chapter.

Present perfect with *avere*

Verbs that use **avere** as the helping verb (or auxiliary verb) in the present perfect tense are generally transitive verbs or verbs that use a direct object and answer the question **Chi?** (*Who?*) or **Che cosa?** (*What?*). The past participle of regular transitive verbs is formed by dropping the infinitive ending and adding:

- **-ato** to the infinitive root of **-are** verbs
- **-uto** to the infinitive root of **-ere** verbs
- **-ito** to the infinitive root of **-ire** verbs

infinitive	past participle
parl**are**	parl**ato**
vend**ere**	vend**uto**
sent**ire**	sent**ito**

In English the present perfect is translated either with the simple past tense or the present perfect.

Ho telefonato alle nove.	*I called at nine o'clock.*
Ho telefonato tardi.	*I have called late.*

There are some intransitive verbs, or verbs that cannot be used with a direct object, that take **avere**. Some of these verbs are: **camminare, dormire, parlare,** and **viaggiare**.

> **Ho camminato** per due ore.　　　*I **walked** for two hours.*

The negative present perfect is formed by placing **non** in front of the auxiliary **avere**.

> **Non** ho mangiato niente.　　　*I **didn't** eat anything.*

Many **-ere** verbs have an irregular past participle. The following list is an example of some of the most commonly used:

accendere	*to turn on*	acceso	*turned on*
aprire	*to open*	aperto	*opened*
bere	*to drink*	bevuto	*drunk*
chiedere	*to ask*	chiesto	*asked*
chiudere	*to close*	chiuso	*closed*
conoscere	*to know*	conosciuto	*known*
cuocere	*to cook*	cotto	*cooked*
dire	*to say, tell*	detto	*said, told*
fare	*to make; do*	fatto	*made; done*
leggere	*to read*	letto	*read*
mettere	*to put*	messo	*put*
morire	*to die*	morto	*died*
nascere	*to be born*	nato	*born*
perdere	*to lose*	perso	*lost*
piangere	*to cry*	pianto	*cried*
prendere	*to take*	preso	*taken*
promettere	*to promise*	promesso	*promised*
rimanere	*to remain*	rimasto	*remained*
rispondere	*to answer*	risposto	*answered*
scendere	*to descend*	sceso	*descended*
scrivere	*to write*	scritto	*wrote*
spegnere	*to turn off*	spento	*turned off*
spendere	*to spend*	speso	*spent*
spingere	*to push*	spinto	*pushed*
vedere	*to see*	visto	*seen*
vincere	*to win*	vinto	*won*
vivere	*to live*	vissuto	*lived*

Exercise 156

Fill in the blanks with the present perfect tense of the verbs in parentheses.

1. Io _____ (parlare) con tua sorella.

2. Tu _____ (giocare) al tennis tutta la mattina.

3. Il tenore _____ (cantare) molto bene.

4. Noi _____ (vedere) un bel film.

5. Voi _____ (piantare) molti fiori.

6. Loro _____ (leggere) tutti i libri.

7. Tu e Maria _____ (mangiare) molti gelati.

8. Io e Carla _____ (capire) bene.

9. Luigi _____ (suonare) il campanello.

10. Alberto _____ (bere) molto.

11. Loro _____ (chiedere) dove eri.

12. Io _____ (dormire) fino a tardi.

Past participle agreement of verbs conjugated with *avere* in the present perfect tense

As previously mentioned, for verbs that use *avere* the past participle does not agree with the subject in gender and number. Here are some cases that differ from this rule, however:

- Regardless of which auxiliary is being used, the past participle must agree with the direct object pronouns: **lo** (*him*), **la** (*her*), **li** (*them*, m.), and **le** (*them*, f.).

Avete visto il vostro amico?	*Did you see your friend?*
No, non **lo** abbiamo visto.	*No, we didn't see **him**.*
Avete visto la mia amica?	*Did you see my girlfriend?*
Sì, **la** abbiamo vista.	*Yes, we saw **her**.*
Hai comprato le banane?	*Did you buy the bananas?*
Sì, **le** ho comprate.	*Yes, I bought **them**.*
Hai comprato i pantaloni?	*Did you buy the pants?*
No, non **li** ho comprati.	*No, I didn't buy **them**.*

- The past participle must agree with the pronoun **ne** when it means *some*, or *part of*.

Avete visitato molti posti in Italia?   *Did you visit many places in Italy?*
Sì **ne** abbiamo visitati molti.   *Yes, we visited many of them.*

- The agreement is optional with the direct object pronouns **mi**, **ti**, **ci**, and **vi**, and when a sentence is introduced by **che**, **il quale**, **la quale**, **i quali**, **le quali**.

Non **ci** hanno visto/visti.   *They did not see us.*

- But, the past participle *never* agrees with the indirect object in a sentence.

Le abbiamo portato tanti giocattoli.   *We brought her many toys.*

Exercise 157

Translate the following sentences into Italian.

1. I wrote many letters.

_____.

2. I wrote her many letters.

_____.

3. You (pl.) have seen the animals at the zoo.

_____.

4. You (sing.) have seen them.

_____.

5. You (pl.) didn't see us.

_____.

6. She called her father.

_____.

7. She called her parents.

_____.

8. He called us.

_____.

9. We sent her a package.

_____ .

10. You (sing.) bought beautiful dresses.

_____ .

11. She bought them at the market.

_____ .

12. Your (sing.) mother cleaned the house.

_____ .

Present perfect with *essere*

The present perfect tense of intransitive verbs—verbs that do not take a direct object—is formed by using the present tense of **essere** and the past participle of the verb showing the action. Many of these verbs express movement (**andare**, *to go*), lack of movement (**stare**, *to stay*), a mental or physical state (**zoppicare**, *to limp*), or a process of change (**invecchiare**, *to age*).

Regular past participles of verbs conjugated with **essere** are formed the same as those conjugated with **avere**, and they agree in gender and number with the subject of the verb.

	andare	*cadere*	*partire*
	to go	**to fall**	**to leave**
io	sono andato(-a)	sono caduto(-a)	sono partito(-a)
tu	sei andato(-a)	sei caduto(-a)	sei partito(-a)
lui/lei	è andato(-a)	è caduto(-a)	è partito(-a)
noi	siamo andati(-e)	siamo caduti(-e)	siamo partiti(-e)
voi	siete andati(-e)	siete caduti(-e)	siete partiti(-e)
loro	sono andati(-e)	sono caduti(-e)	sono partiti(-e)

Carlo è **arrivato** tardi. *Carlo **arrived** late.*
Carla è **arrivata** tardi. *Carla **arrived** late.*

The following list of verbs are conjugated with **essere** in the present perfect tense.

infinitive		**past participle**	
andare	*to go*	andato	*gone*
arrivare	*to arrive*	arrivato	*arrived*
cadere	*to fall*	caduto	*fell*

diventare	*to become*	diventato	*became*
entrare	*to enter*	entrato	*entered*
essere	*to be*	stato	*was*
morire	*to die*	morto	*died*
nascere	*to be born*	nato	*born*
partire	*to leave*	partito	*left*
restare	*to remain*	restato	*remained*
ritornare	*to return*	ritornato	*returned*
salire	*to go up*	salito	*went up*
scendere	*to descend*	sceso	*descended*
stare	*to stay*	stato	*stayed*
tornare	*to return*	tornato	*returned*
uscire	*to go out*	uscito	*went out*
venire	*to come*	venuto	*came*
vivere	*to live*	vissuto	*lived*

Exercise 158

Translate the following sentences into Italian using the present perfect tense.

1. I was in Italy for three weeks.

_____.

2. She went on the airplane.

_____.

3. He returned home late.

_____.

4. We left at dawn.

_____.

5. They came to see the baby.

_____.

6. Her mother left yesterday for her trip.

_____.

7. All the students returned to class.

_____.

8. Giovanni arrived on time.

_____.

9. The train left late.

_____.

10. His mother and father remained at home.

_____.

11. He came home for Easter.

_____.

Exercise 159

Rewrite the following sentences changing them into the present perfect tense.

1. Erica ritorna da scuola.

_____.

2. Lara sale sull'ascensore.

_____.

3. Noi ritorniamo a letto.

_____.

4. I bambini vengono a casa mia.

_____.

5. La nonna scende con il bastone.

_____.

6. Voi partite per l'America del Sud.

_____.

7. Le piante muoiono.

_____.

8. Lei nasce in Africa.

_____.

9. Gli amici arrivano con il treno.

_____.

10. Io (f.) vado all'aeroporto.

_____.

11. Tu (f.) sei dalla tua vecchia zia.

_____.

Additional rules for using *essere* in the present perfect

All reflexive verbs use **essere** in the present perfect tense.

Mi sono svegliato tardi questa mattina.	*I **woke up** late this morning.*
Mi sono vestito in fretta.	*I **got dressed** in a hurry.*

Impersonal verbs also require **essere** in the present perfect tense. Some impersonal verbs in Italian are:

accadere	*to happen*
bastare	*to be enough*
capitare	*to happen*
costare	*to cost*
dispiacere	*to regret, to be sorry*
sembrare	*to seem*
succedere	*to happen*

Vi **sono sembrati** intelligenti?	*Did they **seem** intelligent to you?*
Mi è **dispiaciuto** molto non venire.	*I **was very sorry** not to have come.*

The auxiliary **essere** is used in the present perfect when referring to the weather. However, today it is also common to hear the use of **avere**.

È piovuto tutto il pomeriggio.	*It **has rained** all afternoon.*
Ha piovuto tutto il pomeriggio.	*It **has rained** all afternoon.*

With the modal verbs **dovere**, **volere**, and **potere**, it is preferable to use **essere** if the following infinitive requires **essere**. This rule is especially used in writing. In speech, however, **avere** is used more frequently.

Sono dovuta stare in casa tutto il giorno.	*I **had to stay** at home all day long.*
Non **sono potuti venire** da noi.	*They **could not come** to our house.*

Some verbs can use either **essere** or **avere** depending on whether they are used transitively or intransitively.

Transitive:

I negozianti **hanno aumentato** tutti   *The store owners **have raised** all the prices.*
   i prezzi.

Intransitive:

Tutti i prezzi **sono aumentati**.   *All prices **have gone up**.*

Exercise 160

Translate the following sentences into Italian using the present perfect.

1. I saw what happened to Pietro.

   _____.

2. I didn't see what happened.

   _____.

3. The prices at the supermarket have gone up a lot.

   _____.

4. I have increased the dose of medicine.

   _____.

5. We had a great time.

   _____.

6. They went up on the elevator.

   _____.

7. The last trip cost too much.

   _____.

8. She had to stay home because the car was broken.

   _____.

9. They got up late and arrived late at work.

   _____.

10. This past winter it didn't snow.

   _____.

13

Other Past Tenses

Imperfect tense

The imperfect tense expresses past events that are customary or habitual, or describes an action that happened in the past and is continuing while another takes place. The imperfect tense also describes actions or situations that lasted for an indefinite period of time in the past with no indication of the beginning or the end of the action. It is an easy tense to learn, but not so easy to use. It corresponds to the English use of *used to* or *was* + the *-ing* form of a verb.

Guardavo la televisione tutti i giorni.	*I used to watch television every day.*
Guardavo la televisione.	*I was watching television.*
Ero a Roma, quando è morto il Papa.	*I was in Rome when the Pope died.*

The imperfect tense is usually preceded or followed by expressions such as: **di solito** (*usually*), **qualche volta** (*sometimes*), **spesso** (*often*), **la domenica** (*on Sundays*), **il lunedì** (*on Mondays*), **di frequente** (*frequently*), **mentre** (*while*), and so on.

Di solito, **andavo** in palestra.	*Usually, I went to the gym.*

The imperfect tense is formed by adding the same endings to all three verb types.

- The imperfect indicative of **-are** verbs is formed by dropping the infinitive **-are** ending and adding the endings **-avo, -avi, -ava, -avamo, -avate,** and **-avano** to the verb root.

parlare	*to speak*	parlavo	*I used to speak, I was speaking*

- The imperfect indicative of **-ere** verbs is formed by dropping the **-ere** ending and adding the endings **-evo, -evi, -eva, -evamo, -evate,** and **-evano** to the verb root.

scrivere	*to write*	scrivevo	*I used to write, I was writing*

- The imperfect indicative of **-ire** verbs is formed by dropping the **-ire** ending and adding the endings **-ivo, -ivi, -iva, -ivamo, -ivate,** and **-ivano** to the verb root.

partire   *to leave*   partivo   *I used to leave, I was leaving*

The following table shows an example of the imperfect tense conjugations for **-are**, **-ere**, and **-ire** verbs:

	parlare to speak	*scrivere* to write	*partire* to leave
io	parlavo	scrivevo	partivo
tu	parlavi	scrivevi	partivi
lui/lei	parlava	scriveva	partiva
noi	parlavamo	scrivevamo	partivamo
voi	parlavate	scrivevate	partivate
loro	parlavano	scrivevano	partivano

The verbs **fare** (*to do; make*), **dire** (*to say, tell*), **bere** (*to drink*), **produrre** (*to produce*), and **porre** (*to place*) take their roots for the imperfect tense from the original Latin infinitives, but the conjugations are regular. For these verbs, add the imperfect endings to: **fac-** (for **fare**), **dic-** (for **dire**), **bev-** (for **bere**), **produc-** (for **produrre**), and **pon-** (for **porre**). The conjugated forms look like this:

facevo, facevi, faceva, etc.
dicevo, dicevi, diceva, etc.
bevevo, bevevi, beveva, etc.
producevo, producevi, produceva, etc.
ponevo, ponevi, poneva, etc.

Exercise 161

Change the following sentences to the imperfect tense.

1. Di solito io vado a letto presto.

_____.

2. Noi andiamo spesso in Italia.

_____.

3. Il sabato dormiamo tutti fino a tardi.

_____.

4. Vediamo di frequente la partita di pallone.

_____.

5. Ogni giorno facciamo i compiti.

_____.

6. Mangiamo sempre pane e formaggio.

_____.

7. Di solito non bevo molta acqua.

_____.

8. Penso spesso ai giorni della mia infanzia.

_____.

9. Di solito faccio tante fotografie.

_____.

10. Spesso parlano con i loro nipoti.

_____.

11. Di tanto in tanto ricevo lettere dai miei amici.

_____.

Additional rules for the imperfect tense

The imperfect is used when two or more actions are going on at the same time.

Io **parlavo**, mio fratello **studiava** e mio padre **guardava** la televisione.	*I was speaking, my brother was studying, and my father was watching television.*

The imperfect is used to express age, time of day, and weather conditions in the past.

Ieri **faceva** bel tempo.	*Yesterday the weather was good.*
Quanti anni **aveva** quando è morta?	*How old was she when she died?*
Che ore **erano** quando sei rientrata?	*What time was it when you came back?*

The imperfect is used with color, size, and personal qualities to describe people and objects in the past.

Tua madre **era** molto ambiziosa.	*Your mother was very ambitious.*
Il tetto della tua casa **era** nero.	*The roof of your house was black.*

The imperfect is also used with the preposition **da** to express an ongoing action in the past. (In English this requires the pluperfect tense.)

Pioveva da tre giorni.   *It **had been** raining for three days.*
Lei **era** a letto da un mese.   *She **had been** in bed for three months.*

Exercise 162

Translate the following sentences into Italian using the imperfect tense.

1. Yesterday it was very cloudy.

_____.

2. What was the weather like in Italy?

_____?

3. It was cold and it rained.

_____.

4. It had been raining for a week.

_____.

5. My mother was cooking, and I was playing piano.

_____.

6. He used to read the newspaper every day.

_____.

7. She was taking a shower every morning.

_____.

8. Usually, on Sunday afternoon, we went to the park.

_____.

9. What were you (sing.) writing when I came in?

_____?

10. You (sing.) called me often.

_____.

Comparison of the present perfect and imperfect tenses

Both the present perfect and the imperfect are past tenses. They can be used in the same sentence to express something that was going on when something else happened. Deciding whether the imperfect or the present perfect is needed is not always easy, since in English there is no distinction between the two tenses. In Italian they express different types of actions and cannot be used interchangeably. Following are the instances when one or the other needs to be used:

The present perfect tense expresses events or actions that happened at a specific time.

Ieri sera siamo andati al ristorante con degli amici.

Last night we went to the restaurant with some friends.

The imperfect describes ongoing actions or events in the past.

Per Pasqua, eravamo sempre tutti a pranzo da mia mamma.

At Easter, we were always at my mother's for lunch.

The present perfect expresses an action or an event that was repeated for a definite number of times.

Lei **ha lavorato** in Svizzera **per quattro anni.**

She worked in Switzerland for four years.

The imperfect describes repeated or habitual actions in the past.

Lei **studiava tutti i giorni della settimana.**

She used to study every day of the week.

In addition, the imperfect is used to describe two different actions going on at the same time in the past.

Io **dormivo mentre** lui **studiava.**

I was sleeping while he was studying.

The imperfect tense describes an action that was going on in the past when another action or event took place. This last action or event takes the present perfect tense.

Voi **tagliavate** l'erba **quando è suonato** il telefono.

You were cutting the grass when the phone rang.

Exercise 163

Translate each of the following sentences into Italian using the correct forms of the imperfect and present perfect tenses.

1. I used to ski every year./I skied a lot.

_____.

_____.

2. I went to Africa with my parents./I used to go to Africa often for work.

_____.

_____.

3. You (sing.) went to the dentist./You (sing.) used to go to the dentist.

_____.

_____.

4. She called her children on Sunday./She used to call her children every Sunday.

_____.

_____.

5. I wrote her a long letter./I used to write her long letters.

_____.

_____.

6. We went to a great party./We used to go to some great parties.

_____.

_____.

7. You (pl.) used to listen to classical music./You (pl.) listened to the classical music.

_____.

_____.

8. Last night I didn't sleep well./I used to sleep very well.

_____.

_____.

9. Yesterday she went to the hairdresser./She used to go to the hairdresser every Saturday.

_____.

_____.

10. He used to like eating late./He didn't like eating in that restaurant.

_____.

_____.

Exercise 164

Fill in the blanks using the imperfect or the present perfect tense for the verbs in parentheses.

1. Io _____ (essere) a casa quando tu

   _____ (telefonare).

2. Noi _____ (dormire) quando

   _____ (venire) una scossa di terremoto.

3. Lui non _____ (avere) l'ombrello quando

   _____ (piovere).

4. Loro _____ (essere) a sciare quando

   _____ (venire) una valanga.

5. Mentre lei _____ (dormire) qualcuno

   _____ (bussare) alla porta.

6. Noi _____ (giocare) al tennis quando

   _____ (cominciare) a piovere.

7. Io _____ (avere) mal di testa quando tu mi

   _____ (chiamare).

8. Lui _____ (giocare) al pallone quando

   _____ (avere) un incidente.

9. Mio marito _____ (essere) preoccupato perché non gli

   _____ (telefonare).

10. Noi _____ (dovere) partire, ma l'aereo non

    _____ (arrivare).

Exercise 165

Fill in the blanks using the imperfect or the present perfect tense for the verbs in parentheses.

1. Stamattina _____ (io-ritornare, f.) a casa e

   _____ (io-chiudere) la porta del garage.

2. Ieri sera _____ (lei-andare) al cinema e poi

   _____ (lei-venire) a casa mia.

3. Quando _____ (io-essere, f.) a Roma

   _____ (io-abitare) presso una famiglia.

4. Carla non _____ (comprare) il vestito che desiderava perché

   _____ (costare) troppo.

5. Ieri non _____ (noi-fare) niente perché

   _____ (noi-essere) stanchi.

6. Mentre _____ (loro-salire) sul treno

   _____ (io-vedere) suo fratello.

7. Che cosa _____ (tu-fare) quando

   _____ (tu-andare, m.) a trovare i tuoi nonni?

8. Noi _____ (mangiare) molto bene quando

   _____ (andare) in vacanza.

9. L'anno scorso _____ (io-andare, m.) per una settimana a Parigi

   e poi _____ (io-andare, m.) in Inghilterra.

10. Ieri sera _____ (io-lavorare, f.) fino alle otto e quando

    _____ (uscire), c'_____ (essere)

    la nebbia.

11. Quando _____ (noi-finire) la festa, la nostra casa

    _____ (essere) molto sporca.

12. In Italia, mi _____ (sedere, f.) ad un caffè e

    _____ (guardare) la gente che

    _____ (passeggiare).

Preterit tense

The preterit is also called the historical past. It is mostly used in narrative writing to describe events occurring in the past. In speech and informal letter writing, however, the preterit has been replaced by the present perfect tense by those in northern Italy, but people in southern and central Italy seem to still prefer using the preterit, even if speaking about recent events. Both the present perfect and the preterit are usually translated into English by the simple past tense (*I slept, I ate*).

The preterit of regular verbs is formed by dropping the infinitive endings **-are, -ere, -ire** and adding to the root the following endings:

- -are

  -ai, -asti, -ò, -ammo, -aste, -arono

- -ere

  -ei, esti, è, -emmo, -este, -erono

(Some verbs ending in-**ere** also have the following alternate endings in the **io, lui/lei,** and **loro** forms: -etti, -ette, -ettero.)

- -ire

  -ii, -isti, -ì, -immo, -iste, -irono

	comprare **to buy**	*vendere* **to sell**	*sentire* **to hear**
io	comprai	vendei (vendetti)	sentii
tu	comprasti	vendesti	sentisti
lui/lei	comprò	vendè (vendette)	sentì
noi	comprammo	vendemmo	sentimmo
voi	compraste	vendeste	sentiste
loro	comprarono	venderono (vendettero)	sentirono

The following expressions are often used with the preterit:

all'improvviso	*suddenly*
l'anno scorso	*last year*
l'estate scorsa	*last summer*
ieri	*yesterday*
ieri pomeriggio	*yesterday afternoon*
ieri sera	*last night*
l'inverno scorso	*last winter*
il mese scorso	*last month*

molto tempo fa	*long time ago*
poco fa	*a little while ago*
la settimana scorsa	*last week*

Exercise 166

Complete the verb in each sentence with the correct ending of the preterit tense.

1. Io parl_____ troppo in classe.

2. Tu arriv_____ con due valige.

3. Lei cammin_____ per tante ore.

4. Noi ven_____ al cinema con voi.

5. Voi cant_____ molto bene.

6. Loro lavor_____ con molto zelo.

7. Io lavor_____ molto svogliatamente.

8. I bambini gioc_____ tutto il giorno.

9. Lei compr _____ una bella casa.

10. Lui arriv_____ tardi.

Exercise 167

Fill in the blanks using the preterit tense of the verbs in parentheses.

1. Io _____ (parlare) con sua madre.

2. Tu _____ (cantare) molto bene.

3. Lei _____ (pagare) il conto dell'albergo.

4. Noi _____ (pagare) le vacanze.

5. Voi _____ (preparare) la cena.

6. Loro ci _____ (telefonare) molto tardi.

7. Noi _____ (parlare) in classe.

8. Tu _____ (cenare) in un ristorante elegante.

9. Carla _____ (camminare) con le stampelle.

10. Io _____ (sentire) molti rumori.

11. Lei non _____ (sentire) bene.

Common verbs with irregular roots in the preterit

Many common Italian verbs have irregular roots in the preterit. There is no easy way to learn them; they must be memorized. The endings for the irregular verb roots are the same in the preterit as those shown for regular verbs only in the **tu, noi,** and **voi** forms. These **-ere** verbs are irregular in the **io, lui/lei,** and **loro** forms. The following list shows some common irregular -ere verbs and their complete conjugations in the preterit tense:

accendere (*to turn on*)	**accesi**, accendesti, **accese**, accendemmo, accendeste, **accesero**
bere (*to drink*)	**bevvi** (**bevetti**), bevesti, **bevve** (**bevette**), bevemmo, beveste, **bevvero** (**bevettero**)
chiedere (*to ask*)	**chiesi**, chiedesti, **chiese**, chiedemmo, chiedeste, **chiesero**
chiudere (*to close*)	**chiusi**, chiudesti, **chiuse**, chiudemmo, chiudeste, **chiusero**
conoscere (*to know*)	**conobbi**, conoscesti, **conobbe**, conoscemmo, conosceste, **conobbero**
dare (*to give*)	**diedi**, desti, **diede**, demmo, deste, **diedero**
decidere (*to decide*)	**decisi**, decidesti, **decise**, decidemmo, decideste, **decisero**
dovere (*to have to, must*)	**dovei** (**dovetti**), dovesti, **dovè** (**dovette**), dovemmo, doveste, **doverono** (**dovettero**)
fare (*to make; do*)	**feci**, facesti, **fece**, facemmo, faceste, **fecero**
leggere (*to read*)	**lessi**, leggeste, **lesse**, leggemmo, leggeste, **lessero**
mettere (*to put*)	**misi**, mettesti, **mise**, mettemmo, metteste, **misero**
nascere (*to be born*)	**nacqui**, nascesti, **nacque**, nascemmo, nasceste, **nacquero**
prendere (*to take; get*)	**presi**, prendesti, **prese**, prendemmo, prendeste, **presero**
ridere (*to laugh*)	**risi**, ridesti, **rise**, ridemmo, rideste, **risero**
rimanere (*to remain*)	**rimasi**, rimanesti, **rimase**, rimanemmo, rimaneste, **rimasero**
sapere (*to know how*)	**seppi**, sapesti, **seppe**, sapemmo, sapeste, **seppero**
scegliere (*to choose*)	**scelsi**, scegliesti, **scelse**, scegliemmo, sceglieste, **scelgero**
scendere (*to descend*)	**scesi**, scendesti, **scese**, scendemmo, scendeste, **scesero**
scrivere (*to write*)	**scrissi**, scrivesti, **scrisse**, scrivemmo, scriveste, **scrissero**
spegnere (*to turn off*)	**spensi**, spegnesti, **spense**, spegnemmo, spegneste, **spensero**
stare (*to stay*)	**stetti**, stesti, **stette**, stemmo, steste, **stettero**
tenere (*to keep*)	**tenni**, tenesti, **tenne**, tenemmo, teneste, **tennero**
vedere (*to see*)	**vidi**, vedesti, **vide**, vedemmo, vedeste, **videro**
vincere (*to win*)	**vinsi**, vincesti, **vinse**, vincemmo, vinceste, **vinsero**
vivere (*to live*)	**vissi**, vivesti, **visse**, vivemmo, viveste, **vissero**
volere (*to want*)	**volli**, volesti, **volle**, volemmo, voleste, **vollero**

Some common irregular -ire verbs in the preterit are:

dire (*to say, tell*)	**dissi,** dicesti, **disse,** dicemmo, diceste, **dissero**
divenire (*to become*)	**divenni,** divenisti, **divenne,** divenimmo, diveniste, **divennero**
venire (*to come*)	**venni,** venisti, **venne,** venimmo, veniste, **vennero**

Exercise 168

Fill in the blanks with the preterit tense of the verbs in parentheses.

1. Io _____ (sapere) che tu eri partita.

2. Lara _____ (cadere) dalla bicicletta.

3. La settimana scorsa _____ (noi-bere) il vino nuovo.

4. Anni fa, _____ (noi-comprare) l'olio d'oliva in Toscana.

5. Due anni fa _____ (noi-andare) per una settimana in Grecia.

6. L'anno scorso _____ (noi-noleggiare) una macchina e _____ (noi-potere) visitare molti posti.

7. Loro _____ (vendere) la casa per pochi soldi.

8. _____ (Noi-invitare) anche Carla, ma lei _____ (preferire) rimanere a casa.

9. Io gli _____ (telefonare) molte volte, ma non lo _____ (trovare) mai.

10. Ieri _____ (io-arrivare) con molto ritardo.

Exercise 169

Fill in the blanks with the conjugated forms of the irregular -ire verbs in the preterit.

1. Io _____ (dire) la verità al giudice.

2. Tu _____ (venire) a casa nostra con i tuoi amici.

3. I miei amici _____ (venire) a cena da noi.

4. Lui _____ (divenire) una persona molto importante.

5. Lei non mi _____ (dire) che sarebbe partita.

6. Noi _____ (venire) a casa con la macchina nuova.

7. Chi _____ (venire) a casa con voi?

8. Io non _____ (dire) niente a nessuno.

9. Loro _____ (venire) da noi.

Exercise 170

Rewrite the sentences below using the preterit tense.

1. Ho mangiato bene.

_____.

2. Hai visitato Milano.

_____.

3. Non ha capito niente.

_____.

4. Carlo ha chiesto la ricetta per il dolce.

_____.

5. Noi non abbiamo fatto niente tutto il giorno.

_____.

6. Lei ha scelto dei bei fiori.

_____.

7. Lui ha letto la lettera.

_____.

8. Io e Luisa abbiamo spento il fuoco.

_____.

9. Monica mi ha dato un bel regalo.

_____.

10. Voi siete ritornati dalle vacanze.

_____.

Preterit tense of *essere* and *avere*

Essere and **avere** have irregular forms in the preterit. The complete conjugation of each of these verbs looks like this:

	essere	*avere*
io	fui	ebbi
tu	fosti	avesti
lui/lei	fu	ebbe
noi	fummo	avemmo
voi	foste	aveste
loro	furono	ebbero

Exercise 171

Fill in the blanks with the preterit tense conjugations of either **essere** or **avere**.

1. Io _____ (essere) contento di vederti.

2. Io _____ (avere) molta fortuna.

3. Tu _____ (essere) molto bravo.

4. Lui _____ (essere) un grande artista.

5. Lei _____ (avere) molti soldi.

6. Noi _____ (essere) in viaggio per molti mesi.

7. Noi _____ (avere) dei bei voti a scuola.

8. Voi _____ (essere) molto contenti.

9. Voi _____ (avere) sempre delle caramelle.

10. Loro _____ (essere) molto coraggiosi.

11. Loro _____ (avere) molta ambizione.

Past perfect, preterit perfect, and future perfect tenses

Each of the simple past tenses already discussed has one of these corresponding compound tenses. You are already familiar with the simple past tense of the present perfect. Its corresponding compound tense is the past perfect. The compound tenses are formed by combining a conjugation of the auxiliary verb **avere** or **essere** in the required tense with the past participle of the verb showing the action.

present	io parlo	*I speak*
imperfect	io parlavo	*I spoke, I was speaking*
present perfect	io ho parlato	*I have spoken*

past perfect	io avevo parlato	*I had spoken, I had been speaking*
preterit	io parlai	*I spoke*
preterit perfect	io ebbi parlato	*I had spoken*
future	io parlerò	*I will speak*
future perfect	io avrò parlato	*I will have spoken*

Past perfect tense

The past perfect tense is used to express an action that began and was completed in the past. It is used in Italian the same way as it is used in English. It corresponds to the English use of *had* + past participle (*I had spoken*). It is formed by using the imperfect tense conjugation of the auxiliary **essere** or **avere** + the past participle of the verb.

	studiare	*vedere*	*capire*	*arrivare*
	had studied	**had seen**	**had understood**	**had arrived**
io	avevo studiato	avevo visto	avevo capito	ero arrivato(-a)
tu	avevi studiato	avevi visto	avevi capito	eri arrivato(-a)
lui/lei	aveva studiato	aveva visto	aveva capito	era arrivato(-a)
noi	avevamo studiato	avevamo visto	avevamo capito	eravamo arrivati(-e)
voi	avevate studiato	avevate visto	avevate capito	eravate arrivati(-e)
loro	avevano studiato	avevano visto	avevano capito	erano arrivati(-e)

Io **avevo camminato** tutto il giorno.	*I had walked all day long.*
Io **ero arrivato** a casa tardi.	*I had arrived home late.*

Past participles using **essere** as an auxiliary verb agree in gender and number with the subject. Past participles that use **avere** agree in gender and number with the direct object pronouns **lo, la, li,** and **le,** but it is optional with **mi, ti, ci,** and **vi.**

Le signore **erano andate** a fare la spesa.	*The ladies **had gone** shopping.*
Li **avevo comperati**.	*I **had bought** them.*

To form a negative sentence in the past perfect tense, place **non** in front of the auxiliary.

Tu **non avevi guardato** la televisione.	*You **had not watched** television.*

Exercise 172

Translate the following sentences into Italian using the past perfect tense.

1. I answered the letters that I had received.

_____.

2. Pietro received a good grade because he had studied.

_____.

3. He had not received our letters, so he didn't answer.

_____.

4. He had not arrived home yet.

_____.

5. When I (f.) arrived, he had already left.

_____.

6. You had not finished your job yet.

_____.

7. Rosa had not called us yet.

_____.

8. You had already left, when I (m.) came back.

_____.

9. We had sold our house a year ago.

_____.

Exercise 173

Change the present perfect into past perfect in the following sentences.

1. Io ho vinto.

_____.

2. Tu hai parlato.

_____.

3. Lei ha dormito.

_____.

4. Noi abbiamo comperato.

_____.

5. Voi siete arrivati.

_____.

6. Loro sono partiti.

_____.

7. Io ho letto.

_____.

8. Tu non hai capito.

_____.

9. Lui non è partito.

_____.

10. Noi non ci siamo alzati.

_____.

Preterit perfect tense

The preterit perfect is used with the preterit conjugation of **essere** or **avere** combined with the past participle of the verb. This tense is mainly used in writing and literature when the verb in the main clause is in the preterit. The preterit perfect tense is much less used than the present perfect and in speech is replaced by the present perfect. The translation is the same as that of the past perfect. The following table shows the **-are**, **-ere**, and **-ire** conjugations for the preterit perfect tense:

	cantare **had sung**	*vedere* **had seen**	*finire* **had finished**	*andare* **had gone**
io	ebbi cantato	ebbi visto	ebbi finito	fui andato(-a)
tu	avesti cantato	avesti visto	avesti finito	fosti andato(-a)
lui/lei	ebbe cantato	ebbe visto	ebbe finito	fu andato(-a)
noi	avemmo cantato	avemmo visto	avemmo finito	fummo andati(-e)
voi	aveste cantato	aveste visto	aveste finito	foste andati(-e)
loro	ebbero cantato	ebbero visto	ebbero finito	furono andati(-e)

Lui **ebbe cantato** con il coro e poi andò a casa.

*He **had sung** with the choir, then he went home.*

Noi **fummo andati** a casa appena venne buio.

*We **had gone** home as soon as it became dark.*

Exercise 174

Fill in the blanks with the preterit perfect tense of the verbs in parentheses.

1. Appena _____ (loro-vedere) la casa, decisero di comprarla.

2. Appena _____ (io-arrivare) all'aeroporto, l'aereo atterrò.

3. Io non _____ (finire) di ascoltare la musica, perché dovetti uscire.

4. Lei _____ (piantare) molti fiori, ma lo scoiattolo li mangiò tutti.

5. Appena lei _____ (finire) di mangiare, andò a dormire.

6. Dopo che lui _____ (vestirsi), andammo al ristorante.

7. Quando lui _____ (parlare) tutti applaudirono.

8. Appena _____ (noi-vendere) la macchina, cominciammo ad usare l'autobus.

9. Quando _____ (io-andare) in Cina, mi ammalai.

Exercise 175

Translate the following sentences into Italian using the preterit perfect tense.

1. The students had understood the lesson.

_____.

2. You (sing.) had slept for many hours.

_____.

3. She had spoken with him for a long time.

_____.

4. He wrote a letter, but he did not mail it.

_____.

5. As soon as we had taken a bath, we went out.

_____.

6. As soon as they had finished the exams, they left on vacation.

_____.

7. After I had read the book, I gave it to Lia.

_____.

8. After we had eaten, we went to rest.

_____.

9. I had thought about you.

_____.

Future perfect tense

The future perfect tense expresses an action that will be completed in the future. It is formed by using the future tense of the auxiliary **avere** or **essere** combined with the past participle of the verb. The following table shows the complete conjugation of the future perfect tense with each of the three verb types:

	cantare **will have sung**	*vendere* **will have sold**	*finire* **will have finished**	*andare* **will have gone**
io	avrò cantato	avrò venduto	avrò finito	sarò andato(-a)
tu	avrai cantato	avrai venduto	avrai finito	sarai andato(-a)
lui/lei	avrà cantato	avrà venduto	avrà finito	sarà andato(-a)
noi	avremo cantato	avremo venduto	avremo finito	saremo andati(-e)
voi	avrete cantato	avrete venduto	avrete finito	sarete andati(-e)
loro	avranno cantato	avranno venduto	avranno finito	saranno andati(-e)

Avrete dato gli esami prima di partire per le vacanze?	*Will you have taken the exams before leaving for vacation?*

Usually the future perfect is used after expressions such as: **quando, appena, finché,** or **finché non.**

Ti scriverò **appena mi sarò sistemato.**	*I will write you **as soon as I get settled.***

The future perfect is also used to express possibility, supposition, and doubt in reference to the past.

Avranno già **finito** la partita?	*Could they have already **finished** the game?*

When **se** is used, the future perfect expresses an action that happens before another future action.

> **Se avrete finito** i compiti, vi porterò al cinema.   ***If you will have finished*** *the homework, I will take you to the movies.*

Exercise 176

Translate the following sentences into Italian using the future perfect tense.

1. I will have opened the door.

_____.

2. We will have gotten married.

_____.

3. All the stores will have been closed.

_____.

4. I will have finished cleaning.

_____.

5. She will have given me the book.

_____.

6. He will have called her.

_____.

7. They will have gone to the beach.

_____.

8. We will have turned on the air-conditioning.

_____.

9. They will have rented a villa.

_____.

10. He will have been fired.

_____.

Exercise 177

Fill in the blanks with the future perfect tense of the verbs in parentheses.

1. Io _____ (venire, f.) in montagna con te.

2. Lui _____ (ritornare) all'università.

3. Lei _____ (compare) un vestito nuovo per la festa.

4. Noi _____ (andare) al lago.

5. Loro _____ (ritornare) dalle vacanze.

6. Voi _____ (telefonare) a tutti i vostri amici.

7. Io _____ (rivedere) il mio paese.

8. Loro _____ (studiare) le regioni d'Italia.

9. Tu _____ (divertirsi) in montagna.

10. Noi _____ (partire) quando vi alzerete.

Conditional Tense

14

In both English and Italian the present conditional tense is generally used to express an action that depends on another fact that may or may not happen. It is used to refer to an action or state that *may* happen if something else occurred, or if some condition were present.

English forms the present conditional by using the auxiliary word *would*. Italian forms the present conditional tense by adding the appropriate conditional verb endings to the infinitive. The present conditional tense drops the final -e of all three types of verb infinitives and adds the endings: **-ei, -esti, -ebbe, -emmo, -este, -ebbero.** In addition, the **-a-** of the **-are** infinitives changes to **-e-** before the endings are added. The following table shows the conjugations of all three types of verbs in the conditional tense:

	cantare **would sing**	*vendere* **would sell**	*sentire* **would hear**
io	canterei	venderei	sentirei
tu	canteresti	venderesti	sentiresti
lui/lei	canterebbe	venderebbe	sentirebbe
noi	canteremmo	venderemmo	sentiremmo
voi	cantereste	vendereste	sentireste
loro	canterebbero	venderebbero	sentirebbero

Andrei in Italia, ma i viaggi in aereo sono troppo costosi.

I would go to Italy, but plane trips are too expensive.

Verbs ending in **-care** (**cercare**, *to look for*) and **-gare** (**pagare**, *to pay*) require the addition of an **-h-** in order to keep the hard sound of the infinitive. Verbs ending in **-ciare** (**cominciare**, *to begin*) and **-giare** (**mangiare**, *to eat*) drop the **-i-** of the root since it is not needed to maintain the soft sound of the infinitive: **comincerei** (*I would begin*), **mangerei** (*I would eat*).

The conditional is also used to add kindness or politeness to wishes or demands.

Vorrei un cappuccino.

I would like a cappuccino.

Verbs that have an irregular root in the future tense use the same irregular root in the conditional. Following are some common Italian verbs that have irregular roots with the conjugation of the present conditional tense:

andare	andr-	andrei, andresti, andrebbe, etc.
bere	berr-	berrei, berresti, berrebbe, etc.
dare	dar-	darei, daresti, darebbe, etc.
dovere	dovr-	dovrei, dovresti, dovrebbe, etc.
essere	sar-	sarei, saresti, sarebbe, etc.
fare	far-	farei, faresti, farebbe, etc.
potere	potr-	potrei, potresti, potrebbe, etc.
sapere	sapr-	saprei, sapresti, saprebbe, etc.
vedere	vedr-	vedrei, vedresti, vedrebbe, etc.
venire	verr-	verrei, verresti, verrebbe, etc.
volere	vorr-	vorrei, vorresti, vorrebbe, etc.

Note that the conditional of **dovere** (*to have to, must*) is translated as *should* in English.

Exercise 178

Translate the following sentences into English.

1. Comprerei una casa in Italia.

_____.

2. Inviterei tutti i miei amici e parenti.

_____.

3. Lei ascolterebbe sua madre.

_____.

4. Lui andrebbe a sciare.

_____.

5. Daremmo le chiavi a Roberta.

_____.

6. Voi comprereste molti regali.

_____.

7. Tu dovresti camminare.

_____.

8. Lei dovrebbe alzarsi presto.

_____.

9. Noi potremmo andare.

_____.

10. Voi sapreste la verità.

_____.

11. Maria e Carlo andrebbero in Florida.

_____.

12. Io vorrei fare un regalo a Luisa.

_____.

Exercise 179

Fill in the blanks using the conditional tense of the verbs in parentheses.

1. Mi _____ (piacere) andare al cinema.

2. Tu _____ (andare) volentieri a fare la spesa.

3. Lei _____ (potere) prendere l'autobus.

4. Lui _____ (dormire) tutto il giorno.

5. Noi _____ (arrivare) in orario.

6. I ragazzi _____ (andare) a scuola.

7. Erica _____ (fare) ginnastica.

8. Noi _____ (chiedere) suggerimenti.

9. Erica e Lara _____ (correre) in giardino.

10. Kyria _____ (vedere) il concerto.

11. Cristina _____ (preferire) parlare al telefono.

12. Voi _____ (essere) contenti.

Special verbs in the conditional tense

The following verbs may be used in a variety of ways to achieve different meanings:

- **Dovere** can be used to ask or give advice, to say what one must do or is supposed to do, and to express probability.

Dovresti andare a casa perché non stai bene.	*You should go home because you are not feeling well.*
Dovresti pulire la casa.	*You should clean the house.*

- **Essere** can be used to express irritation or skepticism.

> E che cosa **sarebbe** questo foglio?   *And what **would** this sheet **be**?*

- **Potere** can be used to express a polite request, a definite possibility, or something that could or is likely to happen.

> **Potremmo** andare al ristorante.   *We **could** go to the restaurant.*
> Non c'è nebbia, **potreste** essere a   *There is no fog, you **could** be in Rome*
>   Roma in due ore.   *in two hours.*

- **Sapere** can be used to express a polite request, an ability, or inability to do something.

> Penso che Erica **saprebbe** tradurlo.   *I think Erica **would know how** to translate it.*

- **Volere** expresses wishes and desires.

> Noi **vorremmo** parlare bene l'italiano.   *We **would like** to speak Italian well.*

Exercise 180

Fill in the blanks with the conditional tense of the verbs in parentheses.

1. Io _____ (volere) andare in California.
2. Erica _____ (volere) una bicicletta nuova.
3. Lui _____ (potere) andare con noi.
4. Noi _____ (volere) sapere dove hai messo i libri.
5. Tu _____ (sapere) dirmi come andare in centro?
6. Lei _____ (sapere) tradurre la conversazione.
7. Voi _____ (potere) comprarmi la frutta?
8. Noi _____ (dovere) mettere poca roba nella valigia.
9. Io _____ (dovere) scrivere una lettera.
10. Io non _____ (sapere) dove comprare i francobolli.
11. Noi _____ (potere) chiamarvi quando usciamo.
12. Loro _____ (volere) studiare.

Past conditional tense

The past conditional tense is formed by using the conditional tense of the auxiliary verb **avere** or **essere** plus the past participle of the main verb. As with the present perfect, the past participle agrees with the subject when **essere** is used as the auxiliary verb. It corresponds to the English use of *would have*.

	cantare **would have sung**	*vendere* **would have sold**	*sentire* **would have heard**	*arrivare* **would have arrived**
io	avrei cantato	avrei venduto	avrei sentito	sarei arrivato(-a)
tu	avresti cantato	avresti venduto	avresti sentito	saresti arrivato(-a)
lui/lei	avrebbe cantato	avrebbe venduto	avrebbe sentito	sarebbe arrivato(-a)
noi	avremmo cantato	avremmo venduto	avremmo sentito	saremmo arrivati(-e)
voi	avreste cantato	avreste venduto	avreste sentito	sareste arrivati(-e)
loro	avrebbero cantato	avrebbero venduto	avrebbero sentito	sarebbero arrivati(-e)

> **Avrei scritto** la lettera ai tuoi genitori.　　*I would have written the letter to your parents.*

Very often the past conditional is used for wishes or events that might have happened, but did not.

> Io **sarei venuto** prima.　　*I would have come sooner.*

Piacere and **volere** are used and translated in the conditional the same way as in English.

> **Mi sarebbe piaciuto** venire con voi.　　*I would have liked going with you.*
> **Avrei voluto** andare con voi.　　*I would have liked going (I would have wanted to go) with you.*

The past conditional tense is also used in dependent clauses to express a future event with reference to the past. English uses the simple conditional to express this. For example:

> Ero certa che **sarebbero ritornati** tardi.　　*I was sure that they **would return** home late.*

The past conditional is used with the past perfect subjunctive (see Chapter 15) to express something that could not have happened.

> **Sarei venuta** con te se non avessi dovuto lavorare.　　*I would have gone with you if I had not had to work.*

The past conditional is used to report news that has not been confirmed and rumors or facts that may or may not be true.

> Secondo il giornale, la ragazza **sarebbe sparita** all'improvviso.
>
> *According to the newspaper, the girl* ***would have suddenly disappeared.***

When the past tense of verbs such as **credere**, **dire**, **immaginare**, **pensare**, and **sperare** is needed, in Italian the past conditional is the preferred tense.

> **Pensavo** che **sarebbero ritornati** per le vacanze.
>
> *I was thinking that they would return for their vacation.*

The past conditional is used after the verbs **sapere che** (*to know that*), **promettere che** (*to promise that*), and **dire che** (*to say that, tell that*).

> Hai promesso che **avresti scritto** una lettera.
>
> *You promised that you* ***would write*** *a letter.*

If the dependent clause following a conditional clause is introduced by **ma** (*but*), Italian uses the indicative in the dependent clause. If it is introduced by **se** (*if*), Italian uses the subjunctive, which is discussed in Chapter 15.

> **Avrei studiato, ma ho lasciato** i libri a scuola.
>
> *I would have studied, but I left the books at school.*
>
> **Avrei studiato se avessi avuto** i libri.
>
> *I would have studied if I had had the books.*

Exercise 181

Translate the following sentences into Italian.

1. I would have studied Italian.

_____.

2. You (sing.) would have gone to the movies.

_____.

3. She would have bought a sweater.

_____.

4. You (pl.) would have read the book.

_____.

5. He would have spoken.

_____.

6. We would have traveled.

_____.

7. They would have planted the flowers.

_____.

8. I would have called you.

_____.

9. You (sing.) would have listened to the radio.

_____.

10. We would have gone to the meeting.

_____.

11. They would have called you.

_____.

12. She would have cut her hair.

_____.

Exercise 182

Change the following sentences from the present conditional tense to the past conditional.

1. Io (f.) andrei in piscina.

_____.

2. Tu telefoneresti alla tua amica.

_____.

3. Lui andrebbe a casa del suo amico.

_____.

4. Lei arriverebbe in orario.

_____.

5. Noi scriveremmo una poesia.

_____.

6. Voi fareste una relazione.

_____.

7. Loro andrebbero dal dentista.

_____.

8. Io farei una festa.

_____.

9. Tu compreresti la televisione.

_____.

10. Loro comprerebbero una maglia.

_____.

11. Voi scrivereste una cartolina.

_____.

12. Noi studieremmo molto.

_____.

Compound tenses with reflexive verbs

Compound reflexive verbs are formed by using the auxiliary verb **essere** and the past participle of the reflexive verb. The past participle of a reflexive verb agrees in gender and number with the subject.

Il ragazzo **si è svegliato**.	*The boy **has woken up**.*
I ragazzi **si erano svegliati**.	*The boys **had woken up**.*

The following tables show the compound tense conjugations for the reflexive verb **alzarsi**.

	present perfect	**past perfect**
	have gotten up	*had gotten up*
io	mi sono alzato(-a)	mi ero alzato(-a)
tu	ti sei alzato(-a)	ti eri alzato(-a)
lui/lei	si è alzato(-a)	si era alzato(-a)
noi	ci siamo alzati(-e)	ci eravamo alzati(-e)
voi	vi siete alzati(-e)	vi eravate alzati(-e)
loro	si sono alzati(-e)	si erano alzati(-e)

	future perfect	**past conditional**
	will have gotten up	*would have gotten up*
io	mi sarò alzato(-a)	mi sarei alzato(-a)
tu	ti sarai alzato(-a)	ti saresti alzato(-a)
lui/lei	si sarà alzato(-a)	si sarebbe alzato(-a)
noi	ci saremo alzati(-e)	ci saremmo alzati(-e)
voi	vi sarete alzati(-e)	vi sarete alzati(-e)
loro	si saranno alzati(-e)	si sarebbero alzati(-e)

In compound tenses the reflexive pronoun in a sentence precedes the auxiliary verb. In a negative sentence **non** precedes the reflexive pronoun.

Maria **si è svegliata** tardi.	*Maria **woke up** late.*
Maria **non si è svegliata** tardi.	*Maria **didn't wake up** late.*

Exercise 183

Rewrite the following sentences using the present perfect and the past perfect tenses.

1. Maria si fa la doccia tutte le mattine.

_____.

_____.

2. Luigi si lava i capelli.

_____.

_____.

3. Io (f.) mi metto il cappello.

_____.

_____.

4. Giovanna si alza presto.

_____.

_____.

5. Erica e Lara si divertono molto.

_____.

_____.

6. Pietro si pettina prima di uscire.

_____.

_____.

7. I nonni si sentono bene.

_____.

_____.

8. Voi vi incontrate al mercato.

_____.

_____.

9. Le due donne si salutano dalla finestra.

_____.

_____.

10. Gli innamorati si baciano.

_____.

_____.

11. Le bambine si svegliano alle otto.

_____.

_____.

12. Il sabato tu ti alzi tardi.

_____.

_____.

13. Lei si addormenta davanti alla televisione.

_____.

_____.

14. Luisa si laurea in medicina.

_____.

_____.

15. Tu ti curi la pelle.

_____.

_____.

15

Subjunctive Mood

So far, except for the conditional tense, this book has covered the indicative mood of verbs. This chapter covers the subjunctive mood. The subjunctive is used much more in Italian than in English. The subjunctive mood expresses opinions, uncertainty, supposition, possibility, wishes, and doubts. There is a simple rule that helps in learning the subjunctive: The *subjunctive* expresses *subjectivity*. If there is a chance that the action being expressed has not or may not happen, use the subjunctive. If it is a fact that an action has been realized or will definitely happen, the indicative is used.

So che ti piace andare al cinema.	*I know that you like to go to the movies.*
Spero che ti piaccia andare al cinema.	*I hope that you like going to the movies.*

The first sentence expresses certainty, so it must be in the indicative. The second sentence expresses uncertainty, so the subjunctive should be used. The subjunctive is mainly found in a dependent clause and it is used after the following verbs: **pensare** (*to think*), **credere** (*to believe*), **sperare** (*to hope*), **dubitare** (*to doubt*), **non sapere** (*to not know*), **avere paura** (*to be afraid*), **volere** (*to want*), and **desiderare** (*to wish*). The verb in the main clause is in the indicative and is then followed by a **che** clause expressed in the subjunctive.

Spero che voi **parliate** con loro.	*I hope that you speak with them.*
Lui ha paura che voi vi **perdiate.**	*He is afraid that you will get lost.*

Present subjunctive

The present subjunctive in Italian is used with actions that may take place in the present or in the future.

È necessario che tu beva molto.	*It is necessary that you drink a lot.*
È impossibile che loro arrivino presto.	*It is impossible that they'll arrive early.*

The present subjunctive is formed by adding the required subjunctive endings to the root of the verb. It is never used independently and is usually preceded by a main clause connected by **che**.

	main clause	+	*che*	+	dependent clause
Io	credo		che		lei studi legge.
I	*think*		*that*		*she studies law.*

To create the subjunctive mood with a verb, the -o- of the present tense conjugation in the first person singular (**io** form) is replaced by the endings of the present subjunctive. The following table shows the complete subjunctive conjugation for each of the three verb types. All -are, -ere, and -ire verbs that are regular in the present indicative are conjugated the same as **cantare, vedere, sentire,** and **capire** in the present subjunctive shown in this table.

	cantare	*vedere*	*sentire*	*capire*
	to speak	**to see**	**to hear**	**to understand**
che io	canti	veda	senta	capisca
che tu	canti	veda	senta	capisca
che lui/lei	canti	veda	senta	capisca
che noi	cantiamo	vediamo	sentiamo	capiamo
che voi	cantiate	vediate	sentiate	capiate
che loro	cantino	vedano	sentano	capiscano

If the subject in the **che** clause is the same as the subject of the main clause, the infinitive **di** + is used in place of **che** + the subjunctive.

Penso di ritornare a casa con l'ultimo aereo.

I am thinking of going back home with the last plane.

Exercise 184

Fill in the blanks with the conjugated forms of the present subjunctive for the verbs in parentheses.

1. Credo che tu _____ (dormire) a casa mia.

2. Desidero che voi _____ (camminare) con noi.

3. Lui vuole che io _____ (cantare) in chiesa.

4. Abbiamo paura che lei _____ (perdere) il treno.

5. Vogliamo che lui _____ (scrivere) un libro.

6. Credo che i bambini _____ (guardare) la partita.

7. Penso che loro _____ (sentire) tutti i rumori.

8. Mio marito ha paura che io _____ (spendere) troppo.

9. Penso che voi _____ (ballare) molto bene.

10. Mia madre vuole che noi _____ (telefonare) tutte le settimane.

Verbs ending with -**care** and -**gare** add an -**h**- in all forms of the present subjunctive.

	giocare **to play**	*pagare* **to pay**
che io	gio**chi**	pa**ghi**
che tu	gio**chi**	pa**ghi**
che lui/lei	gio**chi**	pa**ghi**
che noi	gio**chi**amo	pa**ghi**amo
che voi	gio**chi**ate	pa**ghi**ate
che loro	gio**chi**no	pa**ghi**no

Verbs ending with -**ciare** and -**giare**, however, do not repeat the -**i**-.

	cominciare **to start, begin**	*mangiare* **to eat**
che io	comin**ci**	man**gi**
che tu	comin**ci**	man**gi**
che lui/lei	comin**ci**	man**gi**
che noi	comin**ci**amo	man**gi**amo
che voi	comin**ci**ate	man**gi**ate
che loro	comin**ci**no	man**gi**no

Exercise 185

Fill in the blanks with the conjugated forms of the present subjunctive of the verbs in parentheses.

1. Voglio che tu _____ (mangiare) tutta la minestra.

2. Credi che la lezione _____ (cominciare) subito.

3. Speriamo che voi _____ (giocare) al bridge.

4. Dubito che lei _____ (pagare) i suoi debiti.

5. Voglio che loro _____ (mangiare) la colazione.

6. Penso che lui _____ (cominciare) a lavorare.

7. Spero che loro _____ (pagare) il conto.

8. Credo che lei _____ (mangiare) solo frutta.

9. Tu vuoi che io _____ (cercare) un albergo.

10. Spera che voi _____ (cominciare) a fare le valige.

Most verbs with an irregular root in the first person of the present indicative will have an irregular root for the present subjunctive. For example:

	bere to drink	*dire* to say, tell	*fare* to make; do	*potere* to be able
present indicative				
io	bevo	dico	faccio	posso
present subjunctive				
che io	beva	dica	faccia	possa
che tu	beva	dica	faccia	possa
che lui/lei	beva	dica	faccia	possa
che noi	beviamo	diciamo	facciamo	possiamo
che voi	beviate	diciate	facciate	possiate
che loro	bevano	dicano	facciano	possano

The irregular verbs **fare** and **volere** do not double the -i- before the **noi** ending of -iamo. So we have facciamo and vogliamo and not facciiamo and vogliiamo.

Some verbs are irregular in the present subjunctive forms of **io, tu, lui/lei,** and **loro,** but in the **noi** and **voi** forms of the subjunctive they reflect again the root of the present indicative. The verb **dovere** (*must, to have to*), however, is irregular in the **voi** form as shown below:

present indicative		**present subjunctive**	
io	devo (debbo)	che io	deva (debba)
tu	devi	che tu	deva (debba)
lui/lei	deve	che lui/lei	deva (debba)
noi	dobbiamo	che noi	dobbiamo
voi	dovete	che voi	dobbiate
loro	devono (debbono)	che loro	devano (debbano)

Here are the conjugations of the present subjunctive for some common irregular verbs:

	andare to go	*rimanere* to remain	*salire* to ascend, go up
che io	vada	rimanga	salga
che tu	vada	rimanga	salga
che lui/lei	vada	rimanga	salga
che noi	andiamo	rimaniamo	saliamo
che voi	andiate	rimaniate	saliate
che loro	vadano	rimangano	salgano

	tenere to keep	*valere* to be worth	*venire* to come
che io	tenga	valga	venga
che tu	tenga	valga	venga
che lui/lei	tenga	valga	venga
che noi	teniamo	valiamo	veniamo
che voi	teniate	valiate	veniate
che loro	tengano	valgano	vengano

	apparire to appear	*morire* to die	*cuocere* to cook
che io	appaia	muoia	cuocia
che tu	appaia	muoia	cuocia
che lui/lei	appaia	muoia	cuocia
che noi	appariamo	moriamo	cociamo (cuociamo)
che voi	appariate	moriate	cociate (cuociate)
che loro	appaiano	muoiano	cuociano

	sedere to sit	*suonare* to play	*uscire* to go out
che io	sieda	suoni	esca
che tu	sieda	suoni	esca
che lui/lei	sieda	suoni	esca
che noi	sediamo	suoniamo	usciamo
che voi	sediate	suoniate	usciate
che loro	siedano	suonino	escano

Exercise 186

Translate the following sentences into Italian.

1. I want you (pl.) to go home early.

_____.

2. They think that he will arrive late.

_____.

3. I hope that you (sing.) will go home with me.

_____.

4. She doesn't want you (sing.) to keep her cat.

_____.

5. I hope he doesn't die.

_____.

6. He wants them to sit down.

_____.

7. She wants you (sing.) to go up.

_____.

8. I think that she has to study.

_____.

9. We hope that he will play the piano.

_____.

10. He wants you (pl.) to play the violin.

_____.

11. We think that you (sing.) know how to cook well.

_____.

12. They hope that you (sing.) will remain with me.

_____.

The verbs **avere**, **dare**, **essere**, **sapere**, and **stare** are all irregular in the present subjunctive.

	avere	_dare_	_essere_	_sapere_	_stare_
che io	abbia	dia	sia	sappia	stia
che tu	abbia	dia	sia	sappia	stia

che lui/lei	abbia	dia	sia	sappia	stia
che noi	abbiamo	diamo	siamo	sappiamo	stiamo
che voi	abbiate	diate	siate	sappiate	stiate
che loro	abbiano	diano	siano	sappiano	stiano

Exercise 187

Fill in the blanks with the present subjunctive tense of the verbs in parentheses.

1. Spero che tu _____ (avere) molta pazienza.

2. Desidero che lui mi _____ (dare) il suo numero di telefono.

3. Mi sembra che voi gli _____ (dare) troppi regali.

4. Non credo che tu _____ (avere) già fame.

5. Credo che in Italia _____ (fare) freddo in dicembre.

6. Voi pensate che io _____ (avere) molti soldi.

7. Credi che loro _____ (sapere) l'inglese?

8. No, credo che non lo _____ (loro-sapere).

9. Carlo pensa che Maria _____ (essere) troppo magra.

10. Penso che lei mi _____ (dare) molto conforto.

11. Crediamo tutti che lui _____ (essere) un genio.

12. Pensate che _____ (essere) possibile partire prima del previsto?

Subjunctive with impersonal expressions

The subjunctive mood is used in a dependent **che** clause after impersonal expressions of possibility, opinion, and probability. The following expressions use the subjunctive.

Basta che...	*It is enough that . . .*
Bisogna che...	*It is necessary that . . .*
È bene che...	*It is good that . . .*
È difficile che...	*It is difficult that . . .*
È giusto che...	*It is right that . . .*
È importante che...	*It is important that . . .*

È meglio che...	*It is better that . . .*
È necessario che...	*It is necessary that . . .*
È opportuno che...	*It is opportune that . . .*
È peccato che...	*It is a pity that . . .*
È possibile che...	*It is possible that . . .*
È probabile che...	*It is probable that . . .*
È raro che...	*It is rare that . . .*
Non importa che...	*It isn't important that . . .*

Impersonal expressions are followed by an infinitive instead of the subjunctive if no subject is expressed.

È necessario che tu **studi.**	***It is necessary that*** *you* ***study.***
È necessario studiare per imparare.	***It is necessary to study*** *in order to learn.*

When impersonal expressions depict certainty, the indicative is used instead of the subjunctive. The following expressions require the indicative:

È certo che...	*It is certain that...*
È evidente che...	*It is obvious/evident that...*
È ovvio che...	*It is obvious that...*
È chiaro che...	*It is clear that...*

Exercise 188

Fill in the blanks with the present subjunctive of the verbs in parentheses where necessary.

1. È importante che tu _____ (ascoltare) bene quello che dico.

2. È probabile che l'aereo _____ (atterrare) tardi.

3. È difficile che noi _____ (guardare) la televisione.

4. È preferibile che io _____ (stare) in albergo.

5. È raro che loro _____ (andare) in vacanza.

6. È peccato che loro non _____ (venire) questa estate.

7. È ovvio che loro _____ (essere) scontenti.

8. È certo che loro _____ (andare) in Italia.

9. È chiaro che ci _____ (trasferire) il mese prossimo.

10. È ovvio che voi _____ (essere) intelligenti.

11. È meglio che lei _____ (parlare) con il direttore.

12. È difficile che lui _____ (arrivare) in ritardo.

13. È impossibile che gli scienziati _____ (potere) predire i terremoti.

The subjunctive mood is also used with the following subordinate expressions:

a meno che	*unless*
affinché	*in order that*
benché	*although*
così che	*so that*
dopo che	*after*
finché non	*until*
malgrado	*although*
prima che	*before*
purché	*provided that*
sebbene	*even if; although*
senza che	*without*

In addition, the subjunctive is used with the following pronouns, adverbs, and adjectives:

chiunque	*whoever*
dovunque	*wherever*
ovunque	*wherever*
qualunque	*whatever*

Exercise 189

Fill in the blanks with the appropriate forms of the verbs in parentheses.

1. Vengo anch'io malgrado _____ (fare) freddo.

2. Chiunque _____ (io-incontrare) lo saluto.

3. Prima che voi _____ (partire), spero di vedervi.

4. Dovunque lei _____ (andare), la gente la guarda.

5. Sebbene le porte dell'aereo _____ (essere) già chiuse, ancora non si parte.

6. Benché lui _____ (parlare) bene l'inglese, nessuno lo capisce.

7. Vengo con voi, purché mi _____ (fare) pagare.

8. Malgrado _____ (piovere), ci sono molte persone in barca.

9. Parto questa sera a meno che non ci _____ (essere) uno sciopero.

10. Rimango con voi, purché io vi _____ (potere) aiutare.

Imperfect subjunctive

The imperfect subjunctive is used after certain verbs, after impersonal expressions, and after conjunctions. Also, when the action refers to something in the past, the imperfect subjunctive is used. And if the verb of the main clause is expressed in the past tense or in the conditional, the imperfect subjunctive is used.

The imperfect subjunctive of all regular verbs, and almost all the irregular verbs, is formed by adding the endings: -ssi, -ssi, -sse, -ssimo, -ste, -ssero to the first person singular of the imperfect indicative after dropping the -vo.

infinitive	imperfect indicative	imperfect subjunctive
cantare	cantavo	che io cantassi
leggere	leggevo	che io leggessi
sentire	sentivo	che io sentissi

Maria **voleva che noi andassimo a** casa sua.	*Maria **wanted us to go** to her house.*
Maria **vorrebbe che noi dormissimo** a casa sua.	*Maria **would like us to sleep** at her house.*

The following table shows the complete conjugation of the imperfect subjunctive of the regular -are, -ere, and -ire verbs.

	cantare	*scrivere*	*sentire*
che io	cantassi	scrivessi	sentissi
che tu	cantassi	scrivessi	sentissi
che lui/lei	cantasse	scrivesse	sentisse
che noi	cantassimo	scrivessimo	sentissimo
che voi	cantaste	scriveste	sentiste
che loro	cantassero	scrivessero	sentissero

Just as in the previous tenses, these verbs have irregular forms in the imperfect subjunctive:

	dare	*dire*	*essere*	*fare*	*stare*
che io	dessi	dicessi	fossi	facessi	stessi
che tu	dessi	dicessi	fossi	facessi	stessi
che lui/lei	desse	dicesse	fosse	facesse	stesse
che noi	dessimo	dicessimo	fossimo	facessimo	stessimo
che voi	deste	diceste	foste	faceste	steste
che loro	dessero	dicessero	fossero	facessero	stessero

Exercise 190

Rewrite the following sentences in Italian using the imperfect subjunctive. Sometimes the infinitive will be needed.

1. I wanted you (sing.) to come to my house.

_____.

2. You thought you (sing.) could buy the car.

_____.

3. Maria wanted you (sing.) to call her.

_____.

4. I thought he would return.

_____.

5. She would like her to read the letter.

_____.

6. She would like him to read.

_____.

7. I would like them to study more.

_____.

8. She would like me to ask him to come.

_____.

9. I wanted her to invite them to the party.

_____.

10. They did not want him to leave.

_____.

11. Maria did not know he would go.

_____.

12. We thought they would go to the beach.

_____.

Exercise 191

Complete each sentence with the verbs in parentheses putting them in the present subjunctive or imperfect subjunctive as required.

1. Dubito che lui _____ (imparare).

2. Dubitavo che lui _____ (studiare).

3. Volevo che lui _____ (dire) la verità.

4. Lei preferisce che voi _____ (camminare).

5. Vorrebbe che io le _____ (regalare) un anello.

6. Lei pensa che io le _____ (regalare) un anello.

7. Penso che tu ti _____ (dovere) lavare la faccia.

8. Era necessario che tu ti _____ (lavare) le mani.

9. Io preferirei _____ (viaggiare) in aereo.

10. Io preferisco che tu _____ (viaggiare) in macchina.

11. Io preferirei che tu _____ (viaggiare) in treno.

12. Lei ha paura che tu la _____ (sgridare).

Past subjunctive

The past subjunctive is used in a dependent **che** clause to express the speaker's feelings toward a recent past action. The verb in the main clause in this case is in the present indicative. To form the past subjunctive, the present subjunctive of **avere** or **essere** + the past participle of the verb is used. The action in the main clause is in the present tense, while the **che** clause is in the past.

> **Credo che siano arrivati** a casa.
> **Dubito che** lei **abbia vinto.**

> *I believe that they have arrived home.*
> *I doubt that she won.*

The following table shows the complete conjugation of the past subjunctive using **avere** for the three verb types:

	cantare **to sing**	*vendere* **to sell**	*sentire* **to hear**
che io	abbia cantato	abbia venduto	abbia sentito
che tu	abbia cantato	abbia venduto	abbia sentito
che lui/lei	abbia cantato	abbia venduto	abbia sentito
che noi	abbiamo cantato	abbiamo venduto	abbiamo sentito
che voi	abbiate cantato	abbiate venduto	abbiate sentito
che loro	abbiano cantato	abbiano venduto	abbiano sentito

Conjugation of the past subjunctive using **essere** looks like this:

	partire **to leave**	*alzarsi* **to get up**
che io	sia partito(-a)	mi sia alzato(-a)
che tu	sia partito(-a)	ti sia alzato(-a)
che lui/lei	sia partito(-a)	si sia alzato(-a)
che noi	siamo partiti(-e)	ci siamo alzati(-e)
che voi	siate partiti(-e)	vi siate alzati(-e)
che loro	siano partiti(-e)	si siano alzati(-e)

As with the present and the imperfect subjunctive, the past subjunctive is also used after expressions of doubt, emotion, and wishing, and after impersonal expressions.

Dubito che tu **abbia studiato.**	*I doubt that you studied.*
Sono contenta che tu **abbia lavorato.**	*I am happy that you worked.*
È probabile che lui sia già **arrivato.**	*It is possible that he has already arrived.*

The past subjunctive is also used when expressing a past action that has taken place before the action of the main verb. Pay attention to the use of the subjunctive in the following sentences. The past subjunctive is the equivalent of the present perfect in the indicative mood.

present subjunctive	Spero che Luigi **lavori.**	*I hope that Luigi **will work.***
past subjunctive	Spero che Luigi **abbia lavorato.**	*I hope that Luigi **worked.***

| present perfect | Sappiamo che **siete andati** in Italia. | *We know that you **went** to Italy.* |
| past subjunctive | Pensiamo che voi **siate andati** in Italia. | *We think that you **went** to Italy.* |

Exercise 192

Fill in the blanks with the past subjunctive of the verbs in parentheses.

1. Dubito che tu _____ (viaggiare) con il treno.

2. Dubitiamo che lei _____ (accettare) l'invito.

3. Penso che loro _____ (andare) al concerto sinfonico.

4. È probabile che lei _____ (noleggiare) una macchina.

5. Mi dispiace che mio fratello se ne _____ (andare).

6. Penso che lei _____ (piangere) molto.

7. Dubiti che loro _____ (ricordarsi) il regalo.

8. Crediamo che i nostri amici _____ (comprare) una casa nuova.

9. Loro credono che noi _____ (viaggiare) tutta la settimana.

10. È probabile che tu _____ (andare) nel deserto.

11. Luisa crede che loro _____ (andare) a pescare.

12. Carlo pensa che Maria _____ (vendere) molti vestiti.

Exercise 193

Fill in the blanks with the present perfect or the past subjunctive of the verbs in parentheses.

1. È ovvio che loro _____ (partire).

2. Penso che loro _____ (partire).

3. Lei è sicura che voi _____ (leggere) quel libro.

4. Pensiamo che loro _____ (accendere) la luce.

5. Sono certa che lui ti _____ (chiamare).

6. Credi che lei ti _____ (chiamare).

7. Maria sa che Carlo _____ (partire).

8. Maria pensa che Carlo _____ (partire).

9. Crediamo che voi _____ (capire).

10. So dove tu _____ (trovare) quella bella pianta.

11. Non sappiamo dove tu _____ (mettere) il libro.

12. Sono sicura che voi _____ (imparare) a nuotare.

Past perfect subjunctive

The past perfect subjunctive is used when the action of the verb in the dependent clause happened before the action of the verb in the main clause, which is expressed in the past tense. The independent clause is expressed in the subjunctive or in the conditional. It is formed by using the imperfect subjunctive of **avere** or **essere** + the past participle of the verb.

present indicative	perfect subjunctive	imperfect indicative	past perfect subjunctive
Credo che Luigi	sia partito.	Credevo che	Luigi fosse partito.
I think that Luigi	*left.*	*I thought that*	*Luigi had left.*

The following chart shows the conjugations of the past perfect subjunctive for the three verb types using the auxiliaries **avere** and **essere**.

	cantare	*scrivere*	*partire*
che io	avessi cantato	avessi scritto	fossi partito(-a)
che tu	avessi cantato	avessi scritto	fossi partito(-a)
che lui/lei	avesse cantato	avesse scritto	fosse partito(-a)
che noi	avessimo cantato	avessimo scritto	fossimo partiti(-e)
che voi	aveste cantato	aveste scritto	foste partiti(-e)
che loro	avessero cantato	avessero scritto	fossero partiti(-e)

Exercise 194

Fill in the blanks with the past perfect subjunctive of the verbs in parentheses using **essere** or **avere**.

1. Io ero contento che tu _____ (arrivare).

2. Eravamo contenti che voi _____ (venire).

3. Sembrava che loro _____ (capire).

4. Speravo che voi _____ (scrivere) una lettera.

5. Pensavamo che voi _____ già

_____ (partire).

6. Avrei preferito che voi _____ (giocare) al tennis.

7. Era probabile che loro _____ (perdere) la chiave.

8. Pensavate che lui _____ (chiamare) da casa.

9. Pensavo che tu _____ (avere) la macchina.

10. Era impossibile che lui _____ (alzarsi) presto.

11. Sembrava che tutti _____ (andare) in vacanza.

12. Noi eravamo soddisfatti che tu _____ (finire) l'università.

With **come se** (*as if*) the imperfect and the past perfect subjunctive are always used, regardless of the tense of the main verb.

Parlavano come se avessero vinto la partita.	*They were talking as if they had won the game.*
La guardavano come se fosse stata una rarità.	*They were looking at her as if she had been a rarity.*

Exercise 195

Translate the following sentences into Italian using the past perfect subjunctive.

1. It was possible that he had won.

_____.

2. I had hoped that he had waited for me.

_____.

3. She thought that you had spent the money.

_____.

4. We believed that you had gotten sick on the plane.

_____.

5. It was the most interesting book that I had ever read.

_____.

6. You (sing.) hoped that I had found a good job.

_____.

7. He thought that you had bought a new boat.

_____.

8. I doubted that you had seen her.

_____.

9. He hoped that you would have gotten married.

_____.

10. We thought that you had sold the house.

_____.

11. Sara was jumping as if she were a young girl.

_____.

Se clause and the subjunctive

To express a contrary-to-fact statement in the present or future tense, the imperfect subjunctive is used within the **se** clause itself. The conditional is generally used in the main clause to express a conclusion.

Se avessi i soldi, **viaggerei.**   *If I had the money, I would travel.*

To express a contrary-to-fact statement in the past, the past perfect subjunctive is used in the **se** clause and the past conditional is used in the main clause. The conditional is only used in the main clause and never in the **se** clause. The present subjunctive is never used after **se**, only the imperfect or the past perfect subjunctive are used.

Se mi **avessi scritto,** ti **avrei risposto.**   *If you had written me, I would have answered you.*

Se + the imperfect subjunctive is used in exclamations to express wishes that may never materialize.

Se avessi un aereo mio personale!   *If only I had my own personal plane!*
Se potessi vederlo!   *If only I could see him.*

If the hypothesis is real with the **se** clause, the indicative is used.

> **Se vengo**, ti **telefono**.   *If I come, I will call you.*
>
> **Se** lui **torna** in tempo, ci **verremo**.   *If he returns on time, we will come.*

Exercise 196

Fill in the blanks with the appropriate forms of the verbs in parentheses.

1. Vivremmo in Italia se _____ (avere) una casa.

2. Leggerei se ci _____ (vedere) senza occhiali.

3. Comprerebbe la macchina se non ne _____ (avere) una.

4. Avresti parlato se tu _____ (avere) l'occasione.

5. Verrebbe se _____ (sapere) la strada.

6. Sarebbe puntuale se non _____ (perdersi).

7. Comprerei la frutta se _____ (essere) matura.

8. Mangerei la verdura se mi _____ (piacere).

9. Canteresti se _____ (avere) una bella voce.

10. Avreste capito se _____ (ascoltare).

16

Passive Voice

Unlike the active voice studied so far in which the subject *performs* the action, in the passive voice, the subject *receives* the action.

active voice
Carla **scrive** la lettera.
*Carla **writes** the letter.*

passive voice
La lettera è **scritta da** Carla.
*The letter **is written by** Carla.*

Using *essere* in the passive voice

As in English, the passive voice in Italian, when a verb is transitive, is formed by using the verb **essere** + the past participle of the action verb + the preposition **da** if the agent is expressed. However, it is not always necessary to express the agent, in which case **da** is omitted.

La casa è **stata distrutta dal** tornado.
La casa è **stata distrutta**.

*The house **has been destroyed by** the tornado.*
*The house **has been destroyed**.* (destroyed by what is not expressed)

Verbs other than *essere* to express the passive voice

Besides **essere** there are other verbs that are used in the passive voice. **Venire** is one of them. Its use, however, does not change the meaning or translation of a sentence. Usually **essere** is used to emphasize a state of being and **venire** expresses carrying on an action.

La vostra automobile è **riparata**.
La vostra automobile **verrà consegnata** domani.

*You car **is fixed**.* (state of being)
*Your car **will be delivered** tomorrow.* (action)

Exercise 197

Change the following sentences from the active voice to the passive voice in the appropriate tenses.

1. I contadini lavorano la terra.

_____.

2. Mando le lettere per via aerea.

_____.

3. Noi paghiamo l'affitto della casa in anticipo.

_____.

4. Molti seguiranno questa partita.

_____.

5. Il meccanico ripara le macchine.

_____.

6. Luisa invita Carla ogni domenica.

_____.

7. Alessandro Manzoni ha scritto _I Promessi Sposi._

_____.

8. Il dentista ha tolto il dente.

_____.

9. La radio ha già dato questa notizia.

_____.

10. Luigi ha chiuso la porta a chiave.

_____.

11. Dove hai portato le valige?

_____?

12. La fortuna ha baciato quell'uomo.

_____.

Rimanere and **restare** are often used in place of **essere** when the past participle following it describes feelings or emotions such as: **deluso, stupito, sorpreso, meraviglioso, aperto,** and **chiuso.**

Siamo **rimasti molto sorpresi** quando non vi abbiamo visti alla stazione.

*We **were very surprised** when we didn't see you at the station.*

La spiaggia **resterà chiusa** tutto il giorno a causa del mare molto mosso.

*The beach **will remain closed** all day because of the high waves.*

The modal verbs followed by the infinitive of a verb has already been discussed; now take a look at the modal verbs followed by a passive infinitive.

Il biglietto **deve essere acquistato** entro la settimana.

*The ticket **must be purchased** within the week.*

La padrona di casa **vuole essere pagata** subito.

*The landlord **wants to be paid** right away.*

Exercise 198

Translate the following sentences into Italian using the passive voice.

1. The house must be finished.

_____.

2. The house will have to be finished by the owners.

_____.

3. The house was finished in a hurry.

_____.

4. We are surprised that the house has not been finished yet.

_____.

5. The airplane will be (*venire*) finished in a couple of months.

_____.

6. The airplane will have to be fixed.

_____.

7. The concert will be directed by the new orchestra director.

_____.

8. The Oscars will be presented to the best actors and actresses.

_____.

9. The gold medals will be won by the best athletes.

_____.

10. The airplane will be grounded all winter.

_____.

11. The airline ticket will be (*essere*) reimbursed.

_____.

12. The airline ticket will be (*venire*) reimbursed.

_____.

Alternatives to the passive voice

The passive voice in Italian is often used in written language in books, newspapers, and magazines. In the spoken language, however, there are alternatives. Oftentimes, in spoken language, **si** is used to replace *one* when the passive voice is used. This construction is used much more in Italian than in English. **Si** also has a variety of meanings such as *we*, *you*, and *they*.

Si dice che il candidato politico preferito da molti, non vincerà le elezioni.	*They say that the political candidate that everybody likes, will not win the elections.*
Dove **si va** oggi?	*Where **will we go** today?*

A common way to avoid using the passive voice in Italian is to use the passive **si** + the third person singular or plural of the verb.

Dove **si trovano** i biglietti dell'autobus?	*Where does one (do we) buy/find bus tickets? (Where **are** bus tickets **bought**?)*

Exercise 199

Translate the following sentences into English.

1. Si deve finire di imbiancare.

_____.

2. Dove si trova il mercato?

_____?

3. Che cosa si trova al mercato?

_____?

4. A che ora si ritorna a casa?

_____?

5. A che ora si parte?

_____?

6. Qui si parlano tutte le lingue.

_____.

7. Si vende roba di qualità.

_____.

8. Che cosa si dice in Italia della situazione politica?

_____?

9. Si deve finire il lavoro per la fine del mese.

_____.

10. Si deve studiare l'italiano per dieci minuti al giorno.

_____.

17

Verbal Expressions, Idioms, and Special Constructions

Like English, Italian has many expressions, idioms, and special constructions that are commonly used in daily speech. This chapter discusses the most common ones. Commiting them to memory is strongly suggested.

Avere and *fare*

The verb **avere** is used in many idiomatic expressions. Before nouns or adjectives, the infinitive **avere** is abbreviated to **aver**.

avere (aver)... anni	*to be . . . years old*
aver bisogno di	*to need*
aver caldo	*to feel (be) warm*
aver fame	*to be hungry*
aver freddo	*to be cold*
aver fretta	*to be in a hurry*
aver l'impressione (di)	*to have the impression*
aver mal (di)	*to have an ache*
aver paura (di)	*to be afraid*
aver sete	*to be thirsty*
aver sonno	*to be sleepy*
aver voglia (di)	*to feel like doing*

The verb **fare** is also used in idiomatic expressions. The infinitive of **fare** is often abbreviated to **far** before a consonant. Some commonly used expressions with **fare** are:

fare alla romana	*to go dutch*
fare attenzione	*to pay attention*

fare il bagno	*to take a bath*
far bel/brutto tempo	*to be good/bad weather*
fare benzina	*to get gas*
far caldo/freddo	*to be warm/cold*
fare colazione	*to have breakfast*
fare una domanda	*to ask a question*
fare un favore (a)	*to do a favor*
fare fotografie	*to take pictures*
fare male	*to hurt/ache*
fare una passeggiata	*to take a walk*
fare un piacere (a)	*to do a favor*
fare il pieno	*to fill up with gas*
fare presto	*to hurry up*
fare un regalo	*to give a gift*
fare la spesa	*to get groceries*
fare uno spuntino	*to have a snack*
fare un viaggio	*to take a trip*

Exercise 200

Translate the following sentences into Italian using the idiomatic forms of **avere** and **fare**.

1. I need to go to the bank.

_____.

2. I am afraid of dogs.

_____.

3. I am hungry, I need to eat.

_____.

4. They need a new jacket.

_____.

5. She always has a headache.

_____.

6. You (sing.) are thirsty. Would you like a Coke?

_____?

7. She was sleepy. She needed to go to bed.

_____.

8. We go dutch.

_____.

9. I have breakfast with my kids.

_____.

10. We gave her a gift.

_____.

11. He is in a hurry, but he is late all the same.

_____.

12. She took many pictures.

_____.

Special idiomatic constructions with *fare* and *lasciare*

Idiomatic expressions can only be memorized. When an idiomatic expression uses **fare** followed by an infinitive, it corresponds to the English use of *to have something done* or *made*, or to *have someone do something*.

La mamma **fa studiare** i ragazzi.　　*Mother **is having** the kids **study**.*

The direct and indirect object pronouns usually precede **fare**, but follow it only when it is in the infinitive form or when it is conjugated in the familiar second person or formal third person singular form of the imperative.

Faccio cambiare la cucina.	*I am having the kitchen changed.*
La faccio cambiare perché è vecchia.	*I have it changed because it is old.*
Vorrei **far pulire** la casa.	*I would like to have the house cleaned.*
Vorrei **farla pulire**.	*I would like to have it cleaned.*

When the verb **lasciare** is followed by an infinitive, it means *to let, allow,* or *permit*. It is used in the same way as **fare** + the infinitive.

Lasciate entrare la gente!	*Let the people come in!*
Lui non mi **lascia andare** sulla sua bicicletta.	*He doesn't let me go on his bicycle.*

Lasciare may also be followed by che + the subjunctive.

Io **lo lascio andare** in vacanza con gli amici.

*I **let him go** on vacation with his friends.*

Lascio che vada in vacanza con gli amici.

*I **let him go** on vacation with his friends.*

Exercise 201

Translate the following sentences into Italian.

1. You make her study too many hours a day.

_____.

2. I had the ambulance take me to the hospital.

_____.

3. They will have us take care of the children for a week.

_____.

4. You make your kids go to church every Sunday.

_____.

5. She doesn't let her go to the movies.

_____.

6. She doesn't let anybody else talk.

_____.

7. You (sing.) don't let anybody play with your ball.

_____.

8. He doesn't let me go to the party.

_____.

9. I had the tailor make my husband a new suit.

_____.

10. My husband had a tailor in Hong Kong make him a tuxedo.

_____.

Idiomatic expressions using *dare*

Like **fare**, the verb **dare** is used in many idiomatic expressions. Before a consonant, the infinitive of **dare** is abbreviated to **dar**. Some common expressions using **dare** are:

dare ascolto	*to listen to someone*
dare il benvenuto(-a)	*to welcome*
dare un calcio	*to kick*
dar(e) la colpa	*to blame*
dar un esame	*to take a test*
darsi da fare	*to get busy*
dare un film	*to show a movie*
dar(e) da mangiare/bere	*to feed; to give something to eat/drink*
dar(e) la mano	*to shake hands*
dare un passaggio	*to give a lift*
dare una risposta	*to give an answer*
dare i saluti (a)	*to give regards*
dare un sospiro (di)	*to sigh*
darsi per vinto	*to give up*

Exercise 202

Translate the following sentences into Italian using the expressions with **dare**.

1. I have to feed the horses.

   _____.

2. You (sing.) have to give the cat something to drink.

   _____.

3. I like to welcome people.

   _____.

4. Many people do not like to shake hands.

   _____.

5. The students take the tests at the end of the school year.

   _____.

6. The theater is showing the new movie.

_____.

7. He kicked the ball very hard.

_____.

8. They have not given us the answer yet.

_____.

9. I will give him my answer tomorrow.

_____.

10. She sighed with relief.

_____.

11. We have to get busy. Time passes quickly.

_____.

12. I don't like to give up.

_____.

Expressions using *andare*

The verb **andare** is used in many common expressions and is usually followed by a preposition. However, if an adverb follows **andare**, the preposition is omitted. Here are some common expressions using **andare**:

andare d'accordo	*to get along*
andare per affari	*to go on business*
andare bene/male	*to go well/badly*
andare a cavallo	*to go horseback riding*
andare di giorno/di sera	*to go during the day/in the evening*
andare in macchina	*to go by car*
andare a pescare	*to go fishing*
andare a piedi	*to walk/go by foot*
andare a teatro	*to go to the theater*
andare in treno/aereo/bicicletta	*to go by train/plane/bicycle*
andare in vendita	*to go on sale*

Translate the following sentences into Italian using the expressions with **andare**.

1. People in Italy walk a lot.

_____.

2. We like to go to the theater.

_____.

3. Every Sunday she goes horseback riding.

_____.

4. Carlo likes to go fishing with his grandfather.

_____.

5. Everything is going very well.

_____.

6. She thinks that everything is going badly.

_____.

7. My mother is afraid of traveling by plane.

_____.

8. Her house will go on sale soon.

_____.

9. The girls do not get along very well.

_____.

10. You (sing.) prefer to go by train.

_____.

Idiomatic expressions with *stare*

Idiomatic expressions using **stare** are very common. The infinitive of **stare** can be abbreviated to **star** before a consonant. Here are some common expressions using **stare**:

stare attento(-a) (a)	*to pay attention*
star(e) bene/male	*to be/feel well/bad*

stare in casa	*to stay at home*
star(e) con le mani in mano	*to do nothing*
star(e) da...	*to be at somebody's . . .*
star(e) fermo(-a)	*to keep still*
star(e) per...	*to be about to . . .*
stare in piedi	*to be standing*
stare a sedere	*to be sitting*
star(e) seduto(-a)	*to be sitting*
stare a vedere	*to wait and see*
star(e) zitto(-a)	*to be quiet*

Exercise 204

Translate the following sentences into Italian using the idiomatic expressions with **stare**.

1. I told her to pay attention to the curtains.

_____.

2. She pays attention in class.

_____.

3. Boys usually cannot keep still.

_____.

4. Luigi did not feel well last night.

_____.

5. We stayed home all day yesterday.

_____.

6. Many people are standing in the subway.

_____.

7. I don't like to be sitting for a long time.

_____.

8. Erica is never quiet.

_____.

9. You (pl.) are at Maria's for a long time.

_____.

10. I am about to go shopping.

_____.

Verbs and expressions followed by a preposition

In Italian many verbs and expressions are followed by a preposition. Following are the most commonly used expressions followed by the prepositions **a** and **di**:

The preposition **a** is used before a noun or a pronoun with the following verbs:

assistere a	*to attend*
assomigliare a	*to resemble*
credere a	*to believe in*
dare la caccia a	*to chase*
dare un calcio a	*to kick*
dare da mangiare a	*to feed*
dare fastidio a	*to bother*
fare attenzione a	*to pay attention*
fare bene/male a	*to be good/bad*
fare piacere a	*to please*
fare un regalo a	*to give a present to*
far vedere a	*to show*
fare visita a	*to visit*
giocare a	*to play (a game)*
pensare a	*to think about*
ricordare a	*to remind*
servire a	*to be good for*
stringere la mano a	*to shake hands with*
tenere a	*to care about*

Before an infinitive the preposition **a** is used with the following verbs:

abituarsi a	*to get used to*
affrettarsi a	*to hurry*
aiutare a	*to help*
cominciare a	*to begin*
continuare a	*to continue*
convincere a	*to convince*
decidersi a	*to decide*
divertirsi a	*to have fun*
fare meglio a	*to be better off*
fare presto a	*to do quickly*

imparare a	to learn
insegnare a	to teach
invitare a	to invite
mandare a	to send
obbligare a	to oblige
pensare a	to think about
persuadere a	to convince/persuade
provare a	to try
rinunciare a	to give up
riprendere a	to resume
riuscire a	to succeed
sbrigarsi a	to hurry

With verbs of movement use the preposition **a** with the following verbs:

andare a	to go
correre a	to run
fermarsi a	to stop
passare a	to stop by
ritornare a	to return
stare a	to stay
tornare a	to return
venire a	to come

Exercise 205

Translate the following sentences into Italian using the idiomatic expressions.

1. She looks like her father.

_____.

2. I feed the dogs and the cats.

_____.

3. The cat chases the mouse.

_____.

4. Carlo listens to the doctor.

_____.

5. The kids kick the ball.

_____.

6. We pay attention to the lesson.

_____.

7. We play Ping-Pong.

_____.

8. They are invited to the concert.

_____.

9. I am thinking about my mother.

_____.

10. Remind Giovanna to be on time.

_____.

11. I will not give up my airplane ticket to Italy.

_____.

12. I shook hands with the president.

_____.

Many verbs and expressions in Italian are followed by the preposition **di**. Some common verbs followed by the preposition **di** + a noun or pronoun are:

accorgersi di	*to notice*
avere bisogno di	*to need*
avere paura di	*to be afraid of*
dimenticarsi di	*to forget*
fidarsi di	*to trust*
innamorarsi di	*to fall in love*
interessarsi di	*to be interested in*
lamentarsi di	*to complain*
meravigliarsi di	*to be surprised at*
nutrirsi di	*to feed on*
occuparsi di	*to look after*
pensare di	*to think about*
preoccuparsi di	*to worry about*
ricordarsi di	*to remember*
ridere di	*to laugh at*
soffrire di	*to suffer from*
trattare di	*to deal with*
vivere di	*to live on*

Sometimes a conjugated verb is followed by **di** before a verb infinitive. Here are some verbs that are followed by **di** + an infinitive:

accettare di	*to accept*
ammettere di	*to admit*
aspettare di	*to wait for*
augurare di	*to wish*
avere bisogno di	*to need*
chiedere di	*to ask*
confessare di	*to confess*
consigliare di	*to advise*
contare di	*to plan*
credere di	*to believe*
decidere di	*to decide*
dimenticare di	*to forget*
dubitare di	*to doubt*
finire di	*to finish*
ordinare di	*to order*
pensare di	*to plan*
permettere di	*to pemit*
pregare di	*to prohibit*
promettere di	*to promise*
proporre di	*to propose*
ringraziare di	*to thank*
sapere di	*to know*
smettere di	*to stop*
sperare di	*to hope*
suggerire di	*to suggest*
tentare di	*to attempt*

Exercise 206

Translate the following sentences into Italian.

1. I need flour and eggs.

_____.

2. You (sing.) are afraid of mice.

_____.

3. He always forgets his books.

_____.

4. She doesn't trust anybody.

_____.

5. Carla is in love with him.

_____.

6. I am surprised at them.

_____.

7. They constantly worry about him.

_____.

8. You (pl.) suffer a lot because of this.

_____.

9. She laughs at everything.

_____.

10. One doesn't live on bread alone.

_____.

Some verbs are followed by the preposition **su** in an expression. Following are some common expressions using **su**:

contare su	*to count on*
giurare su	*to swear on*
riflettere su	*to reflect on*
scommettere su	*to bet on*

Verbs followed directly by an infinitive

Some commonly used verbs can be followed directly by an infinitive without needing the help of a preposition.

amare	*to love*
desiderare	*to wish*
dovere	*to have to*

fare	to make; do
gradire	to appreciate
lasciare	to let, allow
piacere	to like
potere	to be able
preferire	to prefer
sapere	to know how
volere	to want

Io **desidero conoscere** quella ragazza italiana.	*I **wish to meet** that Italian girl.*
Lei **preferisce parlare** l'inglese con i suoi amici.	*She **prefers to speak** English with her friends.*
Noi **vogliamo imparare** a pattinare.	*We **want to learn** how to skate.*

Exercise 207

Translate the following sentences into Italian.

1. I can count on my family.

_____.

2. He is reflecting on his mistakes.

_____.

3. She loves to plant flowers.

_____.

4. In the morning I appreciate drinking a good cup of coffee.

_____.

5. Italians know how to live well.

_____.

6. I bet on the wrong horse.

_____.

7. We know how to go downtown.

_____.

8. It is enough studying. Now (you pl.) go out to play.

_____.

9. It is necessary to save money.

_____.

10. They prefer speaking with the boss.

_____.

11. You (sing.) like to fly.

_____.

12. We have to remember the needy people.

_____.

13. He can stay as long as he wants.

_____.

14. She knows how to cook very well.

_____.

18

Numbers, Time, and Dates

Italian numbers, times, and dates are easy to learn because they are treated similarly in English. The particulars of each topic are discussed in this chapter.

Cardinal numbers

The cardinal numbers in Italian are:

0	zero	21	ventuno	60	sessanta
1	uno	22	ventidue	70	settanta
2	due	23	ventitré	80	ottanta
3	tre	24	ventiquattro	90	novanta
4	quattro	25	venticinque	99	novantanove
5	cinque	26	ventisei	100	cento
6	sei	27	ventisette	101	centouno
7	sette	28	ventotto	200	duecento
8	otto	29	ventinove	201	duecentouno
9	nove	30	trenta	250	duecentocinquanta
10	dieci	31	trentuno	251	duecentocinquantuno
11	undici	40	quaranta	300	trecento
12	dodici	41	quarantuno	400	quattrocento
13	tredici	48	quarantotto	500	cinquecento
14	quattordici	50	cinquanta	600	seicento
15	quindici			700	settecento
16	sedici			800	ottocento
17	diciassette			900	novecento
18	diciotto				
19	diciannove				
20	venti				

1,000	mille	100,000	centomila
1,001	milleuno	1,000,000	un milione
2,000	duemila	2,000,000	due milioni
3,000	tremila	1,000,000,000	un miliardo

Uno is the only cardinal number to agree in gender with the singular noun it modifies. It has the same forms as the indefinite article.

Mangio **una** mela. *I eat **one** apple.*

When used as a pronoun, **uno** is used for the masculine and **una** for the feminine.

Abbiamo un figlio solo. Ne abbiamo **uno** solo. *We have only a son. We have only **one**.*

The shortened form **un** can be used for **uno** when it is followed by a noun. Otherwise it remains **uno**.

Ho **ventun anni**. *I am **twenty-one years** old.*

But:

Quanti anni hai? Ne ho **ventuno**. *How old are you? I am **twenty-one**.*

Venti, trenta, quaranta, and **novanta** drop the final vowel before combining with **uno** and **otto**. When they combine with **tre**, the final -e takes an accent (**tré**).

trentuno	*thirty-one*
trentatré	*thirty-three*

Mille (*one thousand*) becomes **mila** in the plural.

duemila *two thousand*

When **milione** and **miliardo** are used as nouns, they are joined to the following noun by the preposition **di**. When **milione** and **miliardo** are followed by other numerals **di** is omitted. For example:

In questa città ci sono **dieci milioni di abitanti**. *Ten million people live in this city.*

La casa costa **un milione settecentomila** dollari. *The house costs **one million seven hundred thousand** dollars.*

Cento and **mille** are never preceded by the numeral **un**. When saying **cento** or **mille** one is already saying *one* hundred and *one* thousand.

Ho **cento** messaggi da rispondere.	*I have **one hundred** messages to answer.*
Ho **mille** ragioni per non venire.	*I have **one thousand** reasons not to come.*

Multiple numbers are often written as one word.

nel millenovecentonovantanove	*in 1999*

Numbers used as nouns

Certain numbers are used as collective nouns to express a rounded or approximate number. To use a number as a noun or to approximate a number, add **-ina** or **-aio** to the end of the number word. The new word is then followed by **di** + a noun and agrees with the noun it refers to. The most commonly used are:

una decina	*about ten*
una dozzina	*a dozen*
una quindicina	*about fifiteen*
una ventina	*about twenty*
una cinquantina	*about fifty*
un centinaio	*about one hundred*
un migliaio	*a thousand*

Exercise 208

Rewrite the following numbers in Italian.

1. 12.000 dollari

_____

2. 750 franchi svizzeri

_____

3. 221 dinar

_____

4. 835 franchi francesi

_____

5. 5.210 dollari canadesi

_____

6. 3.450.215 yen giapponesi

_____

7. 21 euro

_____

8. 33 franchi svizzeri

_____

9. 48 sterline inglesi

_____

10. 388 marchi tedeschi

_____

Ordinal numbers

Except for the first ten numbers, ordinal numbers are formed by dropping the final vowel of the cardinal number and adding -**esimo**.

primo(-a/-i/-e)	_1st_	undicesimo	_11th_
secondo(-a/-i/-e)	_2nd_	dodicesimo	_12th_
terzo	_3rd_	tredicesimo	_13th_
quarto	_4th_	quattordicesimo	_14th_
quinto	_5th_	ventesimo	_20th_
sesto	_6th_	ventunesimo	_21st_
settimo	_7th_	ventitreesimo	_23rd_
ottavo	_8th_	trentesimo	_30th_
nono	_9th_	centesimo	_100th_
decimo	_10th_	millesimo	_1000th_

Ordinal numbers agree in gender and number with the noun they modify.

Questa è la **prima** volta che vado *This is my **first** time to Italy.*
    in Italia.
Lui è il **primo** della classe. *He is the **first** of the class.*

In Italian the use of ordinal numbers is similar to that in English, except before numbers of popes and rulers. In this instance, Italian omits the definite article.

Papa Giovanni Paolo **secondo** *Pope John Paul **the Second***
Enrico **quinto** *Henry **the Fifth***

Cardinal numbers ending in **tré** form the ordinal number by dropping the accent and retaining the final -e before the **-esimo** ending.

ventitreesimo(-a/-i/-e) *twenty-third*
trentatreesimo(-a/-i/-e) *thirty-third*

The following forms of the ordinal numbers refer to centuries from the thirteenth century on. These are mostly used when referring to literature, art, and history rather when than referring to numbers.

il Duecento	*the 13th century (i.e., the 1200s)*
il Trecento	*the 14th century*
il Quattrocento	*the 15th century*
il Cinquecento	*the 16th century*
il Seicento	*the 17th century*
il Settecento	*the 18th century*
l'Ottocento	*the 19th century*
il Novecento	*the 20th century*
il Duemila	*the 21st century*

Exercise 209

Fill in the blanks with the ordinal numbers that correspond to the numbers in parentheses.

1. È la _____ (1) volta che vado a cavallo.

2. È la _____ (3) volta che ti dico di stare zitta.

3. È la _____ (2) volta che mangio le rane.

4. È la _____ (6) volta che andiamo a sciare.

5. È la _____ (4) volta che vedo il film: «La vita è bella».

6. Sono le _____ (1) volte che cammina da solo.

7. È il _____ (1) ad arrivare al traguardo.

8. Il cavallo è arrivato al _____ (1) posto.

9. Sono nella _____ (15) brigata militare.

10. Sono i _____ (10) in coda.

The adjective **mezzo(-a/-i/-e)**, meaning *half*, can precede or follow a noun. When it precedes the noun it modifies, **mezzo** agrees with the noun. When it follows the noun it modifies, **mezzo** will not usually agree with it.

una mezz'ora   *half an hour*

But:

un'ora e mezzo (*or* mezza)   *an hour and a half*

Exercise 210

Fill in the blanks with the words for the numbers in parentheses.

1. Il _____ (XVIII) secolo.

2. Vittorio Emanuele _____ (II).

3. Il _____ (4°) piano.

4. Il _____ (15°) anniversario.

5. Papa Pio _____ (XII).

6. Ho comprato _____ (12) uova.

7. Io guido _____ (60) chilometri al giorno.

8. Nel _____ (900) c'erano poche macchine.

9. Sono venuta a casa tua _____ (3) volte.

10. Roberto è il _____ (2°) figlio.

11. Questo è _____ (¼) del terreno.

12. Ci saranno una _____ (15) di ragazzi.

Time

There are two ways in Italian to ask for the time.

Che ora è?	*What time is it?*
Che ore sono?	*What time is it?*

The answer is singular if it is one o'clock, noon, or midnight. It is plural with all the other hours.

È l'una.	*It is one o'clock.*
Sono le due.	*It is two o'clock.*
Sono le due e dieci.	*It is ten after two.*
Sono le tre meno dieci.	*It is ten to three.*
Sono le sei e un quarto.	*It is a quarter after six.*
Sono le tre e quindici.	*It is three fifteen.*
Sono le otto e mezzo (mezza).	*It is half past eight.*
Sono le otto e trenta.	*It is eight thirty.*
Sono le due meno un quarto.	*It is a quarter to two.*
È l'una e quarantacinque.	*It is one forty-five.*
È mezzogiorno.	*It is noon.*
È mezzanotte.	*It is midnight.*

To express time after the hour, Italian uses **e** (*and*) + the number of minutes. **Un quarto** expresses *a quarter* of an hour, **mezzo** (**mezza**) or **trenta** expresses *half past* the hour.

To express time before the hour, **meno** (*less, minus*) is used. The verb **mancare** (*to lack*) may be used in place of **meno**.

Sono le sette **meno** cinque.	*It is five minutes to seven.*
Mancano cinque minuti alle sette.	*It is five minutes to seven.*

To ask *at what time* something will happen, **A che ora?** is used. The answer is expressed with the preposition **a** (*at*) before **mezzogiorno** (*noon*) and **mezzanotte** (*midnight*). And **a** + the definite article is used before all other times, except for one o'clock which takes **all'**.

all'una precisa	*at exactly one o'clock*
all'una in punto	*at exactly one o'clock*
alle due	*at two o'clock*
alle tre	*at three o'clock*

Some more time expressions are:

le sette del mattino (di mattina)	*seven o'clock in the morning*
le due del pomeriggio	*two o'clock in the afternoon, 2:00 P.M.*
le sette di sera	*seven in the evening, 7:00 P.M.*
verso le otto	*about eight o'clock*
mezzogiorno e mezzo	*half past noon*
mezzanotte e trenta	*half past midnight*
un quarto d'ora	*a quarter of an hour*
una mezz'ora	*a half hour*

Il mio orologio è avanti di dieci minuti.	*My watch is ten minutes fast.*
Il mio orologio è indietro di dieci minuti.	*My watch is ten minutes slow.*

In Italian the expressions A.M. and P.M. are expressed with **di mattina** (A.M.), **di pomeriggio** (P.M., from 1:00 P.M. to 4:00 P.M.), **di sera** (from 5:00 P.M. to 9:00 P.M.), and **di notte** (from 10:00 P.M. on).

The twenty-four-hour clock (or official time) is commonly used in Italian with midnight as the zero hour. This system is used throughout Italy by banks, businesses, shops, transportation services, the military, movies, TV, and trains, so it is very important to become familiar with it. In the twenty-four-hour clock, all times are expressed in full numbers. The United States refers to this system as military time. The way to express time commonly used at home in Italy is referred to as colloquial time. Colloquial time is the time more commonly used in the United States. Some common official time expressions are:

0,30	*12:30 A.M.*
le 13,00	*1:00 P.M.*
le 20 e 30	*8:30 P.M.*
le 24	*midnight*

In Italian the definite article is *always* used before the hour.

le tre	*3:00 P.M.*
le cinque	*5:00 P.M.*

The definite article is not used before the words **mezzogiorno** and **mezzanotte**.

Exercise 211

Answer the following questions with complete sentences. Use the colloquial time unless otherwise instructed.

1. Che ora è? (*9:00* A.M.)

_____.

2. Che ore sono? (*2:00* P.M. *official time*)

_____.

3. A che ora ti svegli? (*7:00* A.M.)

_____.

4. A che ora vai a lavorare? (*8:00* A.M.)

_____.

5. Quanto mancano alle due? (*10 minutes*)

_____.

6. Quando esci dal lavoro? (*6:00* P.M.)

_____.

7. A che ora prendi il treno? (*5:00* P.M. *official time*)

_____.

8. Che ore sono? (*midnight*)

_____.

9. A che ora andiamo al ristorante? (*9:00* P.M. *official time*)

_____.

10. A che ora arrivi in ufficio? (*8:00* A.M. *sharp*)

_____.

11. A che ora apre la banca? (*8:30* A.M.)

_____.

12. A che ora cenate? (*8:30* P.M. *official time*)

_____.

Dates

Throughout this book the following terms have been used, but it is important to mention them again here, since they are common in Italian. The days of the week, the months, and the seasons are not capitalized in Italian.

il giorno	*the day*
la settimana	*the week*
il mese	*the month*
l'anno	*the year*
oggi	*today*
domani	*tomorrow*
ieri	*yesterday*

There are various ways to ask what day it is in Italian:

Che giorno della settimana è oggi?	*What day of the week is it?*
Qual'è la data oggi?	*What is today's date?*
Quanti ne abbiamo oggi?	*What is today's date?*
Che giorno è oggi?	*What day is today?*

Days of the week

All days of the week in Italian are masculine except Sunday (**la domenica**). The days of the week in the Italian calendar are usually listed starting with Monday and not Sunday and are not capitalized as is done in English. The days of the week are as follows:

lunedì	*Monday*
martedì	*Tuesday*
mercoledì	*Wednesday*
giovedì	*Thursday*
venerdì	*Friday*
sabato	*Saturday*
domenica	*Sunday*

The preposition *on* used in English before days of the week is not expressed in Italian. To express *on Mondays*, *on Tuesdays*, and so on, Italian uses the day of the week preceded by the definite article. The idea of *every*, is expressed by using **ogni**.

Abbiamo la lezione di italiano **il lunedì**.	*We have Italian lessons **on Mondays**.*
Abbiamo la lezione di italiano **lunedì**.	*We have Italian lessons **on Monday**.*
	(but only this Monday)
Abbiamo la ginnastica **ogni** lunedì.	*We have gymnastics **every** Monday.*

When referring to *last week*, *last year*, and so on, Italian uses **scorso(-a/-i/-e)** or **fa** after the noun it modifies. **Scorso** can be placed before or after the noun it modifies, but **fa** can only follow it. **Scorso** agrees in gender and number with the noun it modifies; **fa** does not change. To express time that has not yet elapsed, **prossimo** (*next*) is used. **Prossimo** is placed before or after the noun it modifies and agrees in gender and number with it.

la settimana **scorsa**	*last week*
una settimana **fa**	*a week ago*
la **prossima** settimana	*next week*

Exercise 212

Translate the following sentences into Italian.

1. I went to Italy a month ago.

_____.

2. I saw my parents three weeks ago.

_____.

3. Today we will sleep late.

_____.

4. She was in church last Sunday.

_____.

5. I (f.) am free on Thursday.

_____.

6. They come to see us next week.

_____.

7. Next Monday we will go to Carla's.

_____.

8. Next week we will have a party.

_____.

9. Friday and Saturday are my favorite days.

_____.

10. On Saturday I will go to the market.

_____.

11. He is free only on Wednesdays.

_____.

12. We will see you on Friday.

_____.

13. We play soccer every Saturday.

_____.

14. Erica and Lara have gymnastics every Monday and Thursday.

_____.

Months of the year

All the months of the year are masculine and, just as with the days of the week, are not capitalized.
To express the English word *in* with months, **in** or **a** is used in Italian.

gennaio	*January*
febbraio	*February*
marzo	*March*
aprile	*April*
maggio	*May*
giugno	*June*
luglio	*July*
agosto	*August*
settembre	*September*
ottobre	*October*
novembre	*November*
dicembre	*December*

Dates in Italian are expressed by using the day, then the month, and then the year: **15 maggio, 2006** and not **maggio 15, 2006** as is done in English.

Use **il primo** for the first day of the month (**il primo gennaio,** *January 1*). For the other days of the month, the cardinal numbers (**due, tre, quattro...**) are used. The preposition **di** can follow the number in this expression (**il primo** *di* **gennaio**) but is not necessary. Before numbers beginning with a vowel, like **otto** and **undici,** the definite article is apostrophized.

Il **primo** di maggio in Italia è festa.	*The **first** of May is a holiday in Italy.*
Il **quattro** (di) luglio è la festa dell'indipendenza in America.	*The **fourth** of July is Independence Day in America.*

The word *on* used in English, is not used with dates in Italian. Instead the definite article is used.

il 15 agosto	*on August 15*

If no date is expressed with a month, **in** or **a** can be placed before the name of the month to say *in January, in February,* and so on.

In/a gennaio fa molto freddo.	*In January it is very cold.*
Nel mese di gennaio fa molto freddo.	*The **month** of January is very cold.*

Exercise 213

Translate the following sentences into Italian.

1. It is the first of May.

_____.

2. Today is Monday.

_____.

3. School ends on June 8.

_____.

4. We go to California in July.

_____.

5. August 15 is a big holiday in Italy.

_____.

6. She was born on October 12, 1964.

_____.

7. We got married in August.

_____.

8. January 1 is the first day of the year.

_____.

9. She studied in Italy during July and August.

_____.

Seasons and years

In Italian *spring* and *summer* are feminine, *fall* and *winter* are masculine.

la primavera	*spring*
l'estate	*summer*
l'autunno	*autumn, fall*
l'inverno	*winter*

Unlike English, Italian expresses years only in thousand and hundreds. English will say *nineteen hundred and ninety-nine*, but Italian uses **millenovecentonovantanove** (*one thousand nine hundred ninety-nine*). When referring to a single year, the definite article is always used.

il 1492	*1492*
il millequattrocentonovantadue	*1492*

This is usually shortened in everyday speech to **nel '92** if the century is known.

When expressing decades the preposition (**di**, **in**, or **per**) + the definite article + **anni** is used in front of the year.

Mi piace la musica **degli anni '80**.	*I like the music of the '80s.*
Viaggiavamo molto **negli anni '70**.	*We used to travel a lot in the '70s.*
Mi è piaciuto molto la libertà **degli anni sessanta**.	*I really liked the freedom of the '60s.*

Exercise 214

Translate the following sentences into Italian.

1. He was born on January 1, 1995.

_____.

2. She started school on August 25, 1998.

_____.

3. The movies of the '60s were very good.

_____.

4. My mother doesn't like the music of the '80s.

_____.

5. This is 2007.

_____.

6. He graduated in 1998.

_____.

7. Last year, in January, we had a big snow storm.

_____.

8. The summer of 2003 was very hot.

_____.

9. 1997 was an excellent year for wine.

_____.

10. My life changed completely in July 1999.

_____.

11. What day is today?

_____?

12. Today is Tuesday.

_____.

13. What is today's date?

_____?

14. Today is the 13th.

_____.

19

Exclamations

Exclamations express strong feelings of admiration, disgust, pleasure, satisfaction, dismay, pain, surprise, and horror. They usually consist of one or several words. Exclamation words in Italian are usually used in the beginning of a sentence and followed by a phrase beginning with **che, come,** and **quanto.** The meaning of exclamations changes depending on the tone of voice one uses, on the gestures one makes, or on the phrase that follows the exclamation. The following list shows some common exclamations and how they are used. Some are impossible to translate and it is necessary to understand them by the *way* they are used.

Uncertainty/incredulity	**Boh!** (*Who knows!*); **Mah!, Beh!, Chissà!** (*Who knows!*); **Macché!** (*No way!*)
Surprise/wonder	**Ah!, Oh!, Caspita!** (*Good heavens!*); **Per bacco!** (*By Jove!*); **Diamine!** (*On earth!*)
Joy/goal achieved	**Hurrà!** (*Hurray!*); **Evviva!** (*Hurray!*)
Sorrow/physical pain	**Ah!, Ahia!** (*Ouch!*); **Peccato!** (*Pity!*); **Ahimè** (*Alas!*)
Tiredness/boredom/disgust	**Uffa!** (*Auf!*); **Pugh!** (*Pugh!*); **Bleh!** (*Bleh!*)
Impatience	**Cribbio!** (*Crikey!*); **Accidenti!** (*My goodness!*)
Invocation	**Mamma mia!, Mio Dio!** (*My God!*); **Pietà!** (*Mercy!*)
Greetings	**Ciao!** (*Bye!*); **Salve!** (*Hello!*); **In bocca al lupo!** (*Good luck!*)
Courtesy	**Congratulazioni!** (*Congratulations!*); **Grazie!** (*Thank you!*)

Cribbio che freddo che fa oggi!	*Crikey, how cold is today!*
Caspita come sei pesante!	*Good heavens, how heavy you are!*

Che is usually placed before nouns and is the equivalent of the English use of *How!* and *What!*

Che caldo fa oggi!	*How warm it is today!*
Che bellezza!	*How nice!*

Che is also used with emphatic adjectives such as **Favoloso!** (*Fabulous!*) and **Meraviglioso!** (*Wonderful!*) and must be followed by a noun. It cannot be used with an adjective alone.

Che torta meravigliosa!	*What a wonderful cake!*
Che casa favolosa!	*What a fabulous house!*

Che can be used with a masculine singular adjective to express a general comment.

Che bello!	*How nice!*
Che brutto!	*How ugly!*
Che strano!	*How strange!*

Che can also be used with an adjective, which agrees with the noun it modifies. Sometimes it is replaced by **come + essere**.

Che brava!	*How good she is!*
Che brava bambina!	*What a good girl!*
Che bel vestito!	*What a nice dress!*

Or:

Com'è brava!	*How good she is!*
Com'è bello questo vestito!	*How nice this dress is!*

Che is also used in combination with the relative pronoun **che** (*that*) followed by a verb.

Che male **che** mi fa la gamba oggi!	*How sore is my leg today!*

Come (*how*) as an exclamation is used before a complete sentence.

Come fa freddo in Alaska!	*How cold it is in Alaska!*

Quanto (*what, how much*) is used before a noun, agrees with it, and it emphasizes amount.

Quanto rumore!	*What a lot of noise!*
Quante persone!	*How many people!*

Quanto can also be used before verbs as an invariable adverb that modifies the verb.

| Quanto hai studiato! | *What a lot* you have studied! |
| Quanto ha pianto (lei)! | *How much* (she) cried! |

When **quanto** is used with **essere**, it replaces **come** + **essere**, especially if it expresses quantity.

| Quant'è intelligente tuo figlio! | *How intelligent your son is!* |
| Quant'è sporca questa casa! | *How dirty this house is!* |

Exercise 215

In complete sentences, express your admiration using **che** and the adjectives in parentheses.

1. macchina (bella)

_____!

2. fiori (profumati)

_____!

3. casa (magnifica)

_____!

4. storia (interessante)

_____!

5. film (spaventoso)

_____!

6. panorama (incantevole)

_____!

7. classe (difficile)

_____!

8. viaggio (noioso)

_____!

9. persona (fortunata)

_____!

10. uomo (gentile)

_____!

Exercise 216

Fill in the blanks with **quanto(-a)** or **come**.

1. _____ va veloce quella macchina!

2. _____ bella frutta hai comprato!

3. _____ tempo hai sprecato!

4. _____ è difficile questa lezione!

5. _____ gente c'era al cinema ieri!

6. _____ è bello quel film!

7. _____ parlano quelle donne!

8. _____ parlano forte quelle donne!

9. _____ tempo che non la vedo!

10. _____ è bello il Lago di Como!

20

Additional Exercises for Further Practice

The following exercises will give you extra opportunity to review and reinforce your command of the grammar learned throughout the book. The exercises are grouped by the different parts of speech.

Nouns and Articles

Exercise 217

Add the definite article to each of the following nouns.

1. _____ borsa
2. _____ casa
3. _____ cielo
4. _____ porta
5. _____ portone
6. _____ tazza
7. _____ uccello
8. _____ valle
9. _____ violino
10. _____ zanzara

Exercise 218

Add the definite article to each of the following nouns.

1. _____ cameriere
2. _____ clima
3. _____ colazione

4. _____ crisi

5. _____ fantasma

6. _____ foto

7. _____ oca

8. _____ stazione

9. _____ temporale

10. _____ turista

Exercise 219

Add the indefinite article to each of the following nouns.

1. _____ auto

2. _____ canzone

3. _____ leone

4. _____ mano

5. _____ pappagallo

6. _____ piede

7. _____ settimana

8. _____ stazione

9. _____ storia

10. _____ zio

Exercise 220

Change the following nouns and articles from singular to plural.

1. la cantante _____

2. il fratello _____

3. il giornale _____

4. il lago _____

5. la mano _____

6. la patata _____

7. il poeta _____

8. la poetessa _____

9. il turista _____

10. lo zaino _____

Pronouns

Exercise 221

Complete each of the following sentences with the appropriate subject pronoun.

1. _____ non ho comprato la pasta.

2. _____ hai scritto la lettera.

3. _____ (m.) guida una bella macchina.

4. _____ (f.) è andata al cinema.

5. _____ abbiamo fame e sete.

6. _____ viaggiate spesso.

7. _____ fanno i dolci per le loro amiche.

8. Maria, _____ vai in chiesa oggi?

9. Marco, _____ lavori tutto il giorno?

10. _____ spediamo un pacco in Italia.

Exercise 222

Complete each of the following sentences with the appropriate direct object pronoun.

1. Maria, compri la carne? Sì, _____ compro.

2. Carla invita le sue amiche? Si, _____ invita.

3. Hai capito la lezione? No, non _____ ho capita.

4. Chiudiamo la porta. _____ chiudiamo.

5. Studiano sempre l'italiano. _____ studiano sempre.

6. Visitate i nonni. _____ visitate.

7. Hai comprato la rivista? No, non _____ ho comprata.

8. Ascoltiamo la musica tutte le sere. _____ ascoltiamo.

9. Oggi lavo le tende. Oggi _____ lavo.

10. Mangiate le castagne? Sì, _____ mangiamo.

Exercise 223

Fill in each blank with the appropriate direct object pronoun.

1. Voglio vedere il concerto. _____ voglio vedere *or* voglio

   veder _____.

2. Vuoi leggere questo libro? Sì, _____ voglio leggere *or* voglio

   legger _____.

3. Marco può comprare la Vespa. Marco _____ può comprare *or* può

   comprar_____.

4. Lara vuole fare i compiti. Lara _____ vuole fare *or* vuole

   far_____.

5. Dobbiamo vendere la casa. _____ dobbiamo vendere *or* dobbiamo

   vender_____.

6. Dovreste visitare il museo. _____ dovreste visitare *or* dovreste visitar

   _____.

7. Lui può comprare le riviste. Lui _____ può comprare *or* può

   comprar _____.

8. Vorrei vedere mia figlia. _____ vorrei vedere *or* vorrei

   veder _____.

9. Vuoi pulire i vetri? _____ vuoi pulire *or* vuoi pulir_____?

10. Potete chiamare i ragazzi? _____ potete chiamare *or* potete

    chiamar _____?

Exercise 224

Fill in each blank with the appropriate indirect object pronouns.

1. Io do il libro alla ragazza. Io _____ do il libro.

2. Carla parla con l'insegnante. Carla _____ parla.

3. Tu compri la macchina a tuo figlio. Tu _____ compri la macchina.

4. Giovanni manda un regalo a sua figlia. Giovanni _____ manda un regalo.

5. Noi diciamo tutto a loro. Noi _____ diciamo tutto.

6. Non telefonare alla tua amica così tardi. Non telefonar_____ così tardi.

7. La bambina assomiglia alla nonna. La bambina _____ assomiglia.

8. Preparo la pizza per voi. _____ preparo la pizza.

9. Ho regalato una bambola a mia nipote. _____ ho regalato una bambola.

10. Lei vuole bene a suo marito. _____ vuole bene.

Exercise 225

Rewrite each sentence replacing the noun with the direct and indirect object pronoun combination.

1. Ti do la mia giacca.

   _____.

2. Lei insegna l'italiano a me.

   _____.

3. Lui comprerebbe una macchina nuova a suo figlio.

   _____.

4. Noi vi scriviamo le lettere.

   _____.

5. Loro portano il telefono al padre.

   _____.

6. Paolo regala una palla al bambino.

   _____.

7. Voi date le forbici alla signora.

   _____.

8. Noi vi cantiamo una bella canzone.

   _____.

9. Carla mostra il film a noi.

   _____.

10. Silvia ha mandato un invito a noi.

   _____.

Exercise 226

Complete the following sentences with the appropriate disjunctive pronouns.

1. Il libro è _____ (for me).

2. Abbiamo ricevuto una lettera _____ (from them).

3. Giulia pensa sempre a _____ (*him*).

4. Loro dormono più di _____ (*me*).

5. Vengo a scuola con _____ (*you, sing.*).

6. Vieni a dormire da _____ (*at my house*).

7. Lei compra la casa per _____ (*you, sing.*).

8. Loro abitano nell'appartamento sotto di _____ (*me*).

9. Noi arriviamo dopo di _____ (*you, pl.*).

10. Tuo fratello va in macchina senza di _____ (*us*).

Exercise 227

Fill in each blank with the appropriate reflexive pronoun.

1. A che ora _____ svegli?

2. _____ sveglio molto presto.

3. Che cosa stai facendo? _____ vesto.

4. I bambini _____ lavano le mani quando tornano da scuola.

5. Tu _____ vesti molto in fretta.

6. Isabella _____ addormenta tardi.

7. Lui _____ siede nella poltrona.

8. Roberto e Luigi _____ mettono la giacca e la cravatta.

9. Voi non _____ pettinate mai.

10. Noi _____ divertiamo molto quando andiamo in Italia.

Exercise 228

Translate the sentences into Italian using the appropriate demonstrative adjectives and pronouns.

1. I want that white car.

_____.

2. She wants to read that magazine.

_____.

3. This is mine, and that is yours.

_____.

4. I want to buy these shoes, and you want to buy those.

_____.

5. Who is that man?

_____?

6. Who are those men?

_____?

7. Those children have received many gifts.

_____.

8. That student is very intelligent.

_____.

9. This house is too big.

_____.

10. These boys are studious; those are lazy.

_____.

Exercise 229

Complete each sentence with the pronoun *ci* or *ne* as needed.

1. Quando andate in Brasile? _____ andiamo l'anno prossimo.

2. Vorrei che tu scrivessi delle frasi. Scrivi _____ almeno due.

3. Tu vorresti comprar_____ due.

4. Non comprare questo vestito. Non _____ entri.

5. Quanto tempo _____ mette tuo padre per arrivare qui?

6. _____ mette dieci ore.

7. Hai visto i cervi? _____ ho visti tanti.

8. Con tutto questo rumore non _____ sento molto bene.

9. Devo andare in banca. Ho bisogno di soldi. Non _____ ho più.

10. Vieni con me in palestra? No, voglio andar_____ da sola.

Exercise 230

Complete each sentence with the appropriate indefinite pronoun.

1. Non c'è _____ per la strada dopo mezzanotte.

2. Il ragazzo ha letto _____ libri storici.

3. Lucia fa _____ domande.

4. _____ signore parlano troppo. _____ stanno sempre zitte.

5. Mi piacciono solamente _____ città.

6. Ho visto _____ che non mi ha riconosciuta.

7. _____ venga, deve avvisarmi.

8. _____ giocano al calcio in Italia.

9. Vorrei ascoltare _____ di buono.

10. _____ ha bussato alla porta.

Prepositions

Exercise 231

Fill in each blank with the missing preposition.

1. La chiesa è _____ mezz'ora _____ casa nostra.

2. Stiamo _____ Bologna _____ una settimana.

3. _____ mio marito piacerebbe andare _____ Italia

4. Domani veniamo tutti _____ te.

5. La casa _____ Giovanni è vicino al fiume.

6. Sta _____ casa perchè ha l'influenza _____ due settimane.

7. Il mese prossimo passiamo _____ Roma.

8. Salgono _____ treno all'ultimo minuto.

9. Entrano _____ casa perchè fa freddo.

10. Io pago solo _____ contanti.

Exercise 232

Fill in each blank with the missing preposition.

1. Andiamo _____ casa di mia mamma, ma c'è sempre troppo _____ mangiare.

2. I ragazzi hanno bisogno _____ mangiare bene.

3. Ho sete. Ho bisogno _____ bere qualcosa.

4. Loro vengono _____ Milano.

5. Conosco la mia amica _____ tanti anni.

6. Studia l'Italiano _____ tre mesi.

7. Vuole studiare l'italiano _____ un semestre in Italia.

8. La mia giacca è _____ lana.

9. Lui è sempre _____ buon'umore.

10. Il dottore e sua moglie sono _____ Napoli.

Exercise 233

Complete each sentence with the appropriate preposition.

1. Mio marito ha comprato questo anello _____ me.

2. La mia amica è partita _____ l'Italia e ritorna _____ due settimane.

3. Mandagli il pacco _____ posta.

4. Ti comunicherò il mio itinerario _____ via fax.

5. Gabriele parte _____ l'Italia _____ sua nonna.

6. Forse arrivano domani _____ l'ultimo aereo.

7. La partenza sarà _____ dieci minuti.

8. Io parto _____ macchina _____ un'ora.

9. _____ me e te c'è _____ mezzo il mare.

10. Il cane tiene l'osso _____ i denti.

Exercise 234

Fill in each blank with the appropriate preposition or prepositional contraction.

1. Lui aspetta sua moglie davanti _____ teatro.

2. Luigi oggi va _____ dottore.

3. Marcello è andato _____ stadio _____ vedere la partita _____ Milan.

4. Non conosco il numero di telefono _____ suoi genitori.

5. La vita _____ monaci _____ conventi è molto dura.

6. Vivono vicino _____ lago _____ Ginevra, ma sono lontani _____ centro.

7. Verremo _____ festa, ma dipende _____ tempo.

8. Il nonno passa molte ore _____orto.

9. La polizia cerca qualcosa _____ borsa _____ mia amica.

10. Maria viene _____Italia e John _____ Stati Uniti.

Exercise 235

Complete the following sentences with the appropriate prepositions or prepositional contractions.

1. Siamo invitati a cena _____ vicini.

2. Hanno la casa _____ un grande parco nascosto _____ pini.

3. Davanti _____ casa c'è un magnifico giardino.

4. Portami il libretto _____ le spiegazioni.

5. _____ lunedì _____ venerdì ci sono cinque giorni.

6. Ti ho parlato _____ mia nipotina?

7. Mi piace molto parlare _____ politica italiana.

8. I danni causati _____ temporale sono molto seri. La pioggia è entrata _____ tetto e ha rovinato i mobili _____ sala da pranzo.

9. La vita _____ emigranti è molto difficile.

10. Voi venite _____ Svizzera o _____ Germania? Veniamo _____ Svezia.

Adjectives

Exercise 236

Fill in the blanks using the descriptive adjectives in parentheses.

1. La casa è _____ (*modern*).

2. Le persone anziane sono molto _____ (*wise*).

3. Questo panorama è _____ (*magnificent*).

4. Le ragazze sono _____ (*cheerful*).

5. In Africa ci sono molte persone _____ (*poor*) e poche _____ (*rich*).

6. La mia amica mi ha fatto dei dolci _____ (*delicious*).

7. Il lago è _____ (*clean*). Il mare invece è _____ (*dirty*)

   e _____ (*polluted*).

8. La tua amica è _____ (*intelligent*) ma molto _____ (*talkative*).

9. I gerani sono i miei fiori _____ (*favorite*).

10. Il tuo discorso è _____ (*interesting*) ma troppo _____ (*long*).

Exercise 237

Complete each of the following sentences with the appropriate form of the adjective in parentheses.

1. Il professore è _____ (*Australian*).

2. Il vino _____ (*French*) e quello _____ (*Italian*) hanno molto

   prestigio.

3. Il padre di suo marito è _____ (*Greek*).

4. Ci sono molti _____ (*Chinese*), _____ (*Philippinos*),

   e _____ in Italia (*Africans*).

5. _____ (*His*) padre e _____ (*his*) moglie sono andati in crociera.

6. I _____ (*my*) compagni di scuola vanno a casa con l'autobus.

7. _____ (*My*) figlio è più alto di _____ (*her*) marito.

8. Il _____ (*my*) amico è caduto e l'hanno portato in ospedale.

9. Dove abitano i _____ (*your*) genitori?

10. La _____ (*their*) abitazione si trova in un palazzo antico.

Exercise 238

Complete each sentence with the appropriate indefinite adjective.

1. Io ho dato ai poveri _____ indumento per l'inverno.

2. _____ vicino ha uno o due cani.

3. C'era _____ gente al supermercato dopo il giorno di festa.

4. La pioggia ha causato _____ danni in _____ case.

5. _____ studenti passano _____ ore in biblioteca.

6. Sulle autostrade italiane ci sono _____ incidenti d'automobile.

7. Quest'anno il fiume ha _____ acqua a causa delle piogge.

8. _____ persona dovrebbe studiare una seconda lingua.

9. _____ le mattine vorrei stare a letto anziché alzarmi per andare a scuola.

10. _____ volta che lo vedo, mi batte forte il cuore.

Exercise 239

Fill in each blank with the appropriate word for the comparative of majority, minority, or equality, using the words in parentheses as a guide.

1. Il tennis è _____ interessante _____ golf. (*more . . . than*)

2. I diamanti sono _____ preziosi _____ oro. (*more . . . than*)

3. È _____ difficile parlare _____ leggere un libro straniero.
   (*more . . . than*)

4. Il baseball è _____ interessante _____ calcio. (*less . . . than*)

5. Il sole in inverno è _____ caldo _____ in estate. (*less . . . than*)

6. Io ho _____ energia _____ miei figli. (*less . . . than*)

7. Loro parlano _____ il francese _____ tedesco. (*better . . . than*)

8. La sua vita è _____ interessante _____ mia. (*more . . . than*)

9. La sua vita è _____ interessante _____ mia. (*less . . . than*)

10. La mia vita è _____ interessante _____ la tua. (*as . . . as*)

Exercise 240

Fill in the blanks with the irregular comparatives of the adjectives in parentheses.

1. Questo dolce è _____ (*better*) di quello.

2. Maria è _____ (*older*) di tua sorella.

3. Questa è sua sorella _____ (*younger*).

4. La _____ (*older*) delle tue amiche si sposerà fra un mese.

5. Questo è il ristorante _____ (*better*) della città.

6. La pizza è _____ (*better*) della focaccia.

7. Giovanni è il _____ (*older*) dei due fratelli.

8. I suoi bambini sono _____ (*better*) dei miei.

9. Il suo dolce è _____ (*worse*) del vostro.

10. La nostra vita è _____ (*better*) della loro.

Verbs

Exercise 241

Fill in each blank with the conjugated form of the present tense of the verb in parentheses.

1. Io _____ (fare) un lavoro interessante.

2. Tu _____ (uscire) per andare all'università.

3. Oggi io _____ (stare) male. Quindi _____ (stare) a casa.

4. Lui _____ (rimanere) in montagna un altro mese.

5. Lei _____ (salire) sul primo autobus che viene.

6. Tutti gli operai di questa fabbrica _____ (essere) in sciopero.

7. Noi _____ (aprire) la porta e _____ (chiudere) la finestra.

8. Voi _____ (spingere) la porta per aprirla.

9. Quando loro _____ (salire) tu _____ (scendere).

10. Mi dimentico sempre di _____ (spegnere) la luce del corridoio.

Exercise 242

Fill in each blank with the conjugated form of the present tense of the verb in parentheses.

1. Io _____ (dovere) rinnovare il passaporto.

2. Tu _____ (dovere) fare la fotografia per il passaporto.

3. Lui _____ (volere) mandare un pacco in Italia.

4. Maria _____ (potere) chiamarmi quando ritorna a casa.

5. Noi _____ (volere) venire a trovarti.

6. Se voi _____ (volere) dimagrire, non _____ (dovere) mangiare troppo.

7. Loro _____ (dovere) spegnere le candele prima di uscire.

8. Io e Luigi _____ (volere) conoscere le vostre amiche.

9. Oggi noi _____ (dovere) andare a Milano. Quale treno _____ (dovere) prendere?

10. Tu _____ (volere) venire alla festa con noi domenica sera?

Exercise 243

Fill in the blanks with conjugated forms of the present tense of the verbs in parentheses.

1. _____ (*I like*) camminare nel bosco.

2. Ti _____ (*miss*) pochi giorni alla partenza.

3. Non gli _____ (*to remain*) niente delle belle giornate passate con loro.

4. Che cosa _____ (*to happen*) in questa casa?

5. Che cosa _____ (*to do*) tu a scuola oggi?

6. Mi _____ (*to seem*) una persona molto istruita.

7. Susanna e Michele, vi _____ (*to like*) il nuovo appartamento?

8. Mio fratello _____ (*to know*) molte persone in tutto il mondo.

9. Io non _____ (*to know*) cosa fare quando arrivo all'aeroporto.

10. Se tu _____ (*to know*) qualcuno che _____ (*to know*) l'inglese

    ti può aiutare a tradurre questo documento.

Exercise 244

Complete each sentence with the appropriate form of the formal or informal imperative.

1. (Tu) _____ (chiamare) il dottore!

2. (Lei) _____ (chiamare) il dottore!

3. (Tu) non _____ (scrivere) gli più!

4. Signora, _____ (venire) sotto il mio ombrello!

5. Carla, _____ (venire) sotto il mio ombrello!

6. Lucia e Giovanni, non _____ (partire) così presto!

7. Signori, _____ (accomodarsi)!

8. (Tu) _____ (guardare) che bel panorama!

9. Ragazzi, non _____ (usare) il telefono mentre guidate!

10. Signor Giovanni, _____ (stare) attento quando scende dalle scale!

Exercise 245

Complete each sentence with the appropriate form of the reflexive verb in parentheses.

1. La ragazza _____ (dimenticarsi) sempre tutto quello che studia.

2. Noi _____ (svegliarsi) presto, ma _____ (alzarsi) tardi.

3. Le signore _____ (fermarsi) davanti alle vetrine dei negozi.

4. Dobbiamo _____ (prepararsi) per andare alla festa.

5. Isabella _____ (annoiarsi) se non gioca con le sue amiche.

6. Io _____ (meravigliarsi) quando vedo i laghi americani.

7. I bambini non _____ (lavarsi) le mani prima di cena.

8. Noi _____ (sposarsi) in una bella chiesa.

9. Erano tanti anni che loro non _____ (parlarsi).

10. Loro _____ (chiamarsi) tutte le sere.

Exercise 246

Fill in each blank with the appropriate form of the present perfect or the imperfect tense.

1. Se vedete il vostro amico, ditegli che _____ (chiamare).

2. Loro _____ (comprare) una casa molto grande in campagna.

3. Loro _____ (volere) comprare una casa grande in campagna.

4. Isabella e Eric _____ (volere) venire, ma _____ (fare) brutto tempo.

5. Noi _____ (andare) all'aeroporto, ma l'aereo _____ (essere) in ritardo. Noi _____ (dovere) aspettare per tre ore.

6. Loro _____ (arrivare) molto tardi.

7. Loro _____ (dormire) a lungo perchè _____ (essere) stanchi.

8. Quando noi _____ (essere) piccoli, _____ (andare) spesso a fare dei safari in Africa.

9. Lui _____ (arrivare) sempre in ritardo, ma non ci _____ (avvisare) mai.

10. Mi _____ (dispiacere) molto che tu non _____ (venire) alla mia festa.

Exercise 247

Fill in the blanks using the conditional tense of the verbs in parentheses.

1. Io _____ (andare) a sciare, ma mi fanno male le ginocchia.

2. Tu _____ (comprare) una nuova lavatrice, ma non hai trovato quella che cercavi.

3. Il ragazzo _____ (dovere) alzarsi presto, ma è andato a letto tardi.

4. Voi _____ (portare) il cane con voi, ma non avete posto in macchina.

5. Loro _____ (dare) la macchina al figlio, ma non ha l'assicurazione.

6. Mi _____ (piacere) parlare molte lingue.

7. Lei _____ (essere) molto contenta di vederti.

8. Lui _____ (preferire) avere un lavoro stabile.

9. Noi _____ (cantare) nel coro, ma non sappiamo le parole e non conosciamo la musica.

10. La grandine _____ (potere) rovinare il tetto della casa.

Exercise 248

Rewrite the following sentences, changing the present conditional to the past conditional.

1. Io (f.) andrei con lei al mercato.

   _____.

2. Tu capiresti meglio la matematica.

   _____.

3. Lui spegnerebbe la luce, ma non ha trovato l'interuttore.

   _____.

4. Lisa saprebbe scrivere una poesia in italiano.

   _____.

5. Noi andremmo alla riunione, ma non ci hanno avvisati.

   _____.

6. Voi ci accompagnereste, ma la vostra macchina è rotta.

   _____.

7. Non avrebbero paura del buio.

   _____.

8. Venderebbe tutta la sua proprietà, ma non vuole muoversi.

   _____.

9. Noi consegneremmo il lavoro, ma non è finito.

   _____.

10. Loro si alzerebbero presto, ma sono molto stanchi.

   _____.

Exercise 249

Fill in each blank with the present subjunctive of the verb in parentheses.

1. Ho paura che lei _____ (ammalarsi) perchè starnutisce continuamente.

2. Mi sembra che tutti gli uomini _____ (volere) guardare la partita di calcio.

3. Speriamo che voi _____ (cominciare) a capire la matematica.

4. Voi sperate che Luisa _____ (prendere) la patente.

5. Mi sembra che loro _____ (cantare) molto bene.

6. Penso che voi _____ (venire) da noi per le vacanze di Natale.

7. Credo che loro _____ (parlare) con il capo oggi.

8. Dubito che lui _____ (giocare) d'azzardo.

9. Bisogna che lei _____ (spedire) il pacco al più presto.

10. Carlo pensa che Maria _____ (dovere) dimagrire un po'.

Exercise 250

Fill in each blank with the conjugated form of the imperfect subjunctive.

1. Avevamo paura che loro _____ (essere) ancora in ospedale.

2. La professoressa sperava che lei finalmente _____ (capire) la matematica.

3. Credevo che la ragazza _____ (prendere) la patente di guida.

4. Vorremmo che loro _____ (cantare) durante il pranzo di Natale.

5. Dubitavi che lui _____ (giocare) d'azzardo?

6. Vorresti che _____ (spedire) io il pacco?

7. Tutti vorremmo che lei _____ (dimagrire) un po'.

8. Sarei molto contenta se i miei figli _____ (venire) a casa.

9. Sarebbe molto contenta se suo figlio _____ (guadagnare) di più.

10. Pensavamo che non _____ (essere) così freddo in inverno.

Exercise 251

Fill in each blank with the conjugated form of the past or past perfect of the subjunctive of the verb in parentheses.

1. Sarebbe stato bello se voi _____ (arrivare) a casa per l'ora di cena.

2. Penso che lui non _____ (spegnere) la luce.

3. Pensavo che lui _____ (spegnere) la luce.

4. Dubiti che io _____ (capire) quello che hai detto.

5. Pensavi che io non _____ (capire) quello che avevi detto.

6. Lei era contenta che voi _____ (riposarsi).

7. Penso che lei _____ (acquistare) il biglietto per il viaggio in Brasile.

8. È probabile che voi _____ (chiamare) quando non eravamo a casa.

9. Speravamo che loro _____ (arrivare) in orario.

10. Volevano che noi _____ (rimanere) da loro per un mese.

Exercise 252

Fill in each blank with an idiomatic expression using *avere*, *fare*, or *stare*.

1. Quando i bambini ritornano da scuola _____ (*to be hungry*).

2. Io _____ (*to be hungry*), _____ (*to be thirsty*), e _____ (*to be tired*).

3. Tu _____ (*to be careful*) quando attraversi la strada.

4. Il mio serbatoio è vuoto; devo _____ (*to get gas*).

5. Spero che lei _____ (*to hurry up*), io _____ (*to be in a hurry*).

6. Lei deve _____ (*to feed*) ai bambini.

7. Quando arriva la sera io _____ (*to sigh*) di sollievo.

8. Io _____ (*to be about*) cambiare tutti i mobili in casa mia.

9. Lei dice tutto a tutti, non sa _____ (*keep quiet*).

10. Molte persone devono _____ (*to be standing*) nella metropolitana.

Answer Key

Exercise 1

1. libro 2. fiore 3. finestra 4. porta 5. casa 6. tazza 7. uccello

Exercise 2

1. pianeta 2. clima 3. fantasma 4. papa 5. pilota 6. panorama 7. mano 8. foto 9. auto 10. radio 11. professore 12. dottore

Exercise 3

1. colazione 2. stazione 3. opinione 4. pensione 5. abitudine 6. origine 7. attrice 8. città 9. onestà 10. gioventù 11. verità 12. crisi

Exercise 4

1. caso 2. casa 3. testo 4. testa 5. posto 6. posta 7. pizzo 8. pizza 9. moda 10. menta 11. torta 12. mento 13. porta 14. collo

Exercise 5

1. il turista 2. la collega 3. il nipote 4. la nipote 5. il cantante 6. la paziente 7. il consorte 8. l'elefante maschio 9. il falco 10. la tartaruga 11. la folla 12. la vittima 13. il/la fisiatra

Exercise 6

1. il figlio 2. lo zio 3. la figlia 4. la nonna 5. il signore 6. il poeta 7. la dottoressa 8. l'attore 9. lo sciatore 10. la sciatrice

Exercise 7

1. il cantante 2. il pediatra 3. il lunedì 4. la domenica 5. il gennaio 6. il luglio 7. l'oro 8. il ferro 9. il calcio 10. il melo

Exercise 8

1. la mela 2. la fragola 3. il fico 4. l'ananas 5. Roma 6. la Toscana 7. le Maldive 8. la Svizzera 9. l'Asia 10. il Brasile

Exercise 9

1. le case 2. i libri 3. i programmi 4. i poeti 5. le polveri 6. le mani 7. le auto 8. le foto 9. le crisi 10. le bici 11. le verità 12. le città

Exercise 10

1. gli sci 2. i re 3. i bar 4. le gru 5. i lunedì 6. i caffè 7. le braccia 8. le uova 9. le orecchie 10. le ginocchia 11. le dita 12. le lenzuola 13. centinaia 14. migliaia

Exercise 11

1. le amiche 2. le banche 3. le mosche 4. le dighe 5. i laghi 6. i fichi 7. gli albicocchi 8. i cuochi 9. i cataloghi 10. le maniche 11. le oche 12. i medici 13. i nemici

Exercise 12

1. i film 2. i gas 3. gli zii 4. i fruscii 5. i baci 6. gli specchi 7. gli orologi 8. i giornalai 9. le arance 10. le guance

Exercise 13

1. cacciavite 2. paracaduti 3. portafoglio 4. arcobaleno 5. pomodori 6. capolavori 7. pesce spada 8. capofamiglia 9. cassaforte 10. terracotta 11. francobolli 12. gentiluomo

Exercise 14

1. uccellino 2. casina 3. vecchietta 4. vecchietta 5. pagnotta 6. praticello 7. alberelli 8. pagnotte 9. vecchietta 10. camicina 11. ometto

Exercise 15

1. È un ragazzaccio. 2. È una stanzaccia. 3. È un poetucolo. 4. È un giovinastro. 5. Quello è un cagnaccio. 6. Quella è una casaccia. 7. È una donnaccia. 8. Quella è una stradaccia. 9. È una ragazzaccia.

Exercise 16

1. È un omone. 2. C'è uno stradone davanti alla sua casa. 3. Abitano in un palazzone. 4. È un donnone. 5. Quel'è un gattone. 6. Luigi è un mattacchione. 7. Spesso usano delle parolone. 8. Per favore, chiudi il portone in fondo alle scale. 9. Nel soggiorno ci sono tre finestrone. 10. Abbassa il tendone!

Exercise 17

1. l'ometto	l'omaccio	l'omone
2. la ragazzina	la ragazzaccia	la ragazzona
3. il gattino	il gattaccio	il gattone
4. la parolina	la parolaccia	la parolona
5. il palazzino	il palazzaccio	il palazzone
6. la stanzina	la stanzaccia	la stanzona
7. la vecchietta	la vecchiaccia	la vecchiona
8. la scarpina	la scarpaccia	la scarpona
9. l'uccellino	l'uccellaccio	l'uccellone
10. la sorellina	la sorellaccia	la sorellona
11. la macchinina	la macchinaccia	la macchinona
12. il librino	il libraccio	il librone

Exercise 18

1. I generosi 2. Le francesi 3. Gli avari 4. I belli 5. I piccoli 6. Gli americani 7. Gli aristocratici 8. I timidi 9. I poveri 10. una dozzina 11. una fetta 12. un metro

Exercise 19

1. L' 2. la 3. in 4. in 5. in 6. la, della 7. La 8. in 9. negli 10. in 11. in

Exercise 20

1. I 2. la 3. – 4. I 5. – 6. i 7. Le 8. I 9. Le 10. I 11. – 12. le

Exercise 21

1. I 2. le 3. I 4. I 5. Il 6. le 7. La 8. l' 9. il 10. – 11. – 12. La, gli, l' 13. le

Exercise 22

1. Ieri sera siamo andati a teatro. 2. È andata a fare la spesa a piedi. 3. Il mio cane è in casa. 4. Mi piace andare a scuola in bicicletta. 5. Ho spedito la lettera per via aerea. 6. Ci sono cento studenti in questa scuola. 7. Ha piantato molti fiori in giardino. 8. Gli piace andare in biblioteca. 9. Ci sono molte carte per terra. 10. Ci sono molte persone in chiesa. 11. Ogni fine settimana guidiamo in campagna. 12. Viaggiamo in macchina.

Exercise 23

1. Il 2. Gli 3. I 4. Gli, lo 5. Gli 6. Lo 7. Lo 8. L' 9. Gli, gli 10. Le, la 11. l'

Exercise 24

1. La, il 2. il 3. la 4. il, la 5. il 6. l' 7. i 8. il 9. la 10. i 11. il 12. la 13. i 14. il 15. il

Exercise 25

1. gli, il 2. Gli, il 3. l' 4. il, il 5. la, la, l' 6. i, la 7. gli, gli 8. il, il 9. gli, lo 10. la. 11. Gli, le 12. la 13. le

Exercise 26

1. delle 2. dallo 3. allo 4. con gli 5. al 6. alle 7. della 8. sul 9. dalla, alla 10. dal 11. al 12. negli

Exercise 27

1. un cane 2. una farmacia 3. un albergo 4. un'automobile 5. un parco 6. una piazza 7. un museo 8. un orologio 9. una pianta 10. una valigia

Exercise 28

1. la casa	una casa
2. la tavola	una tavola
3. il museo	un museo
4. il libro	un libro
5. la moglie	una moglie
6. la sera	una sera
7. la famiglia	una famiglia
8. la lettera	una lettera
9. l'avvocato	un avvocato
10. l'architetto	un architetto
11. lo zaino	uno zaino
12. lo zoo	uno zoo

Exercise 29

1. Mette dei soldi nel portafoglio. 2. Compra dei panini. 3. Compra del pane integrale, dei grissini e dei biscotti per la colazione. 4. Poi, la signora Bassani va dal macellaio. 5. I Bassani non mangiano molta carne. 6. Lei compra del vitello. 7. Lei compra degli asparagi, delle carote, dei piselli e delle patate. 8. Va al bar e ordina un caffè. 9. Vuole dello zucchero e del latte. 10. Prima di uscire compra delle paste. 11. Va in banca a prendere dei soldi. 12. Ritorna a casa a cucinare. 13. Quando arriva a casa si ricorda che doveva comprare dei francobolli.

Exercise 30

1. un po' di 2. nessuna 3. del 4. qualche 5. alcune 6. delle 7. dei 8. dei 9. dei 10. alcuni 11. della 12. dell' 13. alcune 14. nessuno 15. nessun

Exercise 31

1. Che cosa hai visto? 2. Ho visto l'eclissi solare. 3. L'hai vista anche tu? 4. No, non l'ho vista. 5. Loro sono cinesi e noi siamo indiani. 6. Vuoi comprare i biglietti? 7. Lui lavora molto, lei dorme molto. 8. Ho fatto questa maglia. 9. Parlano delle elezioni.

Exercise 32

1. la 2. la 3. li 4. La 5. Lo 6. lo 7. La 8. la 9. Le 10. Le 11. Le 12. Lo 13. Vi

Exercise 33

1. vederla, La 2. leggerlo, Lo 3. comprarla, La 4. comprarla, La 5. guardarli, Li 6. pulirli, Li 7. leggerli, Li 8. vederlo, Lo 9. scriverle, Le 10. berlo, Lo

Exercise 34

1. Eccolo 2. Eccoli 3. Eccola 4. Eccoti 5. Eccomi 6. Eccoci 7. firmarla 8. cantarla 9. studiarla 10. vederle

Exercise 35

1. Non l'ho comprato. 2. Laura le ha lette. 3. Laura non le ha lette. 4. Non li comprare! 5. Le ho spedite ieri. 6. Non li abbiamo studiati. 7. Lo lascia andare. 8. La guardo dalla finestra. 9. Lo faccio fare da qualcuno. 10. Signora Fanti, li finisca!

Exercise 36

1. Dallo a Maria! 2. Valla a prendere! 3. Fallo bene! 4. Dalli a Luigi! 5. Dillo forte! 6. Fallo vedere a Giovanna! 7. Dalli a Pietro! 8. Diamolo a Maria! 9. Andiamo a prenderlo! 10. Scriviamole!

Exercise 37

1. Luigi mi guarda. 2. Gli ho scritto una lunga lettera. 3. Le parli. 4. Gli parla. (Parla a loro.) 5. Maria gli scrive una lettera. 6. Le mando un regalo. 7. Gli mandi un regalo. (Mandi loro un regalo.) 8. Gli hai mandato un regalo. (Hai mandato loro un regalo.) 9. Devi mandargli un regalo. (Devi mandare loro un regalo.) 10. Vuole mandarle un regalo. (Le vuole mandre un regalo.)

Exercise 38

1. Gli mando un regalo. 2. Le telefoni. 3. Lui le risponde. 4. Il professore gli fa una domanda. (Il professore fa loro una domanda.) 5. Gli vogliono parlare. 6. Pensiamo di telefonarle. 7. Le diamo il pacco. 8. Tu gli scrivi. (Tu scrivi loro.) 9. Lei le parla. 10. Lui gli parla.

Exercise 39

1. Sì, le ho telefonato. 2. No, non li ho visti. 3. Sì, l'abbiamo comprata. 4. Sì, l'ho portata. 5. Sì, le ho telefonato. 6. No, non l'ho chiesta. 7. Sì, li abbiamo finiti. 8. Sì, l'ho mandato. 9. Sì, li ha ricevuti. 10. Sì, gli vuole bene.

Exercise 40

1. lui 2. me 3. loro 4. lui 5. voi 6. loro 7. noi 8. lui 9. lui 10. lei

Exercise 41

1. mi 2. ti 3. si 4. si 5. ci 6. si 7. vi 8. si 9. si, si 10. ti

Exercise 42

1. Glielo do. 2. Io gliela darei. 3. Maria ce la insegna. 4. Loro glielo insegnano. 5. Io glielo insegno. 6. Lui me le dà. 7. Carla gliele mostra. 8. Luisa ce le mostra. 9. Glielo porto. 10. Maurizio glielo porta.

Exercise 43

1. Io non te lo do. 2. Noi non glielo regaliamo. 3. Non me l'ha regalato. 4. Voi non ce lo avete dato. 5. Loro non te l'hanno portata. 6. Lui non gliele scrive. 7. Io non gliele do. 8. Tu non gliele dai. 9. Tu non glielo compri. 10. Lui non ve lo dice. 11. Io non glielo porto. 12. Tu non glieli compri.

Exercise 44

1. Me lo puoi dare. 2. Lui me lo vuole insegnare. 3. Ve lo preferiamo chiedere. 4. Me li devo comprare. 5. Lei te lo voleva regalare. 6. Te lo devo portare. 7. Te li dobbiamo vendere. 8. Lei non me la poteva mostrare.

9. Me li vuoi dare? 10. Me lo possono regalare. 11. Glielo vogliamo mostrare. 12. Lei te lo può leggere. 13. Gliela volevano vendere.

Exercise 45

1. Gliene parlo questa sera. 2. Gianni me ne porta alcune. 3. Don gliene manderà due o tre. 4. Me ne ha date alcune. 5. Gliene porteremo alcune. 6. Te ne sei andato senza salutare. 7. Non gliene do una(-o). 8. Se ne porta a casa due. 9. Me ne vuole mandare due. 10. Non se ne importa affatto. 11. Gliene deve molti. 12. Se ne compra due. 13. Dovresti comprargliene un paio.

Exercise 46

1. Maria, dagliela! 2. Carlo, portagliela, per favore! 3. Signorina, me ne porti una, per favore! 4. Signorina, non me la porti adesso! 5. Voglio telefonargliela. 6. Signore, me ne porti uno, per favore! 7. Marco, daglieli! 8. Carla, non raccontargliela! 9. Giovanna, chiedi a Paolo di prestartela. 10. Posso mandarglieli. 11. Facciamogliene una! 12. No, non facciamogliela!

Exercise 47

1. Luisa chiama me dalla finestra. 2. Pietro invita te. 3. Luigi non invita voi. 4. Loro invitano noi. 5. Loro telefonano a noi. 6. Tu inviti loro. 7. Io chiamo lui. 8. Noi non vediamo loro. 9. Io amo te. 10. Pietro e Luisa invitano voi.

Exercise 48

1. Questo è mio fratello e queste sono le mie sorelle. 2. Quella casa è mia e questa è di mia sorella. 3. Chi è quello? 4. Quello è un cantante famoso. 5. Quel libro è molto interessante, ma questo è noioso. 6. Questo studente è intelligente, ma quello è molto pigro. 7. Questa gente viene dall'Africa, quella viene dal Sud America. 8. Quelle mele sono più care di queste. 9. Questa rosa è molto bella, ma quella è appassita. 10. Questi bambini sono fortunati, quelli sono trascurati.

Exercise 49

Io non so ciò che ha detto Pietro. Lui parla sempre, ma non capisco ciò che dice. È difficile seguire ciò che Pietro dice e fare ciò che vuole. Preferirei che lui scrivesse ciò che vuole dire. In questo modo, non ci sarebbero malintesi e tutti potrebbero fare ciò che Pietro desidera.

Exercise 50

1. Queste, quelle 2. queste 3. Quelle, queste 4. quello lì 5. quelle 6. Queste, quelle 7. Questi, quelli 8. Questi, quelli 9. quella, Questa, Quella 10. Questo qui 11. Questo

Exercise 51

1. la tua 2. del mio 3. la tua 4. del tuo 5. dei miei 6. il tuo 7. le tue 8. le sue 9. le sue 10. il suo 11. la sua 12. la sua

Exercise 52

1. Sì, ci vado spesso. 2. No, non ci sono stato. 3. No, non ci vado da solo. 4. Sì, ci riesco. 5. Ci vado tre volte al mese. 6. Sì, ci credo. 7. Sì, ci vorrei andare. 8. No, non ci andiamo questa estate. 9. Sì, ci vedo bene. 10. Sì, ci vado spesso.

Exercise 53

1. Ci rifletto 2. Ci occorre 3. ci stanno 4. ci sento 5. ci credo 6. andarci 7. C'è stato 8. Ci sto 9. Ci vogliono 10. ci tengo

Exercise 54

1. Sì, ne preparo due tipi diversi. 2. Sì, ne voglio 1 kg. 3. Sì, ne ho mangiati due. 4. Sì, ne abbiamo due. 5. No, non ne abbiamo. 6. Sì, ne porta due. 7. Sì, ne devi comprare quattro. 8. Sì, ne compro tanti. 9. Sì, me ne occorrono quattro. 10. Sì, ne compro sei. 11. Sì, ne beviamo un po'. 12. Sì, ne conosco tre.

Exercise 55

1. Chi si sposa domenica? 2. Di chi sono queste scarpe? 3. Che cosa vuoi che io faccia? 4. Qual'è il bravo giocatore di calcio? 5. Quali sono i migliori studenti della classe? 6. Quanto vino vuoi? 7. Quanti bambini ci sono al parco? 8. Chi aspetti? 9. Di chi sono questi bambini? 10. Che cosa devo fare? 11. Chi è il più forte? 12. Quali sono i tuoi genitori?

Exercise 56

1. la quale 2. i quali 3. i quali 4. il quale 5. i quali 6. la quale 7. la quale 8. le quali 9. i quali 10. le quali

Exercise 57

1. che 2. cui 3. cui 4. cui 5. cui 6. che 7. che 8. cui 9. che 10. cui 11. cui

Exercise 58

1. in cui (nella quale) 2. di cui (del quale) 3. di cui 4. di cui (della quale) 5. di cui (dei quali) 6. a cui (al quale) 7. con cui 8. a cui (al quale) 9. da cui 10. di cui

Exercise 59

1. tutto quello che 2. quello che 3. tutte quelle 4. quelle che 5. tutte quelle 6. tutto quello che 7. tutti quelli che 8. tutto quello che 9. Quello che 10. tutto quello che 11. quello che 12. Tutti quelli che

Exercise 60

1. uno(-a) 2. qualcuna 3. uno 4. l'uno 5. l'altra 6. gli uni, gli altri 7. Ognuno 8. Ognuno 9. Ognuno 10. Ognuno

Exercise 61

1. Qualcuno 2. qualcuno 3. Qualcuno di 4. qualcun altro 5. qualcuno 6. Chiunque 7. Chiunque 8. Chiunque 9. qualcuno 10. qualcuno

Exercise 62

1. Non ti ha chiamato nessuno. 2. Non ho ricevuto nessuna lettera oggi. 3. Nessuno dei nostri figli vive vicino a noi. 4. Non ho sentito niente. 5. Nessuno vuole mangiare. 6. Non mi piace nessuno dei due. (Non mi piace né l'uno né l'altro) 7. Prometti di non dire niente. 8. Non fa niente. Ritornerò. 9. Nessuno vuole mangiare a casa. 10. Nessuno di noi vuole andare alla spiaggia. 11. Nessuno vuole vederli.

Exercise 63

1. Ho molte cose da fare. 2. Parli l'italiano? No, solo un poco. 3. Lei non ha alcun letto. 4. Loro non dormono molto. 5. So tutto quello che vuoi insegnarmi. 6. Mi piacciono molte case. 7. In quel negozio trovi di tutto. 8. Questa sera, tutti erano in classe. 9. Tutte e due avevano un vestito nuovo. 10. Tutti vanno in Italia questa estate.

Exercise 64

1. Hai molti amici? No, solo alcuni. 2. Vuoi alcune cartoline? Sì, ne voglio alcune. 3. Ognuno di voi (ragazzi) deve scrivere una lettera. 4. Ognuno di loro ha ricevuto un premio. 5. Vorresti dirgli qualcos'altro? 6. No, non ho nient'altro da dirgli. 7. Chi è rimasto in palestra? Non è rimasto nessun altro. 8. Vorresti qualcos'altro da bere? 9. No grazie. Non voglio nient'altro.

Exercise 65

1. Hai comprato questa televisione a buon mercato. 2. Sarà a casa questa sera? 3. Sono in ritardo a causa della nebbia. 4. Fate la colazione a letto. 5. Non mi piace imparare le cose a memoria. 6. La lezione comincia a pagina nove. 7. Ha mangiato tutto il cibo a poco a poco. 8. Crede nell'amore a prima vista. 9. Il vaso è caduto a terra e si è rotto. 10. Metti la maglia al posto della giacca. 11. Ci piace mangiare all'aperto. 12. Abbiamo vissuto all'estero per quattro anni.

Exercise 66

1. Mi piace andare a piedi nel bosco. 2. Non sono mai andato(-a) a cavallo. 3. A mio marito piacerebbe avere una barca a vela. 4. Amo le cose fatte a mano. 5. A scuola dovevamo imparare tutto a memoria. 6. Non sa che parla ad alta voce. 7. Mi piace la carne ai ferri. 8. La chiesa è troppo lontana per andarci a piedi. 9. In biblioteca non possiamo parlare ad alta voce. 10. Il pesce alla griglia è molto buono.

Exercise 67

1. Andremo in crociera a (in) marzo. 2. Vado a letto a mezzanotte. 3. Di solito pranziamo a mezzogiorno. 4. La mia famiglia viene a Natale e a Pasqua. 5. Devo andare. A presto. 6. Ciao, arrivederci a domani. 7. Lui fa la doccia due volte al giorno. 8. La chiamo due volte alla settimana. 9. Lavoro dalle otto alle cinque. 10. Ho comprato un bel vestito a fiori. 11. Le piace solo il gelato alla nocciola. 12. Le chiese chiudono a mezzogiorno.

Exercise 68

1. ad, a 2. a 3. ad 4. ad 5. a 6. a 7. a 8. a 9. a 10. a, ad

Exercise 69

1. Mi piace andare in Svizzera. 2. Gli piace vivere in campagna. 3. Lui va in treno. 4. Ti piace viaggiare in aereo. 5. In marzo andremo in Sud Africa. 6. In estate, viaggiano sempre. 7. Il treno è arrivato in orario. 8. Lei è sempre in ritardo. 9. Non mi piace arrivare a cena in ritardo. 10. Ci piace vedere gli alberi fioriti a primavera.

Exercise 70

1. Ho fatto un dolce in mezz'ora. 2. Ha finito i compiti in quindici minuti. 3. È andato in treno con le valige. 4. Vorrebbero vivere in Italia. 5. Siamo andati in casa a mangiare. 6. Ogni domenica telefono in Italia. 7. La lettera è nella buca della posta. 8. Tu leggi la lezione in treno. 9. Tutti leggono il giornale in treno.

Exercise 71

1. in contanti 2. in famiglia 3. in fretta 4. in mezzo 5. In quanto 6. In quattro e quattr'otto 7. in tempo 8. indietro 9. invano 10. in contanti 11. in ritardo 12. in famiglia

Exercise 72

1. Vengono da Roma. 2. Devo andare dal dottore. 3. Ha un appuntamento dal dentista. 4. Ha comprato delle belle scarpe da sera. 5. Oggi c'era tanto da fare in ufficio. 6. Non ha mai niente da dire. 7. A Natale c'è sempre troppo da mangiare. 8. Vorrei qualcosa da bere. 9. Abbiamo ancora un po' da fare a casa. 10. Vengono dalla partita.

Exercise 73

1. Ho comprato una macchina da poco. 2. Chi è quel giovane dagli occhi azzurri? 3. Da bambino(-a) piangevo molto. 4. Da giovane giocavo alla pallacanestro. 5. È una casa da pochi soldi. 6. Prendo tre francobolli da un euro. 7. Chi è quell'uomo dai capelli grigi? 8. Si comporta da persona matura. 9. Vive da principessa.

Exercise 74

1. Vuoi fare tutto da solo(-a). 2. Porta tutte le valige da solo. 3. Tagliano l'erba da sé stessi. 4. Mangiamo da soli. 5. Lui ha mangiato la cena tutto da sé. 6. Non la vedo da tanto tempo. 7. Non mi parla da un anno. 8. Non vediamo un film da tanto tempo. 9. Vivi in quella casa da quando eri bambino. 10. Non vado a sciare da cinque anni.

Exercise 75

1. Da dove 2. da parte 3. Da un lato 4. da un pezzo 5. dal mattino alla sera 6. da mattina a sera 7. da parte 8. da un pezzo 9. da dove 10. dalla

Exercise 76

1. D'improvviso 2. di nuovo 3. di mala voglia 4. Di che colore 5. di cinquant'anni 6. d'autunno 7. di moda 8. di andata e ritorno 9. di male in peggio 10. di ritardo 11. Di tanto in tanto

Exercise 77

1. Questa è la casa dei miei genitori. 2. Siamo di Napoli. 3. Va di male in peggio. 4. Vorrei fare qualcosa di interessante. 5. Non c'è niente di interessante alla TV. 6. Mio marito è sempre di buon umore. 7. È arrivato in casa di corsa. 8. La sposa non era vestita di bianco. 9. Ha bevuto la birra d'un fiato. 10. Ho perso la mia catena d'oro.

Exercise 78

1. Eravamo contenti del nostro viaggio. 2. Sono molto felice di vederti. 3. Sei sicura di saperlo? 4. Di notte fa ancora freddo. 5. Lei è triste di vederti partire. 6. Lei indossa un bel vestito di lana. 7. Vado al mercato a comprare della frutta. 8. Ci sono dei fiori che fanno un bel profumo. 9. Nella mia classe ci sono delle donne e degli uomini. 10. Voglio leggere dei bei libri.

Exercise 79

1. dal 2. d' 3. di 4. da 5. da 6. di 7. dall' 8. da 9. da 10. di

Exercise 80

1. Lui non ha amici per la sua timidezza. 2. Si lava sempre le mani per paura di malattie. 3. Non mangiano per paura di ingrassare. 4. Per l'influenza, Giacomo non ha mangiato da tre giorni. 5. Venezia è conosciuta per i suoi canali. 6. Napoli è conosciuta per la sua musica. 7. Roma è importante per la sua storia. 8. Comunicherò con te per telefono. 9. Questo materiale è per la scuola. 10. Andiamo in montagna per sciare.

Exercise 81

1. per caso 2. Per conto 3. Per esempio 4. per favore 5. per lo meno 6. Per ora 7. perciò 8. giorno per giorno 9. Mese per mese 10. per lo meno 11. Per conto 12. per caso

Exercise 82

1. con 2. con 3. tra 4. Tra/Fra 5. Con 6. Con 7. fra 8. Tra/Fra 9. fra 10. tra

Exercise 83

1. in Germania 2. negli Stati Uniti 3. in Argentina 4. del Canada 5. della Lombardia 6. in Italia 7. In Giappone 8. Nei Paesi Bassi 9. in Australia 10. in Svizzera

Exercise 84

1. Pietro impara a guidare. 2. Le italiane vanno a fare la spesa tutti i giorni. 3. Il cane si diverte a nuotare nel lago. 4. Silvia esita a parlare davanti alla gente. 5. Lo mando a imparare lo spagnolo. 6. Lei esce a comprare il giornale. 7. Marco impara a leggere. 8. Non rinunciamo ad andare in vacanza. 9. Provano (Proveranno) a chiamarci per via satellite. 10. Lui non riesce ad aprire la porta.

Exercise 85

1. Non dimenticare di telefonare a tua madre. 2. Le ho promesso di portarla allo zoo. 3. Dovrebbe smettere di fumare. 4. Cerca di arrivare in orario. 5. Lei spera di incontrarlo al parco. 6. Mi hanno pregato di andarli a visitare. 7. Lui mi ha promesso di studiare durante l'estate. 8. Sogno di avere una casa vicino al lago di Como. 9. Lei cerca di imparare le poesie a memoria. 10. Mio padre mi ha proibito di andare alla festa.

Exercise 86

1. Maria finisce di leggere la rivista. 2. Giovanna continua a pulire la casa. 3. Pietro comincia a suonare il violino. 4. Noi cerchiamo di telefonare ai nostri nonni. 5. Lei promette di portare sua figlia al cinema. 6. Voglio mettermi a imparare lo spagnolo. 7. Loro si divertono a cantare mentre lavorano. 8. Voglio imparare a sciare. 9. Lei mi aiuta a fare le valige. 10. Loro si preparano ad andare al campeggio.

Exercise 87

1. senza 2. per 3. prima di 4. senza 5. invece di 6. per 7. al 8. con 9. senza 10. prima di 11. per

Exercise 88

1. È necessario pulire tutto. 2. Oggi devi stare a casa. 3. Non possono uscire senza permesso. 4. Lei sa cucinare molto bene. 5. Lui preferisce parlare l'inglese. 6. A voi piace camminare. 7. A noi non piace camminare. 8. È necessario studiare. 9. È necessario spegnere il cellulare. 10. Desidero mangiare le ciliege.

Exercise 89

1. a 2. a 3. a 4. di 5. di 6. di 7. a 8. di 9. di 10. ad

Exercise 90

1. nel 2. allo, con gli 3. dal, alle 4. alla 5. a 6. al 7. al 8. in 9. della 10. dall', alle 11. delle 12. del

Exercise 91

1. delle 2. delle 3. del 4. della 5. dell' 6. dello 7. dei 8. dei 9. delle 10. degli

Exercise 92

1. nuova 2. calda 3. moderni 4. delizioso 5. rosse 6. studiosi 7. alti 8. generosa 9. domestico 10. giovani 11. spaziosa 12. esile

Exercise 93

1. allegri 2. avaro 3. basso, alta 4. fedele 5. delizioso 6. deliziose 7. magnifico 8. moderna, vecchia 9. piatto 10. povero

Exercise 94

1. intelligente 2. importante 3. tristi 4. interessanti 5. eccellenti 6. elegante 7. forte 8. importanti 9. umile 10. verde 11. veloci 12. triste

Exercise 95

1. i vini forti 2. i negozi nuovi 3. i bambini vivaci 4. i cani intelligenti 5. le signore eleganti 6. gli studenti studiosi 7. gli uomini famosi 8. gli animali notturni 9. i vestiti estivi 10. le strade strette

Exercise 96

1. Oggi il cielo è grigio. 2. Lui è uno scrittore poetico. 3. La maglia è larga/grande. 4. Mi piace un mondo magico. 5. Spesso, i ragazzi e le ragazze sono sciocchi. 6. Alla fine della settimana tutti sono stanchi. 7. Mio nonno è molto saggio. 8. Di solito, le persone vecchie sono sagge. 9. In estate mi piace indossare vestiti bianchi. 10. La strada è molto larga. 11. Questo vaso è antico. 12. I bambini non sono stanchi.

Exercise 97

1. pari 2. dispari 3. ciclamino 4. verde pastello 5. antinebbia 6. antifurto 7. antiruggine 8. rosa, viola 9. antifurto 10. verde scuro

Exercise 98

1. buon 2. begli 3. belle 4. bel 5. bella 6. bella, buona 7. gran 8. buono 9. belle 10. buon

Exercise 99

1. Siamo andati ad una bella gita. 2. Lei è una brava insegnante. 3. Hanno studiato la Rivoluzione Americana. 4. Le piace il vestito rosso. 5. Questo libro è facile da leggere. 6. Lui è un mio caro, vecchio amico. 7. Loro hanno dei genitori molto giovani. 8. Dopo il terremoto il tetto è barcollante. 9. Ho trovato un uccello piccolino nel giardino. 10. Il bambino è un po' troppo cicciotto.

Exercise 100

1. È la mia cara amica. 2. Ci sono diverse ragioni per traslocare. 3. Abito in una casa grande. 4. Ho letto diversi libri l'estate scorsa. 5. Ho letto libri diversi questa estate. 6. Nel Nord Italia ci sono dei bei laghi. 7. C'è un muro alto intorno a Lucca. 8. Lui aveva leggere ferite sulle gambe. 9. Tu hai una borsa leggera. 10. Nella camera c'era il massimo silenzio. 11. Questa è l'unica occasione per vederti. 12. Tu sei una persona unica.

Exercise 101

1. La tua bella casa grande è sul lago. 2. Mi piace guardare documentari di posti eleganti e lussuosi. 3. La sua morte è stata tragica e triste. 4. Tuo figlio è magro. 5. Quell'uomo è un mio vecchio amico. 6. Vorrei farti una semplice domanda. 7. Non è importante. È una domanda semplice. 8. Abbiamo un nuovo problema. Abbiamo perso il libro nuovo. 9. Mi piacciono gli anelli di pietre vere. 10. Hanno una bella casa nuova. 11. È un film insignificante e noioso.

Exercise 102

1. spagnola 2. inglese 3. svizzeri 4. francese 5. australiano 6. scozzesi 7. italiana 8. canadesi 9. greca 10. greci

Exercise 103

1. Questo giovane è mio fratello. 2. Quella casa è vecchia. 3. In quella foto puoi vedere la mia famiglia. 4. Quel libro è molto interessante. 5. Quegli studenti vengono da lontano. 6. Quello studente è estremamente intelligente. 7. Quelle persone lavorano molto. 8. Chi è quest'uomo nella fotografia? 9. Queste mele sono molto care. 10. Voglio comprare quei due pompelmi.

Exercise 104

1. il tuo 2. Sua 3. La nostra 4. i loro 5. il tuo 6. Le tue 7. i tuoi 8. i suoi 9. Il tuo 10. tuo

Exercise 105

1. I miei fratelli suonano la chitarra. My brothers play the guitar. 2. Le sue sorelle suonano il violino. His/Her sisters play the violin. 3. Le tue chiavi sono sulla tavola. Your keys are on the table. 4. I nostri zii abitano a Firenze. Our uncles live in Florence. 5. Ho perso i miei libri. I lost my books. 6. I vostri amici sono americani. Your friends are American. 7. Le nostre mamme cucinano molto bene. Our mothers cook very well. 8. A che ora arrivano le nostre sorelle? At what time will our sisters arrive? 9. Le mie macchine sono nuove. My cars are new. 10. I tuoi orologi sono eleganti. Your watches are elegant.

Exercise 106

1. Un mio vecchio amico mi ha telefonato ieri sera. 2. I loro amici hanno da fare. 3. I suoi fratelli sono alti. 4. I loro nonni sono molto simpatici. 5. Le mie due sorelle sono in Italia per un mese. 6. I loro orologi sono indietro. 7. I loro orologi sono molto cari. 8. Il suo libro è nuovo. 9. I suoi libri sono nuovi. 10. Un mio collega ha perso il lavoro.

Exercise 107

1. Non ho mai visto la sua macchina nuova. 2. La sua casa è molto grande. 3. La sua casa ha un grande giardino. 4. Il loro appartamento è in una bella zona. 5. I suoi parenti vivono lontano. 6. Le loro amiche sono molto carine. 7. Hanno dimenticato i suoi libri. 8. Hanno venduto la sua macchina. 9. La sua ragazza non è molto bella. 10. Il suo appartamento è al terzo piano.

Exercise 108

1. Alcune 2. qualche 3. Ogni 4. Degli 5. Tutti 6. Delle 7. altre 8. Ogni 9. molte 10. troppe 11. molti, poche

Exercise 109

1. Le spose indossano i vestiti bianchi. 2. Il mio colore preferito è il rosso. 3. I girasoli sono gialli. 4. Gli ho comprato una camicia rosa. 5. Il cielo è blu. 6. Mi piacciono le rose rosa. 7. Ad alcuni cantanti non piace il viola. 8. I tibetani portano indumenti arancioni. 9. In Svizzera ci sono molti edifici grigi. 10. A mio marito piace l'erba verde.

Exercise 110

1. Quale 2. Quante 3. Quali 4. Che 5. Che 6. Quanti 7. Quale 8. Quanti 9. Quale 10. Quanti 11. Quali 12. Che

Exercise 111

1. Andrò certamente alla partita la prossima settimana. 2. Gli uomini camminavano lentamente. 3. Gli uomini erano molto lenti. 4. La folla era silenziosa. 5. Fortunatamente ero a casa. 6. Era un dolce delizioso. 7. Andiamo frequentemente al cinema. 8. Molti italiani sono gentili. 9. Le ho chiesto gentilmente di sedersi. 10. È follemente inamorato di lei.

Exercise 112

1. molto 2. molte 3. molto 4. molto 5. bene 6. molto 7. troppo 8. abbastanza 9. quasi 10. molto 11. affatto 12. lentamente

Exercise 113

1. In chiesa tutti parlano piano. 2. Il viaggio in Australia costa caro. 3. La gente al mercato parla forte. 4. Lui guida velocemente. 5. Ho lavorato sodo tutto il giorno sabato. 6. Gli ho detto di andare piano. 7. Mi hanno chiesto di parlare piano (lentamente). 8. Deve andare diritto. 9. Non posso camminare veloce. 10. Gina ha speso abbastanza. 11. I tuoi amici sono molto gentili. 12. Loro parlano gentilmente. 13. Il tuo amico è troppo stanco. 14. Non camminare così veloce!

Exercise 114

1. Adesso mangio, poi studio. 2. Appena arrivo a casa, vado (andrò) a dormire. 3. Oggi ho molto da fare. 4. Li vedo raramente. 5. Lei è sempre davanti alla sua casa. 6. I bambini giocano fuori. 7. Fa freddo dappertutto. 8. Mi piace stare sotto le coperte. 9. Adesso vado a letto. 10. Carla è già andata a letto.

Exercise 115

1. Voglio ritornare a vedere di nuovo il film. 2. Le scriverò di certo. 3. L'ho vista di recente. 4. Dimmi in breve che cosa fai. 5. Ti prego di arrivare in orario. 6. Roberta è sempre in ritardo. 7. Lascia che ti guardi da vicino. 8. Lui l'ha guardata a lungo. 9. A distanza, il quadro sembra vero. 10. Lo fanno sempre apposta.

Exercise 116

1. bene 2. molto 3. Ieri 4. sempre 5. Domani 6. andare avanti 7. appena 8. affatto 9. appena 10. appena, già 11. durante 12. Oggi, troppo

Exercise 117

1. ancora 2. mai 3. sempre 4. in ritardo 5. tardi 6. presto 7. sempre 8. già 9. sempre 10. più, mai 11. ancora 12. già

Exercise 118

1. forse 2. probabilmente 3. Francamente 4. economicamente 5. assolutamente 6. veramente 7. proprio 8. certamente 9. assolutamente 10. Forse 11. davvero 12. persino 13. possibilmente

Exercise 119

1. come 2. quanto 3. come 4. quanto 5. quanto 6. quanto 7. tante 8. tanto 9. tanti 10. come

Exercise 120

1. più, del 2. più, delle 3. più , degli 4. più, che 5. più, delle 6. più, di 7. più, di 8. più, che 9. più, di 10. più, delle 11. più, della 12. più, dei

Exercise 121

1. meno, di 2. meno, che 3. meno, di 4. meno, che 5. meno, che 6. meno, che 7. meno, che 8. meno, che 9. meno, dei 10. meno che gli

Exercise 122

1. più, che 2. meno, che 3. più, che 4. più, di 5. così, come 6. così, come 7. meno, della 8. meno, che 9. tanto, quanto 10. più, che

Exercise 123

1. migliore 2. migliore 3. più grande 4. maggiore 5. più piccola 6. maggiore 7. maggiore 8. minore 9. migliore 10. più piccolo

Exercise 124

1. le più grandi 2. più bella 3. migliore 4. più difficile 5. più interessante 6. più interessante 7. più sciocco 8. più studioso 9. più bella 10. più lentamente

Exercise 125

1. Il calcio è uno sport importantissimo in Italia. 2. Il Pascoli è un poeta italiano famosissimo. 3. Il Monte Everest è altissimo. 4. I supermercati americani sono grandissimi. 5. Il caffè italiano è fortissimo. 6. Maria è intelligentissima (molto intelligente). 7. Il Colosseo a Roma è grandissimo. 8. L'aereo vola velocissimo (molto veloce). 9. La mia amica scrive moltissime lettere. 10. La lavanda è profumatissima (molto profumata).

Exercise 126

1. immenso 2. colossale 3. eccellenti 4. meravigliosi 5. infinito 6. divina 7. enormi 8. asperrimi (molto aspri) 9. eterna 10. saluberrima (molto salubre)

Exercise 127

1. bene 2. meglio 3. peggio 4. molto 5. moltissimo 6. bene 7. pochissimo 8. pochissimo 9. peggio 10. bene 11. immensa 12. peggio

Exercise 128

1. lentamente 2. più lentamente 3. estremamente 4. malissimo (molto male) 5. Stranamente 6. molto stranamente 7. più velocemente 8. freddissimamente 9. molto tardi 10. molto stranamente 11. il loro meglio 12. facilmente 13. più facilmente 14. attentamente 15. correttamente, scorrettamente

Exercise 129

1. ballo 2. canti 3. gioca 4. lavora 5. cominciamo 6. aiutate 7. aspettano 8. riposiamo 9. viaggiano 10. suona 11. provate 12. paga

Exercise 130

1. sto 2. dai 3. fa 4. andiamo 5. cerco 6. cerchi 7. paga 8. paghiamo 9. cominciate 10. mangi 11. cominciamo 12. studi

Exercise 131

1. accendo 2. attendi 3. chiede 4. chiude 5. conosciamo 6. crescono 7. insistete 8. leggono 9. metto 10. perde 11. permetto 12. piangono

Exercise 132

1. Rimangono a casa nostra per tre notti. 2. Scelgo il mio libro nuovo. 3. Lei spegne la luce. 4. Spengono il motore. 5. Lui si toglie la giacca. 6. Tieni chiusa la porta. 7. Tiene i gioielli in cassaforte. 8. Questa scatola contiene materiale pericoloso. 9. Mi siedo perché sono stanco. 10. La mamma tiene il bambino sul grembo. 11. Giovanni sceglie i fiori per sua moglie. 12. Rimango (Sto) in Italia per tre settimane.

Exercise 133

1. Devo andare a lavorare. 2. Deve studiare di più. 3. Posso fare una torta per i bambini. 4. Possiamo aspettarti. 5. Puoi andare al cinema con me? Sì, posso. 6. Sai andare all'aeroporto? 7. Sanno parlare diverse lingue. 8. Voglio mandare un pacco ai miei nipoti. 9. Vuole imparare a nuotare. 10. Oggi, dobbiamo andare a fare delle spese. 11. Potete aspettarmi qui. 12. Sai se vogliono andare con noi?

Exercise 134

1. dormo 2. copri 3. parte 4. apre 5. offre 6. offrono 7. partiamo 8. seguono 9. parte 10. sente 11. scoprono 12. partono

Exercise 135

1. finisco 2. preferisce 3. capisce 4. costruisce 5. pulisce 6. spediscono 7. ubbidiscono 8. preferiamo 9. finite 10. ingrandiamo 11. impedisce 12. capisce

Exercise 136

1. Dormo. 2. Lui apre la porta. 3. Lui costruisce un muro. 4. Mi offre una tazza di caffè. 5. Ti seguiamo. 6. Tu gli offri un bicchiere d'acqua. (Tu offri loro un bicchiere d'acqua.) 7. Apriamo il negozio. 8. Preferisco andare in autobus. 9. Preferiscono volare. 10. Lui non capisce l'italiano. 11. Lui pulisce la sua scrivania. 12. Puliscono il pavimento.

Exercise 137

1. applaudisce (applaude) 2. inghiottisce (inghiotte) 3. nutrono (nutriscono) 4. nutriamo 5. starnutiamo 6. tossiscono (tossono) 7. vengono 8. appare 9. muoio 10. muoiono 11. appare 12. odono

Exercise 138

1. Studio da un'ora. 2. Sta uscendo con lui. 3. Lui sta scrivendo un libro. 4. Il ragazzo vende i biglietti per due ore. 5. Voglio uscire, ma sta per piovere. 6. Sto per andare dal dentista. 7. Stanno per andare a letto. 8. Stai ascoltando l'opera. 9. Sto andando a letto. 10. Sta cuocendo la cena. 11. Stiamo chiudendo la porta. 12. Il bambino sta dormendo.

Exercise 139

1. Studi in Italia? 2. Lei va in chiesa tutte le domeniche? 3. Lavora lontano lui? 4. Andiamo in Italia la prossima estate? 5. Vi piace mangiare al ristorante? 6. Dov'è il museo? 7. Come andate a scuola? 8. Quando vai a prendere le bambine da scuola? 9. Dove lavora tuo marito? 10. Chi ti sta chiamando? 11. Quando viene a casa dal lavoro? 12. Quale ti piace? 13. Quante barche ha lui?

Exercise 140

1. Io non vado a Roma. 2. Tu non scrivi molto bene. 3. Lei non studia molto. 4. Lui non vuole una macchina nuova. 5. Noi non abbiamo bisogno di un computer nuovo. 6. Voi non parlate al telefono. 7. I miei amici non mi chiamano tutte le sere. 8. Voi non partite domenica. 9. Loro non aspettano i nonni. 10. Io non arrivo in ritardo. 11. No, non vado al ristorante questa sera. 12. No, non voglio chiamare mia sorella. 13. No, non ritorniamo a casa subito. 14. No, non gioco al tennis domani. 15. No, non ascolto le canzoni nuove. 16. No, non mi piace giocare a carte. 17. No, non voglio vedere un film questa sera. 18. No, i miei figli non vanno a scuola. 19. No, non vogliamo un caffè. 20. No, non ho bisogno di soldi.

Exercise 141

1. sono 2. sei 3. è 4. è 5. siamo 6. siete 7. sono 8. è 9. è 10. siete 11. siamo 12. sono 13. sei

Exercise 142

1. Lei è mia zia. 2. Carlo è molto bello. 3. Domani è sabato e noi siamo a casa. 4. A che ora è il concerto? 5. Il padre di Paola è un dottore. 6. Noi siamo italiani. 7. I miei genitori sono felici. 8. Sono molto stanchi. 9. Il cielo è blu. 10. Lei è molto elegante.

Exercise 143

1. Ho bisogno di andare in biblioteca. 2. Tu hai freddo. 3. Ho fretta. Devo prendere l'autobus. 4. I bambini hanno paura del buio. 5. In estate abbiamo sempre sete. 6. Lei ha paura di parlare davanti alla gente. 7. Ho voglia di avere un gelato. 8. Quanti anni ha tua madre? 9. Ha ottantotto anni. 10. Io non ho pazienza. 11. Vado a letto. Ho molto sonno. 12. Hai ragione. Fa freddo fuori!

Exercise 144

1. è 2. ha 3. ho 4. hanno 5. sono 6. ho 7. siamo 8. avete 9. ha 10. ha

Exercise 145

1. Ci sono 2. C'è 3. Com'è 4. Come sono 5. c'è 6. ci sono 7. Ci sono 8. Com'è 9. Come sono 10. c'è 11. ci sono 12. ci sono

Exercise 146

1. Mi (A me) piace il pesce. 2. Ti (A te) piace andare alla spiaggia. 3. Gli (A lui) piace lavorare al computer. 4. Le (A lei) piace lavorare con i bambini. 5. Ci (A noi) piace viaggiare. 6. Vi (A voi) piace visitare gli amici. 7. Gli (A loro) piace cucinare. 8. A Luisa piace parlare. 9. A Carlo piace giocare al calcio. 10. A Giovanni e Maria piace visitare i loro nipoti. 11. A Giovanni e Maria piacciono i bambini. 12. A me (Mi) piace viaggiare in aereo.

Exercise 147

1. piacciono 2. piacciono 3. piace 4. piacciono 5. piace 6. piace 7. piace 8. piace 9. piacciono 10. piace 11. piace 12. piacciono

Exercise 148

1. accade 2. serve 3. servono 4. dispiace 5. conviene 6. sembra 7. basta 8. tocca 9. succedono 10. sembra 11. interessa 12. rincresce

Exercise 149

1. Marco, ti piace il nuovo capo? Sì, mi piace molto. 2. Signora, le piacciono i fiori? Sì, mi piacciono molto. 3. Luisa, ti piace andare in palestra? Sì, mi piace. 4. Luisa, ti piace andare in palestra? No, non mi piace. 5. Elena, ti piace leggere? Sì, mi piace. 6. Elena e Franco, vi piace il nuovo corso? No, non ci piace. 7. Elena e Franco, vi piace la spiaggia? No, non ci piace. 8. A noi piace sciare, a voi no. 9. Ti piacciono i fagiolini? A noi, sì, ma a Carlo, no. 10. A lui piace il gelato, a noi, no. A lui piace il caffè, a me piace il cappuccino.

Exercise 150

1. Non conosco molte persone. 2. Tu sai suonare il piano. 3. Voi conoscete le opere italiane. 4. Lui sa il mio numero di telefono. 5. Lei conosce molti negozi buoni. 6. Noi sappiamo molte cose. 7. Mio fratello sa l'arabo. 8. Mio fratello conosce molti arabi. 9. Voi sapete dov'è il museo. 10. Voi non conoscete il museo indiano. 11. Loro sanno dipingere. 12. Loro conoscono il nome dell'imbianchino.

Exercise 151

1. Parla!   Parli!
2. Parlate!   Parlino!
3. Cammina!   Cammini!
4. Canta!   Canti!
5. Cantate!   Cantino!
6. Mangia!   Mangi!
7. Va'!   Vada!
8. Bevi!   Beva!
9. Bevete!   Bevano!
10. Pensa!   Pensino!

Exercise 152

1. Mi alzo presto. 2. Tu ti diverti. 3. Si vestono in fretta. 4. Ci sposiamo questa estate. 5. Lei si ferma davanti al museo. 6. Si fa la barba tutte le mattine. 7. Si addormentano in classe. 8. Ci laviamo le mani quando arriviamo a casa. 9. Mi preparo per uscire a cena. 10. Si annoiano. 11. Mi meraviglio. 12. Non si ricorda di niente. 13. Mi dimentico sempre di chiamarla. 14. Il sabato mi alzo tardi.

Exercise 153

1. Voglio alzarmi presto. Mi voglio alzare presto. 2. Lui vuole svegliarsi presto. Si vuole svegliare presto. 3. Vogliono farsi il bagno. Si vogliono fare il bagno. 4. Devi lavarti la faccia. Ti devi lavare la faccia. 5. Dobbiamo svegliarci presto. Ci dobbiamo svegliare presto. 6. Lui vuole addormentarsi. Si vuole addormentare. 7. Lei vuole divertirsi. Si vuole divertire. 8. Vogliamo sposarci questa estate. Ci vogliamo sposare questa estate. 9. Devi ricordarti il passaporto. Ti devi ricordare il passaporto. 10. Non posso dimenticarmi il passaporto. Non mi posso dimenticare il passaporto. 11. Dovete riposarvi. Vi dovete riposare. 12. Può farsi la barba in aereo. Si può fare la barba in aereo. 13. Non voglio mettermi le scarpe nuove. Non mi voglio mettere le scarpe nuove.

Exercise 154

1. Berrò solo l'acqua minerale. 2. Andrai in chiesa. 3. Lui mangerà a casa di sua madre. 4. Si riposerà e berrà una tazza di caffè. 5. Domani, visiterò i miei amici. 6. Gli parleremo. 7. Vedrete il lago di Como. 8. Luigi aspetterà il treno. 9. Carla abiterà in Italia. 10. Le farai una torta per il suo compleanno. 11. Non dormiremo. 12. Pagheranno il conto.

Exercise 155

1. sarò 2. arriverà 3. andrò 4. raccoglierò 5. Respirerò 6. camminerò 7. sporcherò 8. sarà 9. Chiederò 10. vorranno 11. risponderanno 12. verrà 13. andrò

Exercise 156

1. ho parlato 2. hai giocato 3. ha cantato 4. abbiamo visto 5. avete piantato 6. hanno letto 7. avete mangiato 8. abbiamo capito 9. ha suonato 10. ha bevuto 11. hanno chiesto 12. ho dormito

Exercise 157

1. Ho scritto molte lettere. 2. Le ho scritto molte lettere. 3. Avete visto gli animali allo zoo. 4. Li hai visti. 5. Non ci avete visti(-o). 6. Lei ha chiamato suo padre. 7. Lei ha chiamato i genitori. 8. Lui ci ha chiamati(-o).

9. Le abbiamo mandato un pacco. 10. Hai comprato dei bei vestiti. 11. Li ha comprati al mercato. 12. Tua madre ha pulito la casa.

Exercise 158

1. Sono stata in Italia tre settimane. 2. È andata in aereo. 3. È ritornato a casa tardi. 4. Siamo partiti all'alba. 5. Sono venuti per vedere il bambino. 6. Sua madre è partita ieri per il suo viaggio. 7. Tutti gli studenti sono ritornati in classe. 8. Giovanni è arrivato in orario. 9. Il treno è partito in ritardo. 10. Sua madre e suo padre sono rimasti a casa. 11. È venuto a casa per Pasqua.

Exercise 159

1. Erica è ritornata da scuola. 2. Lara è salita sull'ascensore. 3. Noi siamo ritornati a letto. 4. I bambini sono venuti a casa mia. 5. La nonna è scesa con il bastone. 6. Voi siete partiti per l'America del Sud. 7. Le piante sono morte. 8. Lei è nata in Africa. 9. Gli amici sono arrivati con il treno. 10. Sono andata all'aeroporto. 11. Sei andata dalla tua vecchia zia.

Exercise 160

1. Ho visto che cosa è successo a Pietro. 2. Non ho visto che cos'è successo. 3. I prezzi al supermercato sono aumentati molto. 4. Ho aumentato la dose della medicina. 5. Ci siamo divertiti molto. 6. Sono saliti sull'ascensore. 7. L'ultimo viaggio è costato molto. 8. È dovuta stare a casa, perché la macchina era rotta. 9. Si sono alzati tardi e sono arrivati tardi al lavoro. 10. L'inverno scorso, non è nevicato.

Exercise 161

1. Di solito andavo a letto presto. 2. Andavamo spesso in Italia. 3. Il sabato dormivamo tutti fino a tardi. 4. Vedevamo di frequente la partita di pallone. 5. Ogni giorno facevamo i compiti. 6. Mangiavamo sempre pane e formaggio. 7. Di solito non bevevo molta acqua. 8. Pensavo spesso ai giorni della mia infanzia. 9. Di solito facevo tante fotografie. 10. Spesso parlavano con i loro nipoti. 11. Di tanto in tanto ricevevo lettere dai miei amici.

Exercise 162

1. Ieri era molto nuvoloso. 2. Che tempo faceva in Italia? 3. Faceva freddo e pioveva. 4. Pioveva da una settimana. 5. Mia madre cucinava ed io suonavo il piano. 6. Lui leggeva il giornale tutti i giorni. 7. Lei faceva la doccia tutte le mattine. 8. Di solito, la domenica pomeriggio, andavamo al parco. 9. Che cosa scrivevi quando sono entrato(-a)? 10. Mi chiamavi spesso.

Exercise 163

1. Sciavo ogni anno. Ho sciato molto. 2. Sono andato(-a) in Africa con i miei genitori. Andavo spesso in Africa per lavoro. 3. Sei andato dal dentista. Andavi dal dentista. 4. Domenica, lei ha telefonato ai suoi figli. Telefonava ai suoi figli tutte le domeniche. 5. Le ho scritto una lunga lettera. Le scrivevo lunghe lettere. 6. Siamo andati ad una bella festa. Andavamo a delle belle feste. 7. Voi ascoltavate musica classica. Voi avete ascoltato la musica classica. 8. Ieri notte non ho dormito bene. Dormivo molto bene. 9. Ieri è andata dal parrucchiere. Andava dal parrucchiere tutti i sabati. 10. Gli piaceva mangiare tardi. Non gli è piaciuto mangiare in quel ristorante.

Exercise 164

1. ero, hai telefonato 2. dormivamo, è venuta 3. aveva, è piovuto 4. erano, è venuta 5. dormiva, ha bussato 6. giocavamo, è cominciato 7. avevo, hai chiamato 8. giocava, ha avuto, 9. era, ha telefonato 10. dovevamo, è arrivato

Exercise 165

1. sono ritornata, ho chiuso 2. è andata, è venuta 3. sono stata, ho abitato 4. ha comprato, costava 5. abbiamo fatto, eravamo 6. salivano, ho visto 7. hai fatto, sei andato 8. abbiamo mangiato, siamo andati 9. sono andato,

sono andato 10. ho lavorato, sono uscita, c'era 11. abbiamo finito, era 12. sono seduta, ho guardato, passeggiava

Exercise 166

1. -ai 2. -asti 3. -ò 4. -immo 5. -aste 6. -arono 7. -ai 8. -arono 9. -ò 10. -ò

Exercise 167

1. parlai 2. cantasti 3. pagò 4. pagammo 5. preparaste 6. telefonarono 7. parlammo 8. cenasti 9. camminò 10. sentii 11. sentì

Exercise 168

1. seppi 2. cadde 3. bevemmo 4. comprammo 5. andammo 6. noleggiammo, potemmo 7. venderono (vendettero) 8. Invitammo, preferì 9. telefonai, trovai 10. arrivai

Exercise 169

1. dissi 2. venisti 3. vennero 4. divenne 5. disse 6. venimmo 7. venne 8. dissi 9. vennero

Exercise 170

1. Mangiai bene. 2. Visitasti Milano. 3. Non capì niente. 4. Carlo chiese la ricetta per il dolce. 5. Noi non facemmo niente tutto il giorno. 6. Lei scelse dei bei fiori. 7. Lui lesse la lettera. 8. Io e Luisa spegnemmo il fuoco. 9. Monica mi diede un bel regalo. 10. Voi ritornaste dalle vacanze.

Exercise 171

1. fui 2. ebbi 3. fosti 4. fu 5. ebbe 6. fummo 7. avemmo 8. foste 9. aveste 10. furono 11. ebbero

Exercise 172

1. Ho risposto alle lettere che avevo ricevuto. 2. Pietro riceva un buon voto perché aveva studiato. 3. Lui non aveva ricevuto le nostre lettere, perciò non ha risposto. 4. Non era ancora arrivato a casa. 5. Quando sono arrivata, lui era già andato via. 6. Tu non avevi ancora finito il tuo lavoro. 7. Rosa non ci aveva ancora chiamati. 8. Tu eri già andato via, quando io sono ritornato. 9. Noi avevamo venduto la nostra casa un anno fa.

Exercise 173

1. Io avevo vinto. 2. Tu avevi parlato. 3. Lei aveva dormito. 4. Noi avevamo comperato. 5. Voi eravate arrivati. 6. Loro erano partiti. 7. Io avevo letto. 8. Tu non avevi capito. 9. Lui non era partito. 10. Noi non ci eravamo alzati.

Exercise 174

1. ebbero visto 2. fui arrivato(-a) 3. ebbi finito 4. ebbe piantato 5. ebbe finito 6. si fu vestito 7. ebbe parlato 8. avemmo venduto 9. fui andato(-a)

Exercise 175

1. Gli studenti ebbero capito la lezione. 2. Tu avesti dormito per molte ore. 3. Lei ebbe parlato con lui per molto tempo. 4. Lui ebbe scritto una lettera, ma non l'ebbe spedita. 5. Appena avemmo fatto il bagno, uscimmo. 6. Appena ebbero finito gli esami, andarono in vacanza. 7. Dopo che ebbi letto il libro, lo diedi a Lia. 8. Appena avemmo mangiato, andammo a riposarci. 9. Io ebbi pensato a te.

Exercise 176

1. Avrò aperto la porta. 2. Ci saremo sposati. 3. Tutti i negozi saranno chiusi. 4. Io avrò finito di pulire. 5. Mi avrà dato il libro. 6. Lui l'avrà chiamata. 7. Saranno andati alla spiaggia. 8. Avremo acceso l'aria condizionata. 9. Avranno affittato una villa. 10. Sarà stato licenziato.

Exercise 177

1. sarò venuta 2. sarà ritornato 3. avrà comprato 4. saremo andati 5. saranno ritornati 6. avrete telefonato 7. avrò rivisto 8. avranno studiato 9. ti sarai divertito 10. saremo partiti

Exercise 178

1. I would buy a house in Italy. 2. I would invite all my friends and relatives. 3. She would listen to her mother. 4. He would go skiing. 5. We would give the keys to Roberta. 6. You would buy many presents. 7. You should walk. 8. She should wake up early. 9. We could go. 10. You would know the truth. 11. Maria and Carlo would go to Florida. 12. I would like to give a present to Luisa.

Exercise 179

1. piacerebbe 2. andresti 3. potrebbe 4. dormirebbe 5. arriveremmo 6. andrebbero 7. farebbe 8. chiederemmo 9. correrebbero 10. vedrebbe 11. preferirebbe 12. sareste

Exercise 180

1. vorrei 2. vorrebbe 3. potrebbe 4. vorremmo 5. sapresti 6. saprebbe 7. potreste 8. dovremmo 9. dovrei 10. saprei 11. potremmo 12. vorrebbero

Exercise 181

1. Avrei studiato l'italiano. 2. Saresti andato al cinema. 3. Lei avrebbe comprato una maglia. 4. Voi avreste letto il libro. 5. Lui avrebbe parlato. 6. Avremmo viaggiato. 7. Avrebbero piantato i fiori. 8. Ti avrei chiamato. 9. Avresti ascoltato la radio. 10. Saremmo andati alla riunione. 11. Ti avrebbero chiamato. 12. Si sarebbe tagliata i capelli.

Exercise 182

1. Io sarei andata in piscina. 2. Tu avresti telefonato alla tua amica. 3. Lui sarebbe andato a casa del suo amico. 4. Lei sarebbe arrivata in orario. 5. Noi avremmo scritto una poesia. 6. Voi avreste fatto una relazione. 7. Loro sarebbero andati dal dentista. 8. Io avrei fatto una festa. 9. Tu avresti comprato la televisione. 10. Loro avrebbero comprato una maglia. 11. Voi avreste scritto una cartolina. 12. Noi avremmo studiato molto.

Exercise 183

1. Maria si è fatta la doccia tutte le mattine. Maria si era fatta la doccia tutte le mattine. 2. Luigi si è lavato i capelli. Luigi si era lavato i capelli. 3. Io mi sono messa il cappello. Io mi ero messa il cappello. 4. Giovanna si è alzata presto. Giovanna si era alzata presto. 5. Erica e Lara si sono divertite molto. Erica e Lara si erano divertite molto. 6. Pietro si è pettinato prima di uscire. Pietro si era pettinato prima di uscire. 7. I nonni si sono sentiti bene. I nonni si erano sentiti bene. 8. Voi vi siete incontrate al mercato. Voi vi eravate incontrate al mercato. 9. Le due donne si sono salutate dalla finestra. Le due donne si erano salutate dalla finestra. 10. Gli innamorati si sono baciati. Gli innamorati si erano baciati. 11. Le bambine si sono svegliate alle otto. Le bambine si erano svegliate alle otto. 12. Sabato tu ti sei alzato tardi. Sabato tu ti eri alzato tardi. 13. Lei si è addormentata davanti alla televisione. Lei si era addormentata davanti alla televisione. 14. Luisa si è laureata in medicina. Luisa si era laureata in medicina. 15. Tu ti sei curato la pelle. Tu ti eri curato la pelle.

Exercise 184

1. dorma 2. camminiate 3. canti 4. perda 5. scriva 6. guardino 7. sentano 8. spenda 9. balliate 10. telefoniamo

Exercise 185

1. mangi 2. cominci 3. giochiate 4. paghi 5. mangino 6. cominci 7. paghino 8. mangi 9. cerchi 10. cominciate

Exercise 186

1. Voglio che voi andiate a casa presto. 2. Pensano che lui arrivi tardi. 3. Spero che tu vada a casa con me. 4. Lei non vuole che tu tenga il suo gatto. 5. Spero che lui non muoia. 6. Lui vuole che loro si siedano. 7. Lei vuole che tu salga. 8. Penso che lei debba studiare. 9. Speriamo che lui suoni il piano. 10. Lui vuole che voi suoniate il violino. 11. Noi pensiamo che tu sappia cucinare bene. 12. Loro sperano che tu rimanga con me.

Exercise 187

1. abbia 2. dia 3. diate 4. abbia 5. faccia 6. abbia 7. sappiano 8. sappiano 9. sia 10. dia 11. sia 12. sia

Exercise 188

1. ascolti 2. atterri 3. guardiamo 4. stia 5. vadano 6. vengano 7. sono 8. vanno 9. trasferiamo 10. siete 11. parli 12. arrivi 13. possano

Exercise 189

1. faccia 2. incontri 3. partiate 4. vada 5. siano 6. parli 7. facciate 8. piova 9. sia 10. possa

Exercise 190

1. Volevo che tu venissi a casa mia. 2. Pensavi di poter comprare la macchina. 3. Maria voleva che tu la chiamassi. 4. Pensavo che lui ritornasse. 5. Lei vorrebbe che lei leggesse la lettera. 6. Lei vorrebbe che lui leggesse. 7. Vorrei che loro studiassero di più. 8. Lei vorrebbe che io gli chiedessi di venire. 9. Volevo che lei li invitasse alla festa. 10. Non volevano che lui partisse. 11. Maria non sapeva che lui andasse. 12. Pensavamo che loro andassero alla spiaggia.

Exercise 191

1. impari 2. studiasse 3. dicesse 4. camminiate 5. regalassi 6. regali 7. debba 8. lavassi 9. viaggiare 10. viaggi 11. viaggiassi 12. sgridi

Exercise 192

1. abbia viaggiato 2. abbia accettato 3. siano andati 4. abbia noleggiato 5. sia andato 6. abbia pianto 7. si siano ricordati 8. abbiano comprato 9. abbiamo viaggiato 10. sia andato 11. siano andati 12. abbia venduto

Exercise 193

1. sono partiti 2. siano partiti 3. avete letto 4. abbiano acceso 5. ha chiamato 6. abbia chiamato 7. è partito 8. sia partito 9. abbiate capito 10. hai trovato 11. abbia messo 12. avete imparato

Exercise 194

1. fossi arrivato 2. foste venuti 3. avessero capito 4. aveste scritto 5. foste già partiti 6. aveste giocato 7. avessero perso 8. avesse chiamato 9. avessi avuto 10. si fosse alzato 11. fossero andati 12. avessi finito

Exercise 195

1. Era possibile che lui avesse vinto. 2. Avevo sperato che lui mi avesse aspettato. 3. Aveva pensato che tu avessi speso i soldi. 4. Credevamo che tu fossi stato male sull'aereo. 5. Era il libro più interessante che avessi mai letto. 6. Tu speravi che io avessi trovato un buon lavoro. 7. Lui pensava che tu avessi comprato una barca nuova. 8. Dubitavo che tu l'avessi vista. 9. Lui sperava che tu ti fossi sposato. 10. Pensavamo che tu avessi venduto la casa. 11. Sara saltava come se fosse stata una ragazza giovane.

Exercise 196

1. avessimo 2. vedessi 3. avesse 4. avessi avuto 5. sapesse 6. si perdesse 7. fosse 8. piacesse 9. avessi 10. aveste ascoltato

Exercise 197

1. La terra viene lavorata dai contadini. 2. Le lettere vengono mandate per via aerea. 3. L'affitto della casa viene pagato da noi in anticipo. 4. Questa partita verrà seguita da molti. 5. Le macchine vengono riparate dal meccanico. 6. Luisa viene invitata ogni domenica da Carla. 7. *I Promessi Sposi* è stato scritto da Alessandro Manzoni. 8. Il dente è venuto tolto dal dentista. 9. Questa notizia è già stata data dalla radio. 10. La porta è stata chiusa a chiave da Luigi. 11. Dove sono state portate le valige? 12. Quell'uomo è stato baciato dalla fortuna.

Exercise 198

1. La casa deve essere finita. 2. La casa dovrà essere finita dai proprietari. 3. La casa era stata finita in fretta. 4. Siamo sorpresi che la casa non sia ancora stata finita. 5. L'aereo verrà finito fra un paio di mesi. 6. L'aereo dovrà essere riparato. 7. Il concerto verrà diretto dal nuovo direttore d'orchestra. 8. Gli Oscar verranno presentati ai migliori attori e attrici. 9. Le medaglie d'oro verranno vinte dai migliori atleti. 10. L'aereo verrà atterrato per tutto l'inverno. 11. Il biglietto aereo sarà rimborsato. 12. Il biglietto aereo verrà rimborsato.

Exercise 199

1. We have to (One must) finish painting. 2. Where can we (one) find the market? 3. What does one find at the market? 4. At what time do we return home? 5. At what time do we leave? 6. Every language is spoken here. 7. We sell quality merchandise. 8. What do people say in Italy about the political situation? 9. We must finish the work by the end of the month. 10. One should study Italian for ten minutes a day.

Exercise 200

1. Ho bisogno di andare in banca. 2. Ho paura dei cani. 3. Ho fame, ho bisogno di mangiare. 4. Hanno bisogno di una giacca nuova. 5. Lei ha sempre mal di testa. 6. Tu hai sete. Vorresti una Coca Cola? 7. Lei aveva sonno. Aveva bisogno di andare a letto. 8. Facciamo alla romana. 9. Faccio colazione con i miei bambini. 10. Le abbiamo fatto un regalo. 11. Lui ha fretta, ma è in ritardo lo stesso. 12. Lei ha fatto molte fotografie.

Exercise 201

1. La fai studiare troppe ore al giorno. 2. Mi sono fatta portare all'ospedale dall'ambulanza. 3. Ci fanno badare ai bambini per una settimana. 4. Fai andare i bambini in chiesa ogni domenica. 5. Non la lascia andare al cinema. 6. Non lascia parlare nessuno. 7. Non lasci giocare nessuno con la tua palla. 8. Non mi lascia andare alla festa. 9. Ho fatto fare dal sarto un abito nuovo per mio marito. 10. Mio marito si è fatto fare un tuxedo a un sarto a Hong Kong.

Exercise 202

1. Devo dar da mangiare ai cavalli. 2. Devi dare da bere al gatto. 3. Mi piace dare il benvenuto alla gente. 4. A molte persone non piace dare la mano. 5. Gli studenti danno gli esami alla fine della anno accademico. 6. Il teatro dà il nuovo film. 7. Ha dato un calcio forte alla palla. 8. Non ci hanno ancora dato la risposta. 9. Gli darò la mia risposta domani. 10. Lei ha dato un sospiro di sollievo. 11. Dobbiamo darci da fare. Il tempo passa velocemente. 12. Non mi piace darmi per vinto.

Exercise 203

1. La gente in Italia va molto a piedi. 2. Ci piace andare a teatro. 3. Tutte le domeniche va a cavallo. 4. A Carlo piace andare a pescare con suo nonno. 5. Tutto va molto bene. 6. Lei pensa che tutto vada male. 7. Mia madre ha paura di andare in aereo. 8. La sua casa andrà in vendita presto. 9. Le bambine non vanno molto d'accordo. 10. Tu preferisci andare in treno.

Exercise 204

1. Le ho detto di stare attenta alle tende. 2. Lei sta attenta in classe. 3. Di solito, i ragazzi non sanno stare fermi. 4. Luigi non stava bene ieri sera. 5. Siamo stati a casa tutto il giorno ieri. 6. Molte persone stanno in piedi nella metropolitana. 7. Non mi piace stare seduto(-a) (a sedere) per molto tempo. 8. Erica non sta mai zitta. 9. Voi state da Maria per molto tempo. 10. Sto per andare a fare la spesa.

Exercise 205

1. Lei assomiglia a suo padre. 2. Do da mangiare ai cani e ai gatti. 3. Il gatto dà la caccia al topo. 4. Carlo dà ascolto al dottore. 5. I bambini danno un calcio alla palla. 6. Facciamo attenzione alla lezione. 7. Giochiamo al Ping-Pong. 8. Sono invitati al concerto. 9. Penso a mia madre. 10. Ricorda a Giovanna di essere puntuale. 11. Non rinuncerò al mio biglietto per l'Italia. 12. Ho stretto la mano al presidente.

Exercise 206

1. Ho bisogno di farina e uova. 2. Tu hai paura dei topi. 3. Si dimentica sempre del suo libro. 4. Lei non si fida di nessuno. 5. Carla è innamorata di lui. 6. Mi meraviglio di loro. 7. Si preoccupano sempre di lui. 8. Voi soffrite molto di questo. 9. Lei ride di tutto. 10. Non si vive solo di pane.

Exercise 207

1. Posso contare sulla mia famiglia. 2. Lui riflette sui suoi errori. 3. Lei ama piantare fiori. 4. La mattina gradisco bere una buona tazza di caffe. 5. Gli italiani sanno vivere bene. 6. Ho scommesso sul cavallo sbagliato. 7. Sappiamo andare nel centro. 8. Basta studiare. Adesso andate fuori a giocare. 9. È necessario risparmiare. 10. Preferiscono parlare con il capo. 11. A te piace volare. 12. Dobbiamo ricordare le persone bisognose. 13. Può rimanere quanto vuole. 14. Lei sa cucinare molto bene.

Exercise 208

1. dodicimila dollari 2. settecentocinquanta franchi svizzeri 3. duecentoventuno dinar 4. ottocentotrentacinque franchi francesi 5. cinquemiladuecentodieci dollari canadesi 6. tre milioni e quattrocentocinquantamiladuecentoquindici yen giapponesi 7. ventun euro. 8. trentatré franchi svizzeri 9. quarantotto sterline inglesi 10. trecentoottantotto marchi tedeschi

Exercise 209

1. prima 2. terza 3. seconda 4. sesta 5. quarta 6. prime 7. primo 8. primo 9. quindicesima 10. decimi

Exercise 210

1. diciottesimo 2. secondo 3. quarto 4. quindicesimo 5. dodicesimo 6. dodici 7. sessanta 8. Novecento 9. tre 10. secondo 11. un quarto 12. quindicina

Exercise 211

1. Sono le nove. 2. Sono le quattordici. 3. Mi sveglio alle sette. 4. Vado a lavorare alle otto. 5. Mancano dieci minuti. 6. Esco alle sei. 7. Prendo il treno alle diciassette. 8. È mezzanotte. 9. Andiamo al ristorante alle ventuno. 10. Arrivo in ufficio alle otto in punto. 11. La banca apre alle otto e trenta. 12. Ceniamo alle venti e trenta.

Exercise 212

1. Sono andata in Italia un mese fa. 2. Ho visto i miei genitori tre settimane fa. 3. Oggi dormiremo fino a tardi. 4. Lei era in chiesa la domenica scorsa. 5. Sono libera giovedì. 6. Vengono a visitarci la prossima settimana. 7. Il prossimo lunedì andremo da Carla. 8. La prossima settimana faremo una festa. 9. Venerdì e sabato sono i miei giorni preferiti. 10. Sabato andrò al mercato. 11. Lui è libero solo il mercoledì. 12. Ci vedremo venerdì. 13. Giochiamo al calcio tutti i sabati. 14. Erica e Lara fanno ginnastica tutti i lunedì e i giovedì.

Exercise 213

1. È il primo di maggio. 2. Oggi è lunedì. 3. La scuola finisce l'otto giugno. 4. Andiamo in California in luglio. 5. Il quindici agosto è una grande festa in Italia. 6. Lei è nata il dodici ottobre millenovecentosessantaquattro. 7. Ci siamo sposati in agosto. 8. Il primo gennaio è il primo giorno dell'anno. 9. Ha studiato in Italia in luglio e in agosto.

Exercise 214

1. Lui è nato il primo gennaio millenovecentonovantacinque. 2. Ha cominciato la scuola il venticinque agosto millenovecentonovantotto. 3. I film degli anni sessanta erano molto belli. 4. A mia madre non piace la musica degli anni ottanta. 5. Questo è il duemilasette. 6. Si è laureato nel millenovecentonovantotto. 7. L'anno scorso, in gennaio, abbiamo avuto una grande bufera di neve. 8. L'estate del duemilatre è stata molto calda. 9. Il millenovecentonovantasette è stato un ottimo anno per il vino. 10. La mia vita è completamente cambiata in luglio del millenovecentonovantanove. 11. Che giorno è oggi? 12. Oggi è martedì. 13. Quanti ne abbiamo oggi? (Qual'è la data oggi?) 14. Oggi ne abbiamo tredici. (Oggi è il tredici.)

Exercise 215

1. Che bella macchina! 2. Che fiori profumati! 3. Che magnifica casa! 4. Che storia interessante! 5. Che film spaventoso! 6. Che panorama incantevole! 7. Che classe difficile! 8. Che viaggio noioso! 9. Che persona fortunata! 10. Che uomo gentile!

Exercise 216

1. Come 2. Quanta 3. Quanto 4. Com' 5. Quanta 6. Com' 7. Quanto 8. Come 9. Quanto 10. Com'

Exercise 217

1. la 2. la 3. il 4. la 5. il 6. la 7. l' 8. la 9. il 10. la

Exercise 218

1. il 2. il 3. la 4. la 5. il 6. la 7. l' (la) 8. la 9. il 10. il/la

Exercise 219

1. un' 2. una 3. un 4. una 5. un 6. un 7. una 8. una 9. una 10. uno

Exercise 220

1. le cantanti 2. i fratelli 3. i giornali 4. i laghi 5. le mani 6. le patate 7. i poeti 8. le poetesse 9. i turisti 10. gli zaini

Exercise 221

1. Io 2. Tu 3. Lui 4. Lei 5. Noi 6. Voi 7. Loro 8. tu 9. tu 10. Noi

Exercise 222

1. la 2. le 3. l' (la) 4. La 5. Lo 6. Li 7. l' (la) 8. L' (la) 9. le 10. le

Exercise 223

1. Lo, vederlo 2. lo, leggerlo 3. la, comprarla 4. li, farli 5. La, venderla 6. Lo, visitarlo 7. le, comprarle 8. La, vederla 9. Li, pulirli 10. Li, chiamarli

Exercise 224

1. le 2. gli 3. gli 4. le 5. gli 6. le 7. le 8. Vi 9. Le 10. Gli

Exercise 225

1. Te la do. 2. Me lo insegna. 3. Gliela comprerebbe. 4. Ve le scriviamo. 5. Glielo portano. 6. Gliela regala. 7. Gliele date. 8. Ve la cantiamo. 9. Ce lo mostra. 10. Ce l'ha mandato.

Exercise 226

1. per me 2. da loro 3. lui 4. me 5. te 6. me 7. te 8. me 9. voi 10. noi

Exercise 227

1. ti 2. Mi 3. Mi 4. si 5. ti 6. si 7. si 8. si 9. vi 10. ci

Exercise 228

1. Voglio quella macchina bianca. 2. Vuole leggere quella rivista. 3. Questo è mio e quello è tuo. 4. Io voglio comprare queste scarpe e tu vuoi comprare quelle. 5. Chi è quell'uomo? 6. Chi sono quegli uomini? 7. Quei bambini hanno ricevuto molti regali. 8. Quello studente è molto intelligente. 9. Questa casa è troppo grande. 10. Questi ragazzi sono studiosi; quelli sono pigri.

Exercise 229

1. Ci 2. ne 3. ne 4. ci 5. ci 6. Ci 7. Ne 8. ci 9. ne 10. ci

Exercise 230

1. nessuno 2. alcuni 3. molte 4. Alcune, Altre 5. alcune 6. una 7. Chiunque 8. Tutti 9. qualcosa 10. Qualcuno

Exercise 231

1. a, da 2. a, per 3. A, in 4. da 5. di 6. in, da 7. per 8. in 9. in 10. in

Exercise 232

1. a, da 2. di 3. di 4. da 5. da 6. da 7. per 8. di 9. di 10. di

Exercise 233

1. per 2. per, fra 3. per 4. per 5. per, con 6. con 7. fra 8. in, fra 9. Fra, di 10. tra

Exercise 234

1. al 2. dal 3. allo, per, del 4. dei 5. dei, nei 6. al, di, dal 7. alla, dal 8. nell' 9. nella, della 10. dall', dagli

Exercise 235

1. dai 2. in, dai 3. a 4. con 5. Dal, al 6. della 7. della 8. dal, dal, della 9. degli 10. dalla, dalla, dalla

Exercise 236

1. moderna 2. sagge 3. magnifico 4. allegre 5. povere, ricche 6. deliziosi 7. pulito, sporco, inquinato 8. intelligente, chiacchierona 9. favoriti 10. interessante, lungo

Exercise 237

1. australiano 2. francese, italiano 3. greco 4. cinesi, filippini, africani 5. Suo, sua 6. miei 7. Mio, suo 8. mio 9. tuoi 10. loro

Exercise 238

1. qualche 2. Ogni 3. molta 4. molti, molte 5. Alcuni, molte 6. molti 7. molta 8. Ogni 9. Tutte 10. Ogni

Exercise 239

1. più... del 2. più... dell' 3. più... che 4. meno... del 5. meno... che 6. meno... dei 7. meglio... del 8. più... della 9. meno... della 10. tanto... quanto

Exercise 240

1. migliore 2. maggiore 3. minore 4. maggiore 5. migliore 6. migliore 7. maggiore 8. migliori 9. peggiore 10. migliore

Exercise 241

1. faccio 2. esci 3. sto, sto 4. rimane 5. sale 6. sono 7. apriamo, chiudiamo 8. spingete 9. salgono, scendi 10. spegnere

Exercise 242

1. devo 2. devi 3. vuole 4. può 5. vogliamo 6. volete, dovete 7. devono 8. vogliamo 9. dobbiamo, dobbiamo 10. vuoi

Exercise 243

1. Mi piace 2. mancano 3. rimane 4. succede 5. fai 6. sembra 7. piace 8. conosce 9. so 10. conosci, sa

Exercise 244

1. chiama 2. chiami 3. scrivi 4. venga 5. vieni 6. partite 7. si accomodino 8. guarda 9. usate 10. stia

Exercise 245

1. si dimentica 2. ci svegliamo, ci alziamo 3. si fermano 4. prepararci 5. si annoia 6. mi meraviglio 7. si lavano 8. ci sposiamo 9. si parlavano 10. si chiamano

Exercise 246

1. ho chiamato 2. hanno comprato 3. hanno voluto 4. volevano, faceva 5. siamo andati, era, abbiamo dovuto 6. sono arrivati 7. hanno dormito, erano 8. eravamo, andavamo 9. arrivava, avvisava 10. è dispiaciuto, sei venuta

Exercise 247

1. andrei 2. compreresti 3. dovrebbe 4. portereste 5. darebbero 6. piacerebbe 7. sarebbe 8. preferirebbe 9. canteremmo 10. potrebbe

Exercise 248

1. Io sarei andata con lei al mercato. 2. Tu avresti capito meglio la matematica. 3. Lui avrebbe spento la luce, ma non ha trovato l'interuttore. 4. Lisa avrebbe saputo scrivere una poesia in italiano. 5. Noi saremmo andati alla riunione, ma non ci hanno avvisati. 6. Voi ci avreste accompagnati, ma la vostra macchina è rotta. 7. Non avrebbe avuto paura del buio. 8. Avrebbe venduto tutta la sua proprietà, ma non vuole muoversi. 9. Noi avremmo consegnato il lavoro, ma non è finito. 10. Loro si sarebbero alzati presto, ma sono molto stanchi.

Exercise 249

1. si ammali 2. vogliano 3. cominciate 4. prenda 5. cantino 6. veniate 7. parlino 8. giochi 9. spedisca 10. deva (debba)

Exercise 250

1. fossero 2. capisse 3. prendesse 4. cantassero 5. giocasse 6. spedissi 7. dimagrisse 8. venissero 9. guadagnasse 10. fosse

Exercise 251

1. foste arrivati 2. abbia spento 3. avesse spento 4. abbia capito 5. avessi capito 6. vi foste riposati 7. abbia acquistato 8. abbiate chiamato 9. fossero arrivati 10. fossimo rimasti

Exercise 252

1. hanno fame 2. ho fame, ho sete, sono stanca 3. fai (fà) attenzione 4. fare benzina 5. faccia presto, ho fretta 6. fare da mangiare 7. faccio un sospiro 8. sto per 9. stare zitta 10. stare in piedi